Are Bad Jobs Inevitable?

Critical Perspectives on Work and Employment

Series editors:
Irena Grugulis, Durham University Business School, UK
Caroline Lloyd, School of Social Sciences, Cardiff University, UK
Chris Smith, University of Sidney Business School, Australia
Chris Warhurst, University of Sydney Business School, Australia

Critical Perspectives on Work and Employment combines the best empirical research with leading edge, critical debate on key issues and developments in the field of work and employment. Extremely well regarded and popular, the series is linked to the highly successful *International Labour Process Conference.*

Formerly edited by David Knights, Hugh Willmott, Chris Smith and Paul Thompson, each volume in the series includes contributions from a range of disciplines, including the sociology of work and employment, business and management studies, human resource management, industrial relations and organisational analysis.

Further details of the *International Labour Process Conference* can be found at www.ilpc.org.uk.

Published:
Paul Thompson and Chris Smith
WORKING LIFE

Irena Grugulis and Ödül Bozkurt
RETAIL WORK

Maeve Houlihan and Sharon Bolton
WORK MATTERS

Alan McKinlay and Chris Smith
CREATIVE LABOUR

Chris Warhurst, Doris Ruth Eikhof and Axel Haunschild
WORK LESS, LIVE MORE?

Bill Harley, Jeff Hyman and Paul Thompson
PARTICIPATION AND DEMOCRACY AT WORK

Chris Warhurst, Ewart Keep and Irena Grugulis
THE SKILLS THAT MATTER

Chris Warhurst, Françoise Carré, Patricia Findlay and Chris Tilly
ARE BAD JOBS INEVITABLE?

Andrew Sturdy, Irena Grugulis and Hugh Willmott
CUSTOMER SERVICE

Craig Prichard, Richard Hull, Mike Chumer and Hugh Willmott
MANAGING KNOWLEDGE

Alan Felstead and Nick Jewson
GLOBAL TRENDS IN FLEXIBLE LABOUR

Paul Thompson and Chris Warhurst
WORKPLACES OF THE FUTURE

More details of the publications in this series can be found at http://www.palgrave.com/business/cpwe.asp

---

Critical Perspectives on Work and Employment Series

Series Standing Order ISBN 978–0230–23017–0

You can receive future titles in this series as they are published by placing a standing order. Please contact your bookseller or, in case of difficulty, write to us at the address below with your name and address, the title of the series and the ISBN quoted above.

Customer Services Department, Macmillan Distribution Ltd, Houndmills, Basingstoke, Hampshire RG21 6XS, England

---

Are Bad Jobs Inevitable?

Trends, Determinants and Responses to Job Quality in the Twenty-First Century

Edited by

Chris Warhurst
Professor of Work and Organisational Studies, University of Sydney Business School

Françoise Carré
Research Director at the Center for Social Policy, University of Massachusetts, Boston

Patricia Findlay
Professor of Work and Employment Relations, University of Strathclyde

and

Chris Tilly
Professor of Urban Planning, University of California, Los Angeles

Baker College of Clinton Twp Library

palgrave macmillan

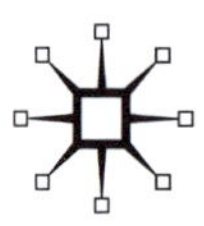

Editorial selection, introduction and chapter 1 © Chris Warhurst, Françoise Carré, Patricia Findlay and Chris Tilly 2012
Individual chapters © Contributors 2012

All rights reserved. No reproduction, copy or transmission of this publication may be made without written permission.

No portion of this publication may be reproduced, copied or transmitted save with written permission or in accordance with the provisions of the Copyright, Designs and Patents Act 1988, or under the terms of any licence permitting limited copying issued by the Copyright Licensing Agency, Saffron House, 6–10 Kirby Street, London EC1N 8TS.

Any person who does any unauthorized act in relation to this publication may be liable to criminal prosecution and civil claims for damages.

The authors have asserted their rights to be identified as the authors of this work in accordance with the Copyright, Designs and Patents Act 1988.

First published 2012 by
PALGRAVE MACMILLAN

Palgrave Macmillan in the UK is an imprint of Macmillan Publishers Limited, registered in England, company number 785998, of Houndmills, Basingstoke, Hampshire RG21 6XS.

Palgrave Macmillan in the US is a division of St Martin's Press LLC, 175 Fifth Avenue, New York, NY 10010.

Palgrave Macmillan is the global academic imprint of the above companies and has companies and representatives throughout the world.

Palgrave® and Macmillan® are registered trademarks in the United States, the United Kingdom, Europe and other countries.

ISBN: 978–0–230–33691–9

This book is printed on paper suitable for recycling and made from fully managed and sustained forest sources. Logging, pulping and manufacturing processes are expected to conform to the environmental regulations of the country of origin.

A catalogue record for this book is available from the British Library.

A catalog record for this book is available from the Library of Congress.

10 9 8 7 6 5 4 3 2 1
21 20 19 18 17 16 15 14 13 12

Printed and bound in Great Britain by
CPI Antony Rowe, Chippenham and Eastbourne

Contents

List of Illustrations

Tables

Figures

Acknowledgements

This book emerged out of the 'Are bad jobs inevitable?' stream organized by the editors at the *27th Annual International Labour Process Conference* at Rutgers University in the US. The editors would like to thank all the contributors who offered papers to that stream – and apologize to those whose papers we have been unable to publish. We would also like to thank the organizers of the conference – Mary Gatta, Heather McKay, David Finegold, Adrienne Eaton and Eileen Appelbaum – for accepting the stream within the conference programme. Ursula Gavin is a long-standing and much appreciated advocate of the Critical Perspectives on Work and Employment series at Palgrave Macmillan, where Ceri Griffiths has been a very helpful editor in seeing this book through to completion. Producing books is time consuming and, as many of our contributors know, often involve working to tight deadlines. As a consequence, there are opportunity costs; in this respect we would also like to thank our respective families (especially Catherine and Anna) for their forbearance.

Notes on Contributors

José Luis Álvarez Galván holds a PhD in Economic Sociology from the London School of Economics and Political Science (LSE), a Master's in Regional Economic and Social Development from the University of Massachusetts and a BA in Economics from the National Autonomous University of Mexico (UNAM). Before pursuing postgraduate education he was a consultant. He has taught at UNAM, the LSE and Brunel University. After completing his PhD he was a visiting researcher in the Department of Political and Social Sciences at the Universitat Pompeu Fabra in Barcelona. He lives in Paris and works as a consultant for the Organisation for Economic Co-operation and Development (OECD).

José-Ignacio Antón is Lecturer in Economics at the University of Salamanca in Spain. His research fields are public and labour economics, on which he has extensively published in books and academic articles in journals such as *European Journal of Health Economics* and *International Journal of Manpower*. His latest book is *Measuring More than Money* (2011).

Mirabai Auer holds a Masters in Urban Planning and Policy from the University of Illinois at Chicago. She is a data analyst at the Program for Environmental and Regional Equity and Center for the Study for Immigrant Integration at the University of Southern California. Her research interests include community economic development strategies, low-wage work and data visualization techniques.

Françoise Carré is Research Director of the Center for Social Policy, University of Massachusetts Boston Graduate School of Policy and Global Studies. She specializes in applied labour economics and comparative employment policy. She has written extensively about temporary and short-term work in the US and in international perspective, low-wage employment and worker representation. She is co-author of 'Working in Large Food Retailers: a France-United States Comparison' (with P. Askezazy, J. Berry, S. Prunier-Poulmaire and C. Tilly) forthcoming in *Work, Employment, and Society*, 'Retail Jobs in Comparative Perspective' (with C. Tilly, M. van Klaveren and D. Voss-Dahm) in *Low-Wage Work in the Wealthy World*, J. Gautié and J. Schmitt (eds) (2010) and 'The United States: Different Sources of Precariousness in a Mosaic of Employment Arrangements' (with J. Heintz) in *Cross-national Perspectives on Precarious Employment*, in L. Vosko, M. MacDonald and I. Campbell (eds) (2009). She received a PhD in Urban and Regional Studies from MIT.

Jennifer Craft Morgan is Scientist at the Institute on Aging in San Francisco and Research Assistant Professor in the Department of Allied Health Sciences in the School of Medicine at the University of North Carolina at Chapel Hill. Her interests include medical sociology, gender stratification, evaluation research, health care workforce and the sociological study of work and careers over the life course. She is working on projects studying the work and careers of three feminized occupational groups: frontline workers, library and information professionals and nurse faculty.

James DeFilippis is Associate Professor in the Bloustein School of Planning and Public Policy at Rutgers University. He is the author of three books and dozens of articles and book chapters on the politics and economics of cities.

Janette S. Dill is a postdoctoral fellow at the Cecil G. Sheps Center for Health Services Research at the University of North Carolina at Chapel Hill. Her current research focuses on the career mobility of low-wage workers in health care settings. Her interests include occupational stratification, gender and work and medical sociology.

Enrique Fernández-Macías is Lecturer in Sociology at the University of Salamanca in Spain. His work focuses on the sociology of labour and industrial relations. He has authored or co-authored several books, book chapters and academic articles on these topics in volumes edited by various publishers and journals such as *European Journal of Industrial Relations* and *Socio-Economic Review*. His latest book is *Measuring More than Money* (2011).

Patricia Findlay is Professor of Work and Employment Relations at the Department of Human Resource Management at the University of Strathclyde Business School and Director of the Scottish Centre for Employment Research. Her research and publications focus on the study of work and the management of the employment relationship and have focused on social innovation in the workplace, skills and skills valuation; workplace and union-led learning; gender and inequality; employment regulation and HR practice, and appear in *British Journal of Industrial Relations*, *Human Relations* and *Work, Employment and Society*. Current research activity is focused on job quality through the Economic and Social Research Council (ESRC) Seminar Series 'Making Bad Jobs Better', co-organized with Chris Warhurst; skills utilization; union-led learning; and the employment implications of devolution. She is a member of the ESRC Peer Review College and of the Editorial Boards of the journals *Work, Employment and Society* and *Industrial Relations Journal*. She has a long-standing association with and has co-organized the International Labour Process Conference.

Janice Fine is Assistant Professor of Labour Studies and Employment Relations at the School of Management and Labor Relations at Rutgers University where she teaches and writes about low-wage immigrant labour in the US, historical and contemporary debates regarding federal immigration policy, dilemmas of labour standards' enforcement and innovative union and community organizing strategies. She is the author of *Worker Centers: Organizing Communities at the Edge of the Dream* (2006).

Jennifer Gordon is Professor of Law at Fordham University School of Law in New York City, where she teaches in the fields of Immigration Law and Labor Law. She writes on the topics of low-wage workers' rights, global labour migration, the intersection of race and immigration, and the role of law in struggles for social justice and has authored a book, *Suburban Sweatshops: The Fight for Immigrant Rights* (2005). Prior to joining the Fordham faculty, Gordon founded the Workplace Project in New York, a nationally recognized immigrant advocacy centre, in 1992. She was awarded a MacArthur Prize Fellowship in 1999.

Douglas D. Heckathorn is Professor of Sociology at Cornell University and Editor-in-Chief of *Rationality and Society*. His research interests include statistical methods for sampling hard-to-reach populations, and formal theories of collective action.

Julia R. Henly is Associate Professor in the School of Social Service Administration at the University of Chicago. Her research focuses on the intersection of employment, parenting, child care and public policy with particular attention to the work–family management strategies of low-income families. Her work has appeared in several peer-reviewed journals, such as *Journal of Urban Affairs*, *Journal of Marriage and Family*, *Early Childhood Research Quarterly* and *Children and Youth Services Review*, as well as several edited book volumes.

Tony Huzzard is Associate Professor at the Department of Business Administration, Lund University and was formerly Visiting Research Fellow at the National Institute for Working Life in Malmö, Sweden. He has researched and published widely on organizational development, work organization and industrial relations. His current research interests are diverse including corporate governance and work organization, process organizing in health care and the branding of business schools.

Susan James is Assistant Director of the ESRC Centre on Skills, Knowledge and Organisational Performance (SKOPE) based in the Department of Education, University of Oxford. Her research interests include theories of learning, school-to-work transitions, VET systems, apprenticeship, work-based learning, on-the-job and off-the-job training, and low skill/low wage work. Susan participated in the US–European research project funded by the Russell Sage Foundation on low-waged work. Her current projects include research on recruitment and selection, developing vocational excellence and apprenticeship, and skills, work and employment in a 'graduatising' industry. She has co-edited *Balancing the Skills Equation* (2004) (with Geoff Hayward) and sits on the board of *Work, Employment and Society.*

Arne L. Kalleberg is Kenan Distinguished Professor of Sociology at the University of North Carolina at Chapel Hill. He has published more than 100 articles and chapters and 11 books on topics related to the sociology of work, organizations, occupations and industries, labour markets and social stratification. His most recent book is *Good Jobs, Bad Jobs: The Rise of Polarized and Precarious Employment Systems in the United States, 1970s–2000s* (2011). He is working on projects that examine the growth of precarious work in Asia and institutional determinants of inequality in the United States.

Ewart Keep is Deputy Director of the ESRC Centre on Skills, Knowledge and Organisational Performance (SKOPE) and is based in the School of Social Sciences at Cardiff University. His research interests include lifelong learning policy, learning organizations, the management of the VET system, employer's attitudes towards skills and what shapes these, and the nature of the relationship between skills and performance (broadly defined). He has published widely on issues to do with bad jobs, particularly developing a typology of incentives for understanding learning and training at the lower end of the labour market. He sits on the expert panel for the UK Commission on Employment and Skills.

Susan J. Lambert is Associate Professor in the School of Social Service Administration at the University of Chicago. She has conducted a series of studies on employer practices and employment conditions in low-level, hourly jobs with the goal of identifying ways to improve workers' economic security, health and well-being. The sites for her research span both production and non-production industries, including retail, hospitality, financial services, transportation and manufacturing, and both publicly held and family-owned companies. Her recent research reveals specific strategies that employers can use to improve schedule predictability, stability and flexibility in hourly jobs, while also meeting business goals.

Ana Luz González is a doctoral candidate in Urban Planning at UCLA. Her research focuses on the labour market status of immigrants and minorities and the role of day labour worker centres in the informal economy.

Ruth Milkman is Professor of Sociology at the City University of New York Graduate Center and Academic Director of the City University of New York's (CUNY) Murphy Labor Institute. Her most recent books are *Working for Justice: The L.A. Model of Organizing and Advocacy* (2010) (co-edited with J. Bloom and V. Narro) and *L.A. Story: Immigrant Workers and the Future of the US Labor Movement* (2006).

Rafael Muñoz de Bustillo is Professor of Applied Economics at the University of Salamanca, Spain, the oldest university in the country and among the oldest in Europe. His research in Welfare State economics, income distribution and labour markets has appeared in more than 100 publications. His latest book is *Measuring More than Money* (2011). He has participated in research projects with the ILO, the European Community and the Spanish Ministry of Labor.

Anne Munro is Professor of Work and Industrial Relations and Associate Dean, Research and Knowledge Transfer in the Business School at Edinburgh Napier University. She has a PhD in Industrial Relations from Warwick University. Her research interests include low-wage workers in the public sector, skills development, equalities issues, workplace learning and union–employer partnerships. She is the author of *Women, Work and Trade Unions* (1999) and co-editor of *Workplace Learning in Context* (2004) (with Helen Rainbird and Alsion Fuller). Her journal publications appear in *British Journal of Industrial Relations* and *New Technology, Work and Employment*. She is Associate Member of the Employment Research Institute in the Business School and Fellow of the Chartered Institute of Personnel and Development.

Victor Narro is Project Director for the UCLA Labor Center. His focus is to provide leadership programmes for Los Angeles' immigrant workers and internship opportunities for UCLA students. Victor is also a lecturer for the Chicano/a Studies Department, where he teaches classes that focus on immigrant workers and the labour movement. Victor is a co-editor of a recent book, *Working for Justice: The L.A. Model of Organizing and Advocacy* (2010) (with Ruth Milkman and Joshua Bloom).

Paul Osterman is the NTU Professor of Human Resources and Management at the MIT Sloan School of Management. His books include *Good Jobs America*

(2011), *The Truth about Middle Managers* (2008), *Gathering Power: The Future of Progressive Politics in America* (2003), *Securing Prosperity: How the American Labor Market Has Changed and What To Do About It* (1999), *Employment Futures: Reorganization, Dislocation, and Public Policy* (1988) and *Getting Started: The Youth Labor Market* (1978). In addition, he has written numerous academic journal articles and policy issue papers on topics such as the organization of work within firms, labour market policy and economic development, and consulted widely to government agencies, foundations, community groups and public interest organizations. His PhD in Economics is from MIT.

Jason Perelshteyn is a manager at Student Agencies, Inc. in Ithaca, New York. He was a graduate student in Sociology at Cornell University.

Barbara Pocock is Inaugural Director of the Centre for Work + Life at the University of South Australia at Adelaide. She initially trained as an economist and completed her doctorate in gender studies. She has been researching work, employment and industrial relations in Australia for over 25 years and has undertaken considerable analysis of work and its complex intersections with households, families and social life. She has published many books, articles and book chapters, and given visiting lectures in the US, Canada, the UK, New Zealand, Switzerland and China. She is actively involved in policy development and public commentary on work issues in Australia, and undertakes many public contributions on these issues each year. Recent books include *Living Low Paid: The Dark Side of Prosperous Australia* (2008) (co-authored with Helen Masterman-Smith), *Kids Count: Better Early Childhood Education and Care in Australia* (2007) (co-edited with Elizabeth Hill and Alison Elliott), *The Labour Market Ate My Babies: Work, Children and a Sustainable Future* (2006) and *The Work/Life Collision* (2003).

Diana Polson is a PhD candidate in Political Science at the City University of New York (CUNY) Graduate Center. Her research focuses on the politics and economics of home-based care work in New York City.

Jeffrey S. Rothstein is Assistant Professor of Sociology at Grand Valley State University near Grand Rapids, Michigan. His research focuses on the changing nature of work in the global economy and the impact of globalization on labour. His work has appeared in a number of journals including *Social Forces, Competition & Change, Research in the Sociology of Work* and *New Labor Forum*. He is working on a manuscript based on fieldwork at General Motors auto plants in the US and Mexico titled *When Good Jobs Go Bad: Globalization, De-unionization, and Declining Labor Standards in the North American Auto Industry*.

Natalie Skinner is Research Fellow at the Centre for Work + Life at the University of South Australia at Adelaide. She is interested in health and well-being in the workplace, with a particular emphasis on psychological health (e.g. stress, burnout, job satisfaction), job quality (work intensity, flexibility, work hours) and work–life interaction. Her interest in well-being extends to the impact of paid work on individuals' capacity to be 'good environmental citizens' – specifically the interaction between paid work arrangements and experiences, gender and other social demographics, and people's willingness and capacity to reduce their environmental impact in their everyday lives.

Michael Spiller is a PhD candidate in Sociology at Cornell University. His research interests include patterns of US educational attainment, causal inference methodology, and social network sampling and analysis.

Mark P. Thomas is Associate Professor in the Department of Sociology and Co-Director of the Centre for Research on Work and Society at York University in Toronto, Canada. His research interests are in the areas of political economy and economic sociology, with a primary focus on the regulation of labour standards at local, national and transnational scales. He is the co-editor of *Power and Everyday Practices* (2011) (with D. Brock and R. Raby) and of *Interrogating the New Economy* (2010) (with N. Pupo) and author of *Regulating Flexibility: The Political Economy of Employment Standards* (2009).

Chris Tilly is Professor of Urban Planning and Sociology and Director of the Institute for Research on Labor and Employment at the University of California, Los Angeles, and an economist specializing in labour, income distribution and local economic development, with research focusing on the United States and Mexico. His books include *The Gloves-Off Economy: Labor Standards at the Bottom of America's Labor Market* (2008), *Stories Employers Tell: Race, Skill, and Hiring in America* (2001), *Glass Ceilings and Bottomless Pits: Women's Work, Women's Poverty, Work Under Capitalism* (1999) and *Half a Job: Bad and Good Part-Time Jobs in a Changing Labor Market* (1995).

Chris Warhurst is Professor of Work and Organisational Studies at the University of Sydney. His interests centre on work and employment, and applying research to policy development. Research includes aesthetic labour, creative labour, graduate labour, skill utilization, union-led learning and low-wage work. He is part of the organizing team for the Annual International Labour Process Conference. His books include *Work Less, Live More?* (2008) (with D. Eikhof and A. Haunschild), *The Skills That Matter* (2004) (with I. Grugulis and E. Keep) and *Workplaces of the Future* (1998) (with P. Thompson). He has published over 40 articles in leading international journals and was co-editor of *Work, Employment and Society* from 2008 to 2010. He is an adviser on skills policy to Skills Australia and the OECD. The task, he believes, is to better understand and thereby help improve jobs.

CHAPTER 1

Job Quality: Scenarios, Analysis and Interventions

Françoise Carré, Patricia Findlay, Chris Tilly and Chris Warhurst

Introduction

Job quality, not just job creation, matters – it contributes to economic competitiveness, social cohesion and personal well-being. In the UK, government recognizes that bad jobs can undermine health and well-being, generate in-work poverty and exacerbate child poverty, create and perpetuate gender inequalities in the labour market and beyond and constrain job and social mobility. Even during the current economic downturn the issue of job quality remains high on government agendas as part of a jobs growth strategy.[1] US policy debates have similarly raised concerns about improving job quality and creating good jobs to deal with social and economic problems (Appelbaum et al., 2008). In Australia, it is recognized that poor job quality has costs for individuals, families and communities, and that the country's social fabric will be frayed without policy intervention to address bad jobs. A similar concern over job quality exists within the EU, with the Lisbon Agreement promoting not just 'more' but also 'better' jobs, attempting to balance the need for increased employment participation with improved job quality. Globally, the ILO is promoting a 'decent work' agenda to raise labour standards, enhance employment and income opportunities, provide social protection and social security and promote social dialogue.

Academic research and debate on job quality have a long history as exemplified by the socio-technical experiments of the Tavistock Institute (e.g. Beirne, 2008), the quality of working life movement (e.g. Davis and Cherns, 1975) and job enrichment initiatives (e.g Hackman et al., 1975). Thereafter, academic attention to job quality waned in some contexts: in the UK, for example, while critical scholars engaged indirectly with job quality through marker of skills, job quality per se was a less explicit concern. More recently, because of its economic and social impacts, academics throughout the advanced economies are once again examining job quality (e.g. Appelbaum, Bernhardt, and Murnane, 2007; Bazen et al., 2005; Bartik and Houseman, 2008; Coats, 2009; Gallie, 2007; Gautié and Schmitt, 2010; Green, 2006). Many think tanks in these countries, using their own and often path-breaking empirical research are pressing governments to do something about bad jobs (e.g. Brookings Institution, 2007; Goulden, 2010; Lawton and Cooke, 2008). However in many cases it is journalists – through national and international bestselling books – who have been most successful in confronting government and raising public consciousness about job quality with damning indictments of the continued existence and consequences of bad jobs (e.g. Aubenas, 2011; Ehrenreich, 2001; Toynbee, 2003; Wynhausen, 2005). As these books graphically portray, workers in bad jobs are often inadequately protected by collective bargaining and employment law. They are frequently vulnerable workers, many of whom are female or ethnic minority workers, with low or no qualifications, often working part-time and in industries that are vitally important, such as health and social care.

This book focuses on these bad jobs. Over recent decades governments in the advanced economies have implicitly assumed that the 'new economy' would generate good jobs while eradicating bad jobs through technological substitution. The reality is somewhat different. Good jobs have been created but bad jobs persist, particularly in services (Holmes, 2011). Not surprisingly there are now demands for a 'new deal' or 'new strategy' for workers in bad jobs (e.g. Kenway, 2008; Grimshaw et al., 2008; Osterman, 2008). Yet while bad jobs are increasingly recognized as a problem, there is little evidence of a coherent policy response.

As the contents of this book recognize, an answer to the question 'are bad jobs inevitable' needs to draw upon new and multidisciplinary approaches, be sensitive to workers' life courses and draw out lessons from a range of countries. The contributions that follow outline debates, developments, issues and trends in job quality; attempt to define and measure bad jobs; explain variation and change in job quality; and identify workplace practices and broader non-workplace strategies for making bad jobs better. This chapter begins by considering a range of job quality scenarios and the debates that underpin them. These debates draw upon varying definitions, components and measures of job quality which, taken together, pose a particular challenge to efforts to chart trends in job quality within and across countries. The chapter then addresses definitional issues before addressing the question of whether bad jobs are inevitable. Thereafter, the various contributors to the book expand and develop these ideas in international, national, sectoral and company contexts.

Potential job quality scenarios

In terms of what is happening to job quality there are a number of possible scenarios. These scenarios can be distinguished by their concern: some focus on changes to the number of good and bad jobs within the labour market; others focus on changes within particular jobs which make these jobs either better or worse. The two dominant scenarios for most of the past 50 years have been of the former type, anticipating that there will be relatively more good or more bad jobs respectively:

Scenario 1: jobs are getting better. In this scenario, bad jobs are eliminated, leaving only good jobs; at the same time, new types of good jobs emerge. As a consequence, the labour market is populated with only good jobs. For much of the latter half of the twentieth century, this possibility seemed more like a probability within some policy and academic circles and across the political spectrum (Darr and Warhurst, 2008). Bad jobs are eradicated as labour is substituted by technology (Holmes, 2011). The number of good jobs increases because technological advances create more complex processes, and the shift to service-based economies requires more educated labour – that is, more skilled workers (with qualifications as the proxy) (e.g. Mills, 1951; Kerr et al., 1960; Bell, 1973). A recent twist on this scenario in the advanced economies is the quest for comparative advantage against developing economies by becoming high-skill economies driven by knowledge and creativity. In such economies the production of high value-added, often intangible, products is carried out by high-skilled workers who are paid commensurately higher wages (Reich, 1993; Florida, 2002 – for an overview see Lloyd and Payne, 2004).

Scenario 2: jobs are getting worse. In this scenario, good jobs deteriorate so that the labour market is populated primarily with bad jobs. As an intentional counter to Scenario 1, some academics argued that the long-term trend over the twentieth century was not better work but a 'degradation of work', most obviously manifest in deskilling (Braverman, 1974). Deskilling resulted from the needs of capitalists to remain competitive and how they used technology to do so, rather than technological determinism. This deskilling applied as much to the emerging white-collar work as to blue-collar work, and would eventually occur to 'brain work' as well as that involving brawn (Braverman, 1974: ch.15; Beirne et al., 1998). Labour process analysis emerged out of this critique, became a key critical account of jobs in the advanced economies in the 1990s (Kitay, 1997) and continues to exercise intellectual influence (see Thompson and Smith, 2010).

Both scenarios rely heavily on skill as a marker of job quality. Interestingly, although acknowledging the role of technology, both scenarios also represent market-based accounts of job quality trends. Scenario 1 assumes that the emergence of particular products and/or positioning in particular product markets can determine job quality – intangible goods and services trigger upskilling and quality-driven products need highly skilled workers. Scenario 2 assumes that competitive pressures from the market drive employers to seek to cheapen production processes leading to the deskilling of workers, starting with blue-collar but eventually spreading to white-collar workers too.

More recently there is an emerging consensus around a third scenario that is still focused on the relative numbers of good and bad jobs:

Scenario 3: polarization of job quality. In this scenario structural economic change triggers two possibilities: first, differential growth expands employment in industries providing good and bad jobs; second, the middle is hollowed out as intermediate jobs either disappear or gravitate into either good or bad jobs or are simply offshored to the developing countries. Both the US and UK labour markets have experienced growth in the number of jobs at the top and bottom of the occupational hierarchy, leading to more managerial, professional and associate professional jobs at the top, and more routine personal and interactive services jobs at the bottom (Levy and Murnane, 2004; Reich, 1993). In this respect, Goos and Manning (2007) argue that the UK labour market is now characterized by what they call 'lovely' and 'lousy' jobs. Using a mix of pay and skill as a proxy for pay, they demonstrate job growth in the lowest two and highest two deciles by pay over 1979–99, and a contraction in all other deciles (for a similar pattern in the US see Wright and Dwyer, 2006). This job polarization however does not form two parallel economies; rather, its parts are structurally interdependent, rising and falling together. Illustratively, more routine workers are required to service cash rich, time poor workers in good jobs facing a time squeeze that disables their capacity to service their own physical reproduction. Florida (2002) refers to these low-wage, low-skill workers as a 'service class' undertaking work pushed out from the home into the market (Warhurst, 2008). These routine service jobs are not easily automated (Holmes, 2011). This phenomenon exists in the larger global (Sassen, 2001) and creative (Florida, 2005) cities; it also exists throughout the Anglo-Saxon economies where relatively deregulated labour markets and highly polarized wage distributions make labour displacement and reconfiguration economically viable (Gautié and Schmitt, 2010).

The above three scenarios largely reflect a quantitative approach, charting the relative number of good and bad jobs in the economy. In contrast, the scenarios below focus on qualitative changes to the characteristics of jobs that make them better or worse. There are two main possibilities. The first possibility envisages the distance between good and bad jobs widening, either as good jobs get better or bad jobs get worse; the second envisages the distance diminishing, as either good jobs get worse or bad jobs get better.

Scenario 4: good jobs are getting better. In this scenario, features that make a job good in the first place become further enhanced. In both the US and UK top earners' pay has increased dramatically as a ratio of low earners' pay and even middle income earners' pay has stagnated relative to that of top earners who have 'continued to move away' from middle and bottom income earners (Plunkett, 2011: 10). If bad jobs are the end of a camel train, to paraphrase Toynbee (2003), the camels at the front of the train are now not just pulling further away but disappearing over the dunes. Stewart (2011) reports that high income earners have pulled even further away during the current economic downturn as monetary quantitative easing policy has boosted share dividends and profits, from which some workers already in good jobs are more likely to benefit (as shareholders), while fiscal and wage restraint has resulted in falling real wages and salaries for workers in poorer quality jobs.

Scenario 5: bad jobs are getting worse. In this scenario, the gap between good and bad jobs also widens but for different reasons. The features that make jobs bad become worse. For example, in the US workers on the lowest wages have seen those wages drop not just in relative but also absolute terms over recent years (Green, 2006). In Australia, as Pocock and Skinner (Chapter 4) note, swathes of already low wage, low skill workers have seen their employment status reconfigured to become 'casual' labour, losing benefits, entitlements and protection as a consequence. By 2010 a quarter of all such employees were employed as casuals, lacking both holiday pay and sick leave entitlements. Eroding standards and weak government enforcement of employment law both in the US (Fine and Gordon in Chapter 12 and Theodore et al. in Chapter 13) and UK (Metcalf, 2007) mean that workers in bad jobs become even more vulnerable.

It is possible that both these scenarios unfold simultaneously, creating an even greater gap and a squeeze on modal job quality. However the other possibility is that the distance diminishes between good and bad jobs:

Scenario 6: good jobs go bad. Under this scenario, the features that made these jobs good deteriorate. A stark illustration of this possibility for good jobs at the top of the occupational hierarchy is provided by Felstead et al. (2007) who note that whilst discretion in work has declined over time for all workers, it has declined most for professional workers. Even within professional jobs, not all workers enjoy high pay and good career prospects, either because of discrimination or because the work is not equally accessible to all workers due to non-work commitments. For example, Eikhof and Warhurst (2010) reveal how nominally good jobs in the audio-visual industries go bad for women and particularly those with dependent children. This occurrence matters because the creative industries are a key feature of governments' beloved 'new economy'. This example also illustrates that who the job-holders are matters in any understanding of job quality, and how workers' particular personal circumstances can influence perceptions and experience of job quality. Moreover, relatively good jobs are not confined to the top of the occupational hierarchy. Some intermediate jobs, particularly in manufacturing, also attained some good jobs' features in the twentieth century; won by trade unions supported by progressive governments. However these gains are under threat, this time through globalization. To save these jobs from being offshored and lost to cheaper wage countries, labour in the advanced economies accepts new and inferior terms and conditions, typically work intensification and lower wages. Health insurance and other benefits too are disappearing (Bartik and Houseman, 2008). This theme is one taken up by Rothstein (Chapter 8). Amid concerns about the relocation of production to Mexico, he reveals a 'hollowing out' of good jobs in the US auto industry. However he also appreciates that those jobs that are relocated to Mexico are relatively good jobs in that country even if comparatively worse than jobs remaining in the US. Clearly geography matters too in understanding job quality.

There are thus a number of possibilities with regard to the job quality trajectory. What can be said with some confidence is that bad jobs still exist, are likely to persist and possibly grow in number and may even be worsening. There is some indication that good jobs might also be worsening. The latter scenario represents a regressive way to reduce the gap between good and bad jobs. A more progressive way forward emerges with the final scenario, that of improving bad jobs:

Scenario 7: bad jobs get better. Under this scenario, the features that make jobs bad are ameliorated. Despite governments' desire for a 'new economy' of good jobs, a wholesale transformation of bad jobs into good jobs is unlikely. As Crouch et al. (1999) and Keep (2000) point out, if product market positioning and consumer purchasing power in the economy drive job quality, there are only so many industries and occupations that can sustain high pay and skills. That bad jobs will persist might not be a problem if they are populated with workers with ready exit options. Students, for example, can work in these jobs to pay their way through study but then move onwards and upwards into good jobs using their acquired educational qualifications as leverage. However for other occupants of these jobs, at least in the US and UK, there is an acute 'bad jobs trap' (Booth and Snower, 1996), particularly for women (Mason and Salverda, 2010), with a range of deleterious economic and social consequences. Interventions to make bad jobs better are therefore desirable, and discretionary space exists for these interventions (Glyn, 2006). These interventions would centre on enforcing, or better still, enhancing existing employment standards – that is levering 'employment enrichment'. They would be driven by a number of actors individually or in concert nationally and internationally: government, unions and employers most obviously. Chapters in this volume, especially in Part II, offer a range of ideas, initiatives and suggestions as to how this discretionary space is being, or could be, exploited. For example, Dill et al. (Chapter 7) discuss specific improvement initiatives aimed at bad jobs in the US health care sector; Lambert and Henly (Chapter 9) show that even in the presence of strong corporate constraints, managers can create more humane scheduling regimes; Fine and Gordon (Chapter 12) explore how worker organizations can be incorporated into workplace inspection. Thus while making bad jobs better is aspirational, there are good examples of how aspiration might be turned into reality.

Analysing job quality

As Antón et al. (Chapter 2) note, despite the best efforts of governments and academics, there is no universally accepted definition of job quality. Instead, analyses typically proceed by focusing on one or a number of components of what might comprise job quality and for which data sets already exist. The scenarios above highlight the reliance on pay and skill in many accounts, and this approach is not unusual (Clark, 2005). However, the scenarios also hint at other potential components of job quality. These components include labour contract type, job security, training and progression opportunities, employee voice and social dialogue, job satisfaction, work organization generally and task discretion particularly, management style and fairness at work, working hours flexibility specifically and work–life balance generally (variously, for example, Coats 2009; Gallie, 2007; Gautié and Schmitt, 2010; Green, 2006; Kalleberg, 2011; Smith et al.2008; Tilly, 1997). Enveloping these markers is an over-arching debate over whether job quality should be measured by job or worker characteristics, objective or subjective measures (Gallie, 2007). A recent addition to this debate is the configuration of good and bad jobs by geography. The varieties of capitalism approach, whilst primarily seeking to differentiate and categorize countries – articulated usually as those with co-ordinated market economies or liberal market economies – also, at least implicitly, assumes that jobs within one of these types – the coordinated market economies – are better than in the others (Crouch, 2009). This assumption is borne out by Green's (2006) analysis. However, good jobs and bad jobs can and do co-exist within the same economy type (even within occupations) and in different regions of the same country, as Green (2009) demonstrates with the UK. Regional differences shape not just average job quality, but also the contours of *inequality* in job quality (McCall, 2001).

Within this debate, academics have a disciplinary bent. Economists prioritize pay and sometimes skill; sociologists focus on skill (and related work and management practices such as autonomy and discretion) and more recently job security (Kalleberg, 2011; Kalleberg et al., 2000) and work–life balance (Kelliher and Anderson, 2008). Psychologists focus on job satisfaction and commitment and, more recently, well-being and happiness (Warr and Clapperton, 2009). Political scientists and geographers emphasize the cross-national and cross-regional distribution of job quality (Crouch, 2009; Green, 2009). This debate on how best to analyse job quality is important. Despite the emphasis on it, data on what workers consider a good job reveal that pay is not the priority. Using two proxy measures of job quality – workers' commitment to their job and the attributes of those jobs (the latter distinguished by extrinsic and intrinsic attributes), Sutherland (2011) shows that, in order of preference, workers most value work that is enjoyable, has job security, provides opportunity to use their abilities, has good social relations in production and allows them to use their initiative. Pay ranks only seventh. These findings are aggregated; a breakdown reveals that women more than men value work with convenient hours or hours that they can choose, that highly qualified workers want jobs that allow them to use their initiative and use their abilities, and that workers with dependent children place more emphasis on pay. This later emphasis is picked up by Pocock and Skinner (Chapter 4). They point out that, although objective minimum standards are required, particularly for casual workers in Australia, what constitutes a good job can vary subjectively by personal circumstance. They argue analysis of job quality requires a new framework, one based on workplace, industry, relevant institutions and wider social contexts plus awareness that what constitutes a good job may change over a workers' life stage.

In addition to identifying and analysing the components of job quality, a key issue implicitly raised by Pocock and Skinner is the standard against which job quality is measured. Absolute standards (such as 'decent work') have some appeal; although in order to generate consensus, they tend to be set low. Further, on closer examination what may appear at face value as an absolute standard can contain relative elements. For example, in the ILO's 'decent work' discourse there is a welcome demand for the banning of child labour but definitions of a 'child' may be contested.

Moreover, sociological and social psychological evidence suggests that beyond a minimum level of job quality, relative rather than absolute assessments of job quality are most salient to people. Highlighting the importance of relative quality, Álvarez-Galván (Chapter 10) examines the apparent paradox that workers in 'bad' call centre jobs in Mexico like their jobs, whereas those in 'good' call centre jobs do not: the explanation lies in the reference point to which they are comparing these jobs. However, there are varied dimensions of relativity: comparisons can be made relative to other jobs and economic alternatives, relative to other life circumstances and stages, relative to past job quality and relative to job quality in other countries. The latter emphasizes the need for international analyses of job quality which recognizes dynamism in the global economy. Job quality can be 'read' differently in different countries at different times. Consider, for example, contemporary China in relation to the US or UK. In China, rural-to-urban migrants begin by comparing jobs to even worse rural alternatives but over time shift the focus of their comparison to their urban peers, leading to different evaluations and expectations of job quality, in this case contributing to the mid-2010 manufacturing strike wave (Piore, 1979; Kennedy and Tilly, 2010). Moreover, because of the participation of companies and countries in global value chains, job quality comparisons (particularly in relation to wages and therefore production costs) become international. In China's case, Chinese labour costs are constantly being compared with those in richer countries ('Is China taking our jobs?') and poorer countries ('Will Vietnam and Bangladesh take China's jobs?').

Similarly, even in the richer countries such as the US and UK, workers make intra-country comparisons with other occupations and over time. Bad jobs look particularly bad in the context of extraordinarily high compensation for managers, bankers and entertainers, and in context of increasing shares of national income going to property income (Toynbee and Walker, 2008). Moreover, there is a strong sense that the quality of bad jobs is worsening over time. As Aubenas (2011) points out in her account of bad jobs in France, these jobs were indeed bad before the current economic downturn but have become considerably worse.

Are bad jobs inevitable?

The co-editors of this volume share the view that disparities among jobs, between so-called bad jobs and the rest, are too large and can be reduced. Given the evidence of worsening job quality in a number of industries and occupations, this section examines the forces that have contributed to eroding the quality of entry- and mid-level jobs. It then goes on to explore avenues for counteracting these forces or remedying the impacts on workers.

What forces are driving changes in jobs, particularly the worsening of jobs?

Three sets of inter-related trends of the past 30 years have undermined job quality. First, in a number of industries, business strategy has essentially shifted to labour cost cutting as a primary competitive strategy. Coupled with this emphasis, firms have reorganized production processes in ways that rely more readily on international supply chains, inter-firm subcontracting, and externalization of some workforces to the end of saving on production costs. Concurrent with these changes, greater penetration of financial actors in firm ownership and finances ('financialization') has generated particular incentives – for example, leveraged buy-outs have inserted great pressure on management to yield high and growing net earnings and shortened the time horizon for management decisions (Batt and Appelbaum, 2010). Second, many of these practices have thrived in a neo-liberal policy environment favouring deregulation of industries and reduction of labour standards protection. Third, pressure on systems has come from more proximate wage competition due to the increased ease of implementation of off-shore production. The intent in analysing these trends is not to argue that jobs have on average become worse but to understand the dynamics that underlie situations in which jobs at lower and middle levels *have* become worse.

Firstly, in industries where job quality has been of concern – often, but not exclusively, labour-intensive industries – the most proximate cause for quality erosion has been changes in labour deployment strategies. Firms have chosen labour strategies, ostensibly to match product market strategies, that emphasize cost cutting, with labour costs reductions expected to support other cost savings achieved through productive efficiency gains. These cost cutting strategies in turn have been further enabled by the choices underpinning the implementation of new technologies, particularly information technologies, that facilitate off-shoring of manufacturing and some services (by facilitating long distance coordination) (Appelbaum et al., 2008). Rothstein's study (Chapter 8) of the downward arc of automotive assembly jobs includes all of these elements.

Additionally, in domestic service industries, firms have implemented information technology in ways that decrease the task autonomy of workers while increasing their responsibility for outcomes, as has been the case with banking and insurance workers (e.g. Adler, 1986; Appelbaum and Albin, 1989). In many industries, management has exhibited a predilection towards maintaining, or reinforcing, habits regarding job design that limit autonomy. Contributions to this volume by Álvarez-Galván (Chapter 10) and Lambert and Henly (Chapter 9) depict cases in point, low end call centre work and retail sales. This pattern of control occurs even in industries where the prevailing competitive strategy is not simply cost cutting but entails competing on product or service quality (Bailey and Bernhardt, 1998; Putton et al. 2008). In this regard, broad groups of entry- and mid-level workers, not solely those with the worst jobs, may have experienced job worsening.

A number of factors have enabled or facilitated these changes within firms: changes in job structures and altered power relations. Traditional avenues for pay progression and job improvement over the work careers that consisted of job ladders within firms have significantly weakened (Cappelli et al., 1997; Osterman, 1996). Employers have greater ability to recruit from outside the firm for intermediate positions. With this pattern of recruitment, entry level jobs are severed from paths of internal promotion and remain low quality. In most countries, the shift to mid-level recruitment from outside has been made possible by the increased availability of credentialed workers and, to some extent, the spread of generic skills (tied to widely used information technologies) that facilitates lateral mobility of mid-level workers (Hartmann, 1987). The decreased emphasis on firm-specific knowledge (Cappelli et al., 1997; Hunter et al., 2001) has played a role in this altered hiring and promotion pattern though it is hard to tell whether this emphasis is inevitable or itself a product of the choice of labour strategy. In industries that do not entail face-to-face contact to deliver the product, even mid-level jobs can be outsourced domestically or off-shored and are thus subject to wage pressure.

At the same time, within firms and industries, worker organizations have lost substantial bargaining power over compensation and job design; again, Rothstein's account of an auto industry once dominated by a mighty union in the US is apposite. This power shift from labour to management has consequences at the firm level and, as discussed below, at the policy level as well. The loss of power of worker organizations is driven by several factors: forces described above, as well as increased geographical mobility of capital within and across national borders. Within national borders, firms may choose to move to regions with low unionization rates or threaten to do so. Flexibility in the location of production is significant for manufacturing, e.g in the auto industry as seen in Rothstein's chapter (Chapter 8) and financial services (banking, insurance, telecommunications, as in the outsourced call centre functions Ávarez-Galván describes (Chapter 10), but is quite limited in the case of in-person services industries. Also, labour bargaining power is weakened by labour market conditions themselves as a result of changes in the geographical distribution of production. In parts of Western Europe, for example, persistent high unemployment and underemployment, particularly among recent labour force entrants, have undermined workers' individual and collective power.

Within each industry, patterns of labour use have spread through dynamics of their own. Labour cost cutting competitive strategies can spread and average job quality may worsen as a result. Spread occurs primarily through price competition: witness the spread of labour cost cutting practices in the food retail sector as a result of the expansion of large chains such as Tesco and Walmart. Importantly, practices that lead to debased job design and low compensation may spread within industries through the adoption of 'standards of practice' by management.

A second trend feeding the worsening of jobs is that, beyond within-sector management practices, changes have taken place in national institutional environments that render easier the spread of cost cutting practices across sectors, with damaging impacts on job quality. (The contributions in Gautié and Schmitt (2010) illustrate how some industries take the lead in low-wage practices that are the 'wedges' in jettisoning practices and standards in other industries.) While the present discussion summarizes these trends schematically, cross-national differences in institutional environments and in interactions between state and market spheres must be borne in mind. The extent of bad jobs and their characteristics depend upon national and regional institutional contexts as well. For example, countries differ greatly in the extent of regulation of a floor of wage and working conditions (an issue spotlighted by Theodore et al. in Chapter 13), of collective bargaining coverage and comprehensiveness of vocational and skill training systems. Additionally, countries differ in the extent to which work organization and design are subjects of collective bargaining. Here, the goal is to identify broad trends that have affected all advanced economies but have been more marked in some countries than others, partly due to these cross-national differences in national models (Gallie, 2007; Gautié and Schmitt, 2010).

What societal and institutional forces have enabled the spread and adoption of strategies that result in 'bad' jobs? An overarching factor has been a progressive loss of interest in a redistributive agenda and a social agenda for policy as well as a reduced sense of social responsibility among leading employers. It is difficult to tell whether this loss of interest is the cause or effect of other changes. Nevertheless, it is related in part to changed power relationships in societies, most notably the loss of union power at the national level, itself another dimension of the diminished role of unions at the workplace level in some countries as well as the reduced share of (heavily unionized) manufacturing in total employment. In the policy arena, this shift is often characterized as neo-liberalism (Gentile, 2011; Harvey, 2005). The ability of unions and other pro-worker organizations to maintain the value of minimum wages, to forestall deregulatory policy moves (youth sub minimum wages or marginal/'mini' jobs operating under different social contribution regimes or nonstandard contracts) and to support training and job creation policies has decreased. A pro-worker agenda is harder to push forward in national environments where state–employer relationships are being re-negotiated and where tri-partite (corporatist) frameworks for policy making are losing legitimacy or simply losing relevance and impact. In one example, Thomas (Chapter 14) shows how governments in the Canadian province of Ontario progressively loosened labour standards in the name of 'efficiency'. Related policy changes extend as well to more macroeconomic policies, so-called free trade agreements, or even foreign exchange policies that affect the price of exports thereby affecting market opportunities for particular sectors (particularly manufacturing), with further consequences for managerial decisions regarding job quality.

Bad jobs have also persisted because firms have been able to externalize some of the costs of bad jobs and shifted them to other parts of the socio-economic system. For example, low-wage workers may access income support programmes to make up for budget shortfalls. Osterman in Chapter 3 notes that even those sympathetic to the needs of workers in the US tend to emphasize the Earned Income Tax Credit – an income supplement – rather than policy directed at improving jobs themselves, a point Toynbee (2003) made about the last New Labour Government in the UK.

Also contributing to a policy environment where the generation of bad jobs is not perceived as a policy problem is the reduction in government's role as an employer, thus diminishing its opportunities to play the role of a trend setter for employment practices and policies as it has historically done in many countries. Fiscal pressures have affected jobs in public organizations, government agencies as well as para-public institutions such as hospitals or public utilities. Munro (Chapter 11) examines the trajectory of government's initiatives to change – or not – the nature of hospital cleaning jobs in the UK and the impact of such changes on the quality of cleaning jobs.

National and regional institutional environments may also enable the spread of bad job strategies by facilitating the migration of practices from one industry to others. 'Race to the bottom' strategies that are enabled by weak worker organization also weaken action to reinforce labour standards, to advocate for workforce training and to put pressure on firms to invest in workforce training and career ladder development.

A third and often mentioned source of downward pressure on job quality has been what some see as the virtual expansion of labour markets due to European integration and the opening of Eastern Europe as well as China and India to global markets. Workforces may travel more easily and directly compete for jobs with each other or may compete indirectly by being involved in cross-border production processes that enable firms to achieve cost savings through wage competition (Freeman, 2006). Actual relocation, or even a threat of relocation, can discourage worker organization, as Bronfenbrenner (2000) notes, and trigger wage pressure. This pressure can affect jobs at all levels. Effects may include a worsening of existing bad jobs or an increase in the number of bad jobs. Exactly how these pressures will play out and affect labour markets is still the subject for industry- and occupation-specific research.

How could bad jobs get better?

The three sets of reasons for worsening jobs also point to three possible leverage points for improving job quality: 'high road' business strategy, shifts in the institutional incentive structure and global regulatory approaches. However, before examining these three avenues, it is necessary to examine a stumbling block to improving jobs: the notion of a 'quality–quantity trade off', meaning that any attempt to raise labour standards will lead to decreases in the quantity of employment, or at least of formal employment.

The quality–quantity trade-off is underpinned by the neoclassical economic propositions that workers get pay equal to their productivity, that the configuration of technology and skills determine productivity levels, and that actions raising unit labour costs above productivity will induce employers to either scale back employment (shedding less productive workers) or evade the raised labour standards by moving into the informal economy. This argument is deployed against minimum wages, unionization and a variety of other worker protections. Perhaps its most notable exposition was the OECD *Jobs Study* (1994), which casts a long shadow over job quality discussions to this day. However, much research has challenged the *Jobs Study* directly (Howell et al. 2007; Bradley and Stevens, 2007), as well as presenting evidence that particular labour standards have little or no negative employment impact (Card and Krueger, 1995; Galli and Kucera, 2008). Indeed, within this volume, Paul Osterman (Chapter 3) mounts a spirited critique of the quality–quantity trade-off and Antón et al. (Chapter 2) show that, within Europe, job quality is positively correlated with employment levels. Overall, the evidence could be summarized as demonstrating that quite a bit of variation in labour standards and institutions is possible with little or no negative effect (and in some cases, it appears, with positive effect) on the quantity of formal jobs.

So what of the three avenues for improving bad jobs? Regarding business strategy, many argue that firms can follow a 'high road' that involves simultaneously improving worker jobs and achieving higher quality and innovation, so that the two processes reinforce each other (Appelbaum and Batt, 1994; Appelbaum et al., 2000; Best, 1990, Lazonick, 1991; Schuler and Jackson, 1987). In this view, diffusing knowledge of high road strategies is in itself an important strategy for better jobs. However, some research suggests that the connection between business strategy and human resource strategy is tighter in manufacturing than in services (Bailey and Bernhardt, 1997; Dutton et al., 2008; Lloyd, 2005) – and of course, at least in the richer countries, service jobs make up the majority of jobs and include a disproportionate share of bad jobs (as Antón et al. document in Chapter 2). Moreover, most high road advocates acknowledge that it is necessary to 'block off the low road' through regulatory measures in addition to 'paving the high road' (Wright and Rogers, 2010, ch. 9).

In this volume, several authors cast a critical eye on high road possibilities. Dill et al. are most sanguine, describing how US health care employers have constructed career ladders offering upward mobility in order to motivate and retain their employees. Munro also examines a health care case (hospital cleaners in the UK), but find a tension between cost-cutting and career path creation. Lambert and Henly, studying a single US retailer, offer evidence that when managers use their limited discretionary power to offer more liveable work schedules, it pays off in reduced employee turnover. Huzzard, contrasting two Swedish automotive suppliers, notes the importance of corporate governance, and specifically 'patient capital', in making high road human resource strategies feasible. Finally Rothstein, comparing auto assembly plants in the US and Mexico, not only explores the downside of employee involvement but also shows that even within the same company and production system, the meaning and implementation of employee involvement can take entirely distinct forms depending on historical and institutional context.

Institutional carrots and sticks represent a second possible avenue towards better jobs. The emphasis here is precisely on paving the high road and closing off the low road. Paving the high road can include strengthening workforce training and retraining (Ashton et al., 2000), and providing assistance for technological or business system upgrading, especially for smaller or informal businesses (Lal, 2008; Tendler, 2002). Closing off the low road, most fundamentally, means setting and enforcing a floor on employment conditions, as Fine and Gordon, Pocock and Skinner, Thomas and Theodore et al. emphasize in this volume. But it can also extend beyond the workplace proper to include rebuilding a social safety net (Standing, 2004) and providing added supports in the reproductive sphere to enable those with unpaid care work and family responsibilities to more effectively negotiate the interface between work and home life (Wagner, 2005); Lambert and Henly's contribution to this volume (Chapter 9) demonstrates how important this interface is to workers, but also to business outcomes. Blocking the low road can also include policies in the market for goods and services, directing competition towards channels other than pure price competition (Askenazy et al. forthcoming; Gautié and Schmitt, 2010).

Although this list of institutional levers has spotlighted state action, worker organizations also play a critically important role in both facilitating the high road and obstructing the low road. Thus innovative labour strategies, especially those that reach marginal, informal and hard-to-organize workers, are part of the prescription for better jobs (Eade and Leather, 2005; Milkman et al., 2010; Silver, 2003). Trades unions and other worker organizations do not loom large in the current volume, perhaps a reflection of their diminished clout. Indeed, Rothstein depicts an autoworkers' union wielding precious little power in the face of competitive threats and the reorganization of production. Nonetheless Carré and Tilly, Huzzard and Pocock and Skinner posit the continuing importance of unions and Thomas's account of legislated employment standards points to the importance of organized labour as an advocate for high road policies.

Importantly, these policy tools can be most effective in combination. To this point, Keep and James (Chapter 15) argue that investing in skills alone has not and cannot substantively change the nature of jobs; rather, what they call 'a multi-level suite of policy interventions' is required – a point amplified by Pocock and Skinner (Chapter 4).

Turning to the third avenue for improving jobs, global labour regulation in many ways reprises the options just discussed, though on the less familiar terrain of the global economy. Backer (2008) and others have pointed to the growing importance of private regulatory channels, such as corporate codes of conduct or fair trade labelling. Bronfenbrenner (2007) highlights the impact of global unions and labour alliances. The ILO (e.g. ILO 1998) has stressed the adoption by states of universal principles, especially the so-called core labour standards. Some observers (Evans, 2010; Hepple, 2005) descry in this accumulating patchwork of regulatory elements the potential for a more comprehensive and powerful global framework for boosting job quality. Rothstein's analysis of the transnational auto industry (Chapter 8) points to the need to develop such a comprehensive framework.

A relevant question about these avenues for improving bad jobs is, will any of them actually happen? This is a difficult question to answer from the cool detachment of social science observation. The viability of these options is largely a matter of political and managerial will as well as the organizing ingenuity and persistence of worker organizations and other progressive forces. What *can* be stated is that these options are real possibilities.

The book before you

This volume explores the inevitability – or not – of bad jobs empirically. Part I, 'International Overviews and Comparative Approaches', starts with reviews of job quality issues in the EU (Antón, Fernández-Macías and Muñoz de Bustillo), the US (Osterman) and Australia (Pocock and Skinner). All three chapters make comparisons: Antón et al. compare two dozen EU countries, while Osterman and Pocock and Skinner contrast their subject countries with other OECD members. Carré and Tilly close the section with a conceptual framework for cross-national comparative analysis of determinants of job quality.

Part II, 'Influences on Job Quality: Sectoral Approaches and Workplace Practices', presents a kaleidoscopic collection of case studies of bad jobs in particular industries and countries. The chapters encompass a broad range of industries. Huzzard and Rothstein scrutinize automotive manufacturing – Huzzard in Sweden, Rothstein in the US and Mexico. Lambert and Henly examine retail in the US. Álvarez-Galván draws contrasts among call centre jobs in Mexico. Munro, along with Dill, Morgan and Kalleberg, investigates health care jobs in the UK and the US respectively. These rich case studies analyse why some jobs are better or worse than others despite similar job content and settings. They emphasize the variability of business human resource strategies.

Part III, 'Influences on Job Quality: The Role of Public Agency', spotlights the state's role in assuring or undermining job quality. James and Keep and Theodore, Bernhardt and DeFilippis (plus co-authors) point to the problems that arise when states set labour standards too low or fail to enforce them. Finally, Thomas as well as Fine and Gordon look at ways that local and regional authorities and national states can more effectively regulate job terms and conditions.

Are bad jobs inevitable? The evidence in this volume suggests that they are not. Particular business strategies, particular market ground rules and particular public policies can make many bad jobs better. This research makes a strong case that, though it is not easy to improve bad jobs, it can be done.

Note

1 For an overview of the UK government's approach see http://www.makingbadjobsbetter.org.uk

REFERENCES

Adler, P. S. (1986) 'New Technologies, New Skills', *California Management Review*, 29:1, 9–29.

Appelbaum E. and Albin P. (1989) 'Computer Rationalization and the Transformation of Work: Lessons from the Insurance Industry', in S. Wood (ed.) *The Transformation of Work? Skill Flexibility and the Labour Process*, London: Unwin Hyman Ltd, pp. 247–265.

Appelbaum, E. and Batt, R. (1994) *The New American Workplace: Transforming Work Systems in the United States*, Ithaca, NY: Cornell University Press.

Appelbaum, E., Bernhardt, A. and Murnane, R. J. (eds) (2003) *Low-wage Work in America*, New York: Russell Sage Foundation.

▶
Ashton, D., Sung, J. and Turbin, J. (2000) 'Towards a Framework for the Comparative Analysis of National Systems of Skill Formation', *International Journal of Training and Development*, 4:1, 8–25.
Askenazy, P., Berry, J-B., Carré, F., Prunier-Poulmaire, S. and Tilly, C. (forthcoming) 'Working in Large Retailers: A US-France Comparison', *Work, Employment and Society*.
Aubenas, F. (2011) *The Night Cleaner*, Cambridge: Polity.
Bailey, T. R. and Bernhardt, A. (1997) 'In Search of the High Road in a Low-wage Industry', *Politics and Society*, 25:2, 179–201.
Bartik, T. J. and Houseman, S. N. (eds) (2008) *A Future of Good Jobs?* Kalamazoo, MI: Upjohn Institute.
Batt, R. and Appelbaum, E. (2010) 'Globalization, New Financial Actors, and Institutional Change: Reflections on the Legacy of LEST.' 40th Anniversary Conference. Laboratoire d'Economie et de Sociologie du Travail, Centre National de La Recherche Scientifique (LEST, CNRS), Aix-en-Provence, U. of Marseille, France. May 27–28.
Bazen, S., C. Lucifora and W. Salverda (eds) (2005) *Job Quality and Employer Behaviour*, Basingstoke: Palgrave Macmillan.
Beirne, M. (2008) 'Idealism and the Applied Relevance of Research on Employee Participation', *Work, Employment and Society*, 22:4, 675–693.
Beirne, M., Ramsay, H. and Panteli, N. (1998) 'Developments in Computing Work: Control and Contradiction in the Software Labour Process', in P. Thompson and C. Warhurst (eds) *Workplaces of the Future*, London: Palgrave Macmillan, pp. 142–162.
Bell, D. (1973) *The Coming of Post-Industrial Society*, New York: Basic Books.
Best, M. (1990) *The New Competition: Institutions of Industrial Restructuring*, Cambridge, MA: Harvard University Press.
Bradley, D. H. and Stevens, J. D. (2007) 'Employment Performance in OECD Countries: A Test of Neo-Liberal and Institutionalist Hypotheses', *Comparative Political Studies*, 40:12, 1486–1510.
Braverman, H. (1974) *Labor and Monopoly Capital*, New York: Monthly Review Press.
Bronfenbrenner, K. (2007) *Global Unions: Challenging Transnational Capital through Cross-Border Campaigns*, Ithaca, NY: Cornell University Press.
Bronfenbrenner, K. (2007) 'Uneasy Terrain: The Impact of Capital Mobility on Workers, Wages, and Union Organizing'. Submitted to the U.S. Trade Deficit Review Commission. September 6.
Brookings Institution (2007) 'Better Workers for Better Jobs: Improving Worker Advancement in the Low-Wage Labor Market', Brookings Institution Policy Brief No 2007–15.
Booth, A. and Snower, D. J. (1996) 'The Low-Skill, Bad-Job Trap', in D. J. Snower and A. Booth (eds) *Acquiring Skills*, Cambridge: Cambridge University Press, pp. 109–124.
Cappelli, P., Bassi, L., Katz, H., Knoke, D., Osterman, P., and Useem, M. (1997) *Change at Work*, New York: Oxford University Press.
▶

▶

Card, D. and Krueger, A. (1995) *Myth and Measurement: The New Economics of the Minimum Wage*, Princeton: Princeton University Press.

Clark, A. (2005) 'What Makes a Good Job? Evidence from OECD Countries', in S. Bazen, C. Lucifora, C. and W. Salverda, W. (eds) *Job Quality and Employer Behaviour*, Houndmills: Palgrave Macmillan, pp. 11–30.

Coats, D. (2009) 'The Sunlit Uplands or Bleak House? Just How Good are Today's Workplaces?' in S. C. Bolton and M. Houlihan (eds) *Work Matters*, London: Palgrave Macmillan, pp. 21–37.

Crouch, C. (2009) 'Typologies of Capitalism', in B. Hanké (ed.) *Debating Varieties of Capitalism*, Oxford: Oxford University Press, pp. 75–94.

Crouch, C., Finegold, D. and Sako, M. (1999) *Are Skills the Answer?* Oxford: Oxford University Press.

Darr, A. and Warhurst, C. (2008) 'Assumptions, Assertions and the Need for Evidence: Debugging Debates about Knowledge Workers', *Current Sociology*, 56:1, 25–45.

Davis, L. E. and Cherns, A. B. (1975) *The Quality of Working Life*, New York: Free Press.

Dutton, E., C. Warhurst, C. Lloyd, S. James, J. Commander and D. Nickson (2008) 'Just Like the Elves in Harry Potter: Room Attendants in UK Hotels', in C. Lloyd, G. Mason and K. Mayhew (eds) *Low Wage Work in the UK*, New York: Russell Sage Foundation, pp. 96–130.

Eade, D. and Leather, A. (eds) (2005) *Development NGOs and Labor Unions: Terms of Engagement*, Bloomfield, CT: Kumarian Press.

Ehrenreich, B. (2001) *Nickel and Dimed*, New York: Metropolitan Books.

Eikhof, D. R. and Warhurst, C. (2010) 'The Creative Industries: You Don't Have to Be Male, White and Middle Class to Work Here – But It Helps', *Work, Employment and Society Conference*, University of Brighton, UK.

Evans, P. (2010) 'Is It Labor's Turn to Globalize? Twenty-First Century Opportunities and Strategic Responses', *Global Labour Journal*, 1:3, 352–379.

Felstead, A., Gallie, D., Green, F. and Zhou, Y (2007) *Skills at Work, 1986 to 2006*, ESRC Centre on Skills, Knowledge and Organisational Performance: Universities of Oxford and Cardiff.

Florida, R. (2002) *The Rise of the Creative Class*, New York: Basic Books.

Florida, R. (2005) *Cities and the Creative Class*, New York: Routledge.

Freeman, R. (2006) 'The Great Doubling: The Challenge of the New Global Labour Market'. U.C. Berkeley lecture. August, http://emlab.berkeley.edu/users/webfac/eichengreen/e183_sp07/great_doub.pdf

Galli, R. and Kucera, D. (2008) 'Labour Standards and Informal Employment in Latin America', in J. Berg and D. Kucera (eds) *In Defence of Labour Market Institutions: Cultivating Justice in the Developing World*, New York: Palgrave Macmillan, pp. 192–217.

Gallie, D. (ed.) (2007) *Employment Regimes and the Quality of Work*, Oxford: Oxford University Press.

Gautié, J. and Schmitt, J. (2010) (eds) *Low Wage Work in the Wealthy World*, New York: Russell Sage Foundation.

▶

Gentile, A. (2011) 'Party Governments, US Hegemony, and a Tale of Two Tillys' Weberian State', in M. Hanagan and C. Tilly (eds) *Contention and Trust in Cities and States*, Amsterdam: Springer, pp. 149–168.

Glyn, A. (2006) *Capitalism Unleashed*, Oxford: Oxford University Press.

Goos, M. and Manning, A. (2007) 'Lousy and Lovely Jobs: The Rising Polarization of Work in Britain', *Review of Economics and Statistics*, 89:1, 118–133.

Goulden, C. (2010) *Cycle of Poverty, Unemployment and Low Pay*, York: Joseph Rowntree Foundation.

Green, A. (2009) *Geography Matters: The Importance of Sub-National Perspectives on Employment And Skills*, Praxis no. 2, UKCES: Wath-upon-Dearne.

Green, F. (2006) *Demanding Work*, Woodstock: Princeton University Press.

Grimshaw, D., Lloyd, C. and Warhurst, C. (2008) 'Low Wage Work in the UK: A Synthesis of Findings, the Institutional Effects and Policy Responses', in C. Lloyd, G. Mason and K. Mayhew (eds) *Low Wage Work in the UK*, New York: Russell Sage Foundation, pp. 284–326.

Hackman, J. R., Oldham, G. R., Janson, R. and Purdy, K. (1975) 'A New Strategy for Job Enrichment', *California Management Review*, 17:4: 57–71.

Hartmann, H. (1987) (ed.) *Computer Chips and Paper Clips*, vol. 2, Washington, DC: National Academy Press.

Harvey, D. (2005) *A Brief History of Neoliberalism*, Oxford: Oxford University Press.

Hepple, B. (2005) *Labour Laws and Global Trade*, Portland, OR: Hart Publishing.

Holmes, C. (2011) 'Implications of Polarisation for UK Policymakers, *SKOPE Issues Paper 26*, Universities of Oxford and Cardiff.

Howell, D. R., Baker, D., Glyn, A. and Schmitt, J. (2007) 'Are Protective Labor Market Institutions at the Root Of Unemployment? A Critical Review of the Evidence', *Capitalism and Society*, 2:1, 1–71.

Hunter, L., Bernhardt, A., Hughes, K. L. and Skuratowicz, E. (2001) 'It's Not Just The ATMs: Technology, Firm Strategies, Jobs, and Earnings in Retail Banking', *Industrial and Labor Relations Review*, 54:2A, 402–424.

International Labour Organization (ILO) (1998) *ILO Declaration on Fundamental Principles and Rights at Work*, http://www.ilo.org/declaration/thedeclaration/textdeclaration/lang--en/index.htm, accessed 9 September 2011.

Kalleberg, A (2011) *Good Jobs, Bad Jobs: The Rise of Polarized and Precarious Employment Systems in the United States, 1970s to 2000s*, New York: Russell Sage Foundation.

Kalleberg, A. L., Reskin, B. and Hudson, K. (2000) 'Bad Jobs in America: Standard and Nonstandard Employment Relations and Job Quality in the United States', *American Sociological Review* 65:2, 256–278.

Keep, E. (2000) *Upskilling Scotland – A New Horizon Report*, Edinburgh: Centre for Scottish Public Policy.

Kelliher C. and Anderson D. (2008) 'For Better or for Worse? An Analysis of How Flexible Working Practices Influence Employees' Perceptions of Job Quality', *International Journal of Human Resource Management*, 19:3, 419–431.

▶
Kennedy, M. and Tilly, C. (2010) 'On Strike in China', *Dollars and Sense* 290, 19–23.

Kenway, P. (2008) *Addressing In-Work Poverty,* York: Joseph Rowntree Foundation.

Kerr, C., Dunlop, J. T., Harbison, F. H. and Meyers, C. A. (1960) *Industrialism and Industrial Man*, Cambridge, MA: Harvard University Press.

Kitay, J. (1997) 'The Labour Process: Still Stuck? Still a Perspective? Still Useful?' *Electronic Journal of Radical Organisation Theory*, 3:1, 1–10.

Lal, R. (2008) 'Macroeconomic Policies to Address Informality: A Two-Pronged Strategy to Foster Dynamic Transformations that Reduce Informality' *IDS Bulletin*, 39:2, 120–129.

Lawton, K. and Cooke, G. (2008) *Working Out of Poverty: A Study of the Low-Paid and the 'Working Poor'*, London: IPPR.

Lazonick, W. (1991) *Business Organization and the Myth of the Market Economy*, Cambridge: Cambridge University Press.

Levy, F. and Murnane, R.J. (2004) *The New Division of Labor*, New York: Russell Sage Foundation.

Lloyd, C. (2005) 'Competitive Strategy and Skill in the Fitness Industry', *Human Resource Management Journal*, 15:2, 15–34.

Lloyd, C. and Payne, J. (2004) 'The Political Economy of Skill: A Theoretical Approach to Developing a High Skills Economy in the UK', in C. Warhurst, E. Keep and I. Grugulis (eds) *The Skills That Matter*, London: Palgrave Macmillan, pp. 207–225.

McCall, L. (2001) *Complex Inequality: Gender, Class and Race in the New Economy*, New York: Routledge.

Mason, G. and Salverda, W. (2010) 'Low Pay, Working Conditions and Living Standards', in J. Gautié, J. and J. Schmitt (2010) (eds) *Low-Wage Work in the Wealthy World*, New York: Russell Sage Foundation, pp. 35–90.

Metcalf, D. (2007) *Why Has the British National Minimum Wage Had Little or No Effect on Employment?* Centre for Economic Performance, London School of Economics.

Milkman, R., Bloom, J. and Narro, V. (eds) (2010) *Working for Justice: The L.A. Model of Organizing and Advocacy*, Ithaca, NY: Cornell University Press.

Mills, C. W. (1951) *White Collar*, Oxford: Oxford University Press.

Organisation for Economic Cooperation and Development (OECD) (1994) *OECD Jobs Study*, http://www.oecd.org/dataoecd/42/51/1941679.pdf . Accessed 7 September 2011.

Osterman, P. (1996) *Broken Ladders: Managerial Careers in the New Economy*, New York: Oxford University Press.

Osterman, P. (2008) 'Improving the Quality of Low-Wage Work: The Current American Experience', *International Labour Review*, 147:2–3, 115–134.

Piore, M. J. (1979) *Birds of Passage: Migrant Labor and Industrial Societies*, New York: Cambridge University Press.

Plunkett, J. (2011) *Growth without Gain? The Faltering Living Standards of People on Low-Middle- Incomes*, London: Resolution Foundation.
▶

▶

Reich, R. (1993) *The Work of Nations*, London: Simon and Schuster.

Sassen, S (2001) *The Global City : New York, London, Tokyo* (2nd edn) Princeton: Princeton University Press.

Schuler, R. and Jackson, S. (1987) 'Linking Competitive Strategies and Human Resource Management Practices', *Academy of Management Executive*, 1:3, 207–219.

Silver, B. (2003) *Forces of Labor: Workers' Movements and Globalization Since 1870*, Cambridge: Cambridge University Press.

Standing, G. (ed.) (2004) *Promoting Income Security as a Right: Europe and North America*, London: Anthem Press.

Stewart, H. (2011) 'Quantitative Easing "Contributes to Social Unrest"', *Observer*, 14 August, p. 40.

Sutherland, J. (2011) 'What Makes a Good Job?' *Spotlight*, Skills Development Scotland, available at http://www.skillsdevelopmentscotland.co.uk/media/374613/spotlightarticlemay2011.pdf

Tendler, J. (2002) 'Small Firms, the Informal Sector, and the "Devil's Deal"', *Institute for Development Studies Bulletin* (University of Sussex), 33:3, 98–104.

Thompson, P. and Smith, C. (2010) *Working Life*, London: Palgrave Macmillan.

Tilly, C. (1997) 'Arresting the Decline of Good Jobs in the USA?' *Industrial Relations Journal*, 28:4, 269–274.

Toynbee, P. (2003) *Hard Work*, London: Bloomsbury.

Toynbee, P. and Walker, D. (2008) *Unjust Rewards*, London: Granta.

Wagner, A. (2005) 'Services and the Employment Prospects for Women', in G. Bosch and S. Lehndorff, *Working in the Service Sector: A Tale from Different Worlds*, New York: Routledge, pp. 103–130.

Warhurst, C. (2008) 'The Knowledge Economy, Skills and Government Labour Market Intervention', *Policy Studies*, 29:1, 71–86.

Warr, P. and Clapperton, G. (2009) *The Joy of Work?* London: Routledge.

Wright, E. and Dwyer, R. (2006) 'The Pattern of Job Expansion in the USA', in G. Wood and P. James (eds) *Institutions, Production and Working Life*, Oxford: Oxford University Press.

Wright, E. O. and Rogers, J. (2010) *American Society: How It Actually Works*, New York: W.W. Norton.

PART

I

International Overviews and Comparative Approaches

CHAPTER 2

Identifying Bad Jobs across Europe

José-Ignacio Antón, Enrique Fernández-Macías and Rafael Muñoz de Bustillo

Introduction

Given the importance of job quality, it is surprising that there is relatively little focus on it in academic and economic policy debate. While there is fairly comprehensive and almost real-time information on the number of jobs created and disappearing, much less is known on the attributes of these jobs. While there is concern over job quality, especially in those jobs at the bottom of the wage distribution (Lucifora and Salverda, 1998; Bazen et al., 1998; Marx and Salverda, 2005; Lucifora et al., 2005; Muñoz de Bustillo and Antón, 2007; Eurofound, 2010; Gautié and Schmitt, 2010; Grimshaw, 2011) beyond wages, understanding of these jobs is very limited.

Jobs represent much more than money – wages are not even the attribute of work most valued by workers (Clark, 2005). However job quality, understood from a multidimensional perspective comprising not only earnings but other conditions of work and employment, has received much less attention. In this respect, government initiatives for measuring job quality have been remarkably absent, while academia and some international organizations – particularly the International Labour Organization – have attempted to develop different indicators (for an review of existing proposals, see Muñoz de Bustillo et al. 2011a). Unfortunately, because it is still an immature field, there is no consensus on what job quality is and how it is to be measured, and thus little understanding of bad jobs.

The aim of this chapter is to try to fill this gap by determining the incidence and identifying the main characteristics of poor quality jobs across EU countries using a multidimensional indicator of job quality developed by the authors. We outline and discuss this measure elsewhere (Muñoz de

Bustillo et al., 2011b) and its application to the 2005 wave of the *European Working Conditions Survey*. This chapter has five sections. After these introductory remarks, the next section is devoted to presenting the main features of our index of job quality. The third section illustrates the overall distribution of job quality across Europe while the fourth uses the measure to estimate the incidence of bad jobs across EU countries according to three different approaches. In the fifth part, the main characteristics of low-quality jobs are explored. The final concluding section summarizes the findings and raises new issues.

A new measure of job quality for the EU

The importance of having a reliable measure of job quality is increasingly recognized in academic and policy circles, and a number of different job quality indexes have been proposed both at national and international levels (see Muñoz de Bustillo et al., 2011a). However, for different reasons related to both conceptual problems and statistical availability, none of these indexes has been accepted as a standard measure of job quality. Measuring job quality remains a difficult task. First, it requires agreeing on what job quality is. Often, indicators of job quality include elements such as productivity or unemployment, important by themselves but clearly unrelated with the quality of jobs. Second, because job quality is multidimensional in nature, consensus is not only difficult to reach but also difficult to transform into a single indicator. Third, the construction of such an indicator is constrained by the lack of suitable data. However, these difficulties need to be seen in context; we should not forget that indicators that we take for granted today (e.g. GDP, the consumer price index or the unemployment rate) had the same problems in the past which were overcome through scientific discussion and the political allocation of resources to generate the data needed.

The index of job quality used in this work, which we have named Job Quality Index (JQI), has been built on the following principles (for more information and a detailed discussion, see Muñoz de Bustillo et al., 2011b):

- It is restricted to information about the attributes of jobs, not of the workers who hold them (even if the information is reported by the workers themselves). It does not include contextual information (on institutional settings, unemployment levels, etc.). Furthermore, it refers to variables that measure results rather than procedures (unless such procedures themselves have a direct impact on the well-being of workers).
- It includes five dimensions that broadly correspond to the five main traditions of the study of job quality (or the impact of job attributes on

the well-being of workers), identified through a detailed literature review (Muñoz de Bustillo et al., 2011b), namely, pay, intrinsic characteristics of the job, terms of employment, health and safety and work–life balance. These five dimensions are in turn formed by different components, subcomponents and finally individual variables taken from the *European Working Conditions Survey 2005* (EWCS 2005) (for details on the survey, see Parent-Thirion et al. 2007), as shown in Figure 2.1. Except at the highest level of aggregation (that is, from the five dimensions to the overall index), the aggregation of information is carried out through weighted arithmetic averages, following the structure of the model shown in Figure 2.1.

- The index is computed at the individual level in order to allow analysis of specific groups of workers, as well as the intersection of the different dimensions and components of job quality at the individual level. In contrast to most of the indicators proposed in the specialized literature, this feature makes it feasible to study the dispersion of job quality and thus to evaluate what happens at the bottom of the distribution.
- The aggregation of these dimensions into a single index is made using a weighted geometric average. This methodology presents two important advantages over the most frequent method of arithmetic averaging: first, the contribution of each dimension to the overall index is not linear but decreasing (that is, an increase in a dimension from a low initial value produces a larger expansion of job quality than the same increase from a high initial value); second, the contribution of each dimension depends on the values of all the other dimensions (that is, even if the sum of scores is the same, a job with more balanced values in the five dimensions would have a higher quality than a job with very high values in two dimensions but very low in the other three). This approach means that our index of job quality assumes decreasing returns for the different work and employment attributes, and imperfect substitutability among the different attributes (with penalization for significant imbalances between them).

The nested structure of the index, including the weights given to the different areas of job quality, is reproduced in Figure 2.1.

The EWCS sample used in this chapter is representative of all employed persons in the EU countries specified in the charts and, unless otherwise specified in the analysis, includes the employed and self-employed and full-time and part-time, male and female workers. The index has two major weaknesses associated with the data used in its application. The first is the subjective nature of some of the variables provided by the EWCS and the second the small sample size, 1000 individuals per country (a lower size in the case of small countries), which limits considerably analysis at the country level, although not the European level. Another potential issue relates to the

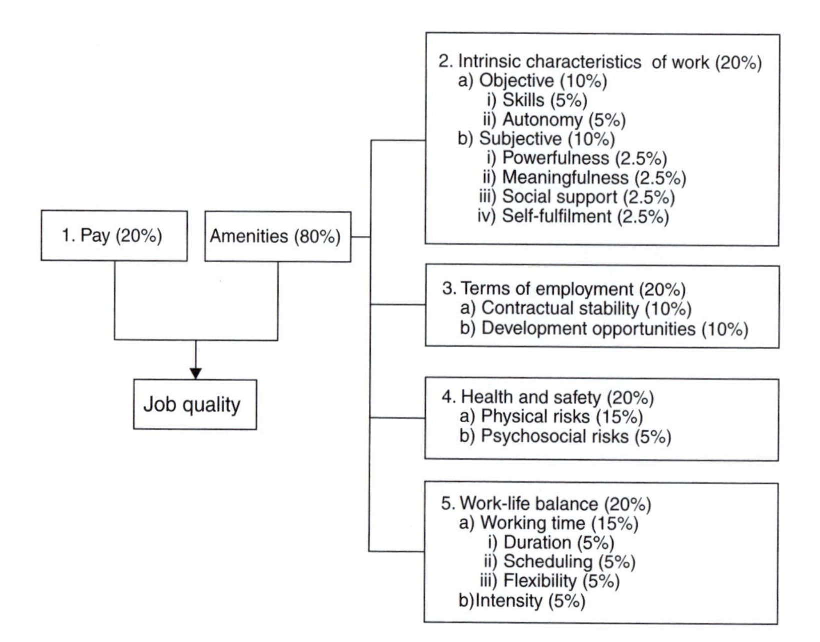

Figure 2.1 The structure of the JQI

arbitrary nature of the weighting of the dimensions. In this respect, and in order to see to what extent the results are contingent on the specific weights applied, we have performed a sensitivity analysis, evaluating the amount of change in the relative position of countries in the overall index resulting from the following changes: first, in the aggregation procedure, using an arithmetic mean instead of a geometric mean; and second, in the weight given to the different dimensions, giving each dimension, in following rounds, a weight of twice the rest of the attributes (0.33 *versus* 0.17). The results obtained suggest that, with a few exceptions limited to some Eastern Europe countries and Portugal and Greece, the ranking of countries is remarkably stable (see Muñoz de Bustillo et al., 2011b, section 6.2.4).

Job quality across the EU

Figure 2.2 depicts the main features of the distribution of job quality across Europe according to our JQI: the thick black bar in the middle of each country line represents the average value, the box around it represents the interquartilic range (the distance between values of job quality in the 25th and the 75th percentiles in each country) and the whiskers represent the distance

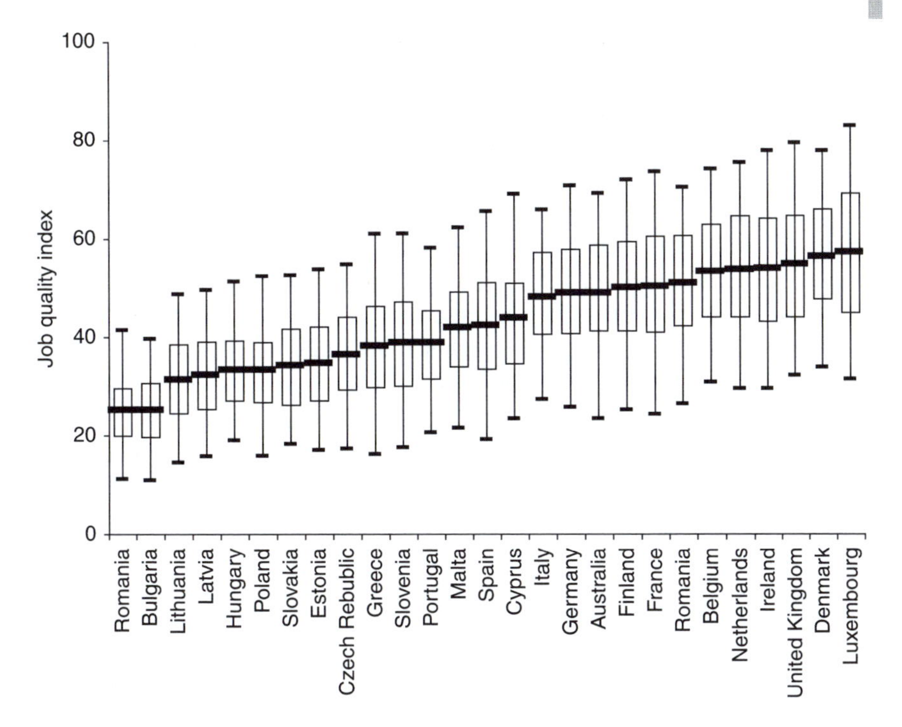

Figure 2.2 Main features of the JQI by country, 2005
Source: Muñoz de Bustillo et al. (2011: 206).

between the values of job quality of the 5th and 95th percentiles in each countries. The countries have been sorted from low to high average job quality, left to right. Those states that occupy the bottom of the job quality ranking displayed in Figure 2.2 are all Eastern European countries that joined the EU in 2004 or later (the two most recent members, Romania and Bulgaria, occupy the very bottom of the list). Southern Europe is next, with mid–low levels of job quality. Continental European countries generally have mid–high values, and the top positions are occupied by Nordic countries, the UK and Ireland. There are some outliers to these general patterns: the value of Slovenia puts it within Southern rather than European countries; Finland has slightly lower values than the other Scandinavian states; Netherlands gets a value as high as the Nordic countries; and the very top of the list is occupied by a very distinct country – Luxemburg. Despite such outliers, our JQI maps well onto the institutional clusters of countries identified previously as 'welfare regimes' or 'institutional families' (Esping-Andersen, 1990, Arts and Gelissen, 2002), with these clusters having clearly differentiated levels of job quality according to our index.

Pay is one of the five top-level dimensions of our index, and although it has been adjusted to Purchasing Power Parity (PPP), the differences between countries in this dimension are much larger than in any of the other four. Hence, it is useful to plot separately the first dimension and the rest, which is done in Figure 2.3. The average value of the pay dimension (which reflects differences in pay levels in PPP across Europe, rescaled to 0–100 with the lowest bound being the lowest decile of pay in the lowest-paying country and the highest bound the highest decile of pay in the highest-paying country) is represented in the horizontal scale, and a reduced index based only on the other four dimensions is represented in the vertical scale. We call this reduced index the 'amenities index' in reference to Adam Smith's theory of compensating wage differentials (since it is a measure of the 'disamenities' of jobs, for which wages are supposed to compensate). We can immediately see that the spread of the pay dimension (in the horizontal axis) is much wider than that of the amenities index (scores of 2 to 55 against 44 to 61), and although the average values of both indices are highly correlated (the value of R^2 is 0.58), there are some important outliers with an interesting interpretation: for instance, the position in terms of amenities for Greece and Spain is much lower than in terms of pay, while the opposite happens in Slovakia, the Netherlands and Denmark. In

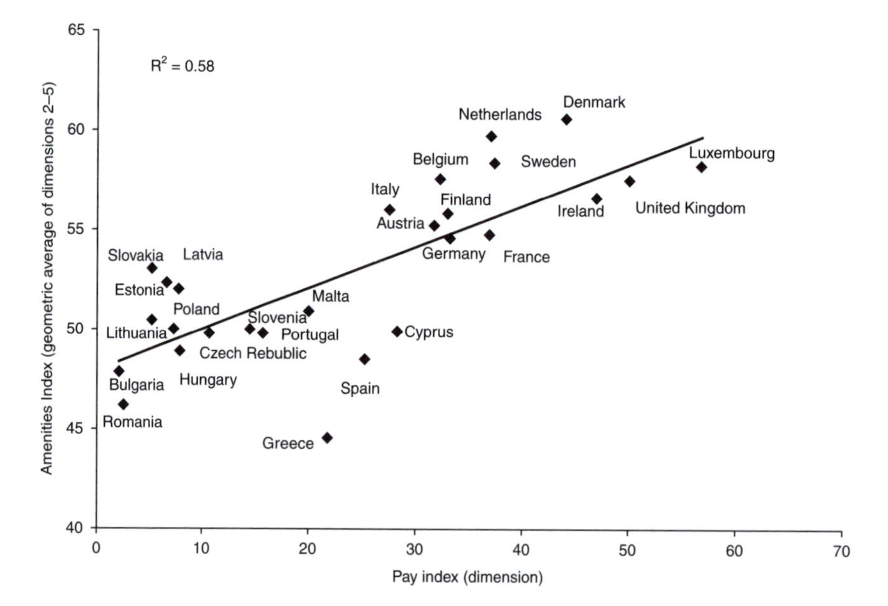

Figure 2.3 Correlation between the average values of the pay dimension and the average values of the amenities index, 2005

Source: Muñoz de Bustillo et al. (2011b: 210).

the rest of this chapter, we refer to both the overall job quality index and the amenities index in order to make our conclusions less dependent on differences in pay across Europe.

As Paul Osterman notes elsewhere in this volume, it is often argued that there is a trade-off between job quantity and job quality, according to which improvements in job quality can lead to a reduction in the rate of job creation and an increase in unemployment. In this respect, the data presented in Figure 2.4 suggests that, at least in the European context, job quantity and job quality go hand in hand, as those countries with higher levels of job quality as measured by the JQI exhibit, on average, lower unemployment rates. It is outwith the scope of this chapter to investigate the causality and rationale behind such a relationship, but it is important to point out that, empirically and at the country level, there is no association between higher job quality and higher unemployment and vice versa.[1] This result is in line with the analysis of job quality carried out in *Employment in Europe* (EC, 2008), according to which,

> ...the higher score [in terms of working conditions] tends to be associated with better labour market outcomes (i.e. higher employment rates and lower youth unemployment ratios) as well as favourable outcomes in terms of productivity levels. These results imply the existence of synergies, instead of a trade-off between qualitative and quantitative outcomes in the labour market. (EC 2008: 156)

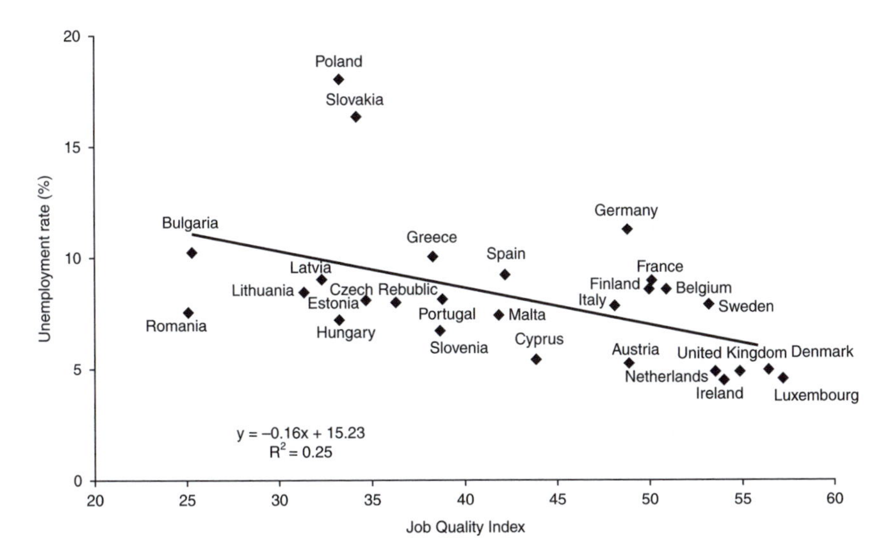

Figure 2.4 JQI and the unemployment rate across the EU, 2005

Identifying bad jobs in Europe

This section draws on the JQI to identify and quantify bad jobs in the different EU countries. Three different strategies are used: first, we adopt a pseudo-absolute approach, considering as bad jobs those held by workers whose job quality value is below 60 per cent of median job quality in the EU; second, we consider a relative measure, based on a threshold of less than 60 per cent of the median job quality in each country and at the individual level; third, a 'job' approach is employed, identifying those jobs that account for the lowest 20 per cent of the labour market in terms of job quality.

The first two strategies are an adaptation of the standard methods used in comparative poverty analysis. The simplest distinction among methodologies for measuring deprivation in any well-being indicator across countries refers to the dichotomy between absolute and relative approaches (Atkinson 1998). In the former case, the researcher establishes a threshold common to all individuals irrespective of the society where they live, whereas, in the latter, the level under which a person is considered to experience deprivation depends on the living standards where he or she lives.

In the particular case of our JQI, there are no *a priori* criteria about which level of job quality is to be considered as minimally acceptable – in contrast to analyses of poverty in which minimum dietary requirements or baskets of basic goods can be inferred. Therefore, in order to establish an absolute *bad job* threshold invariant across countries we simply use the 60 per cent of the median job quality across the whole EU. In other words, our 'absolute' approach is actually relative from a European perspective. Since we want to see how far the results are driven by wages, which is the dimension with the largest variance, we reproduce the analysis using the amenities index, based only on the four non-pecuniary dimensions.

According to this pseudo-absolute definition, the percentage of workers with bad jobs in the EU is 12.7 per cent, a figure which goes down to 4.8 per cent when the earnings dimension is excluded from the calculations (see Figure 2.5). What is really interesting is the proportion of these EU-defined *bad jobs* across countries. Bad jobs are strongly concentrated, firstly, in Eastern Europe, particularly in Bulgaria and Romania, with more than half the employed population holding a bad job according to this first definition and, secondly, in Mediterranean countries such as Greece, Spain, Portugal and Malta (with more than 10% of workers having bad jobs). At the other extreme of the ranking, differences are very narrow and the share of bad jobs very low, with Denmark and Luxemburg at the bottom. When carrying out the analysis without the earnings dimension, the picture is slightly different. Firstly, there is a remarkable compression and reduction of the figures, which are much lower and less dispersed than when considering the overall index (because the dispersion of the pay dimension is considerably higher than the rest). Secondly,

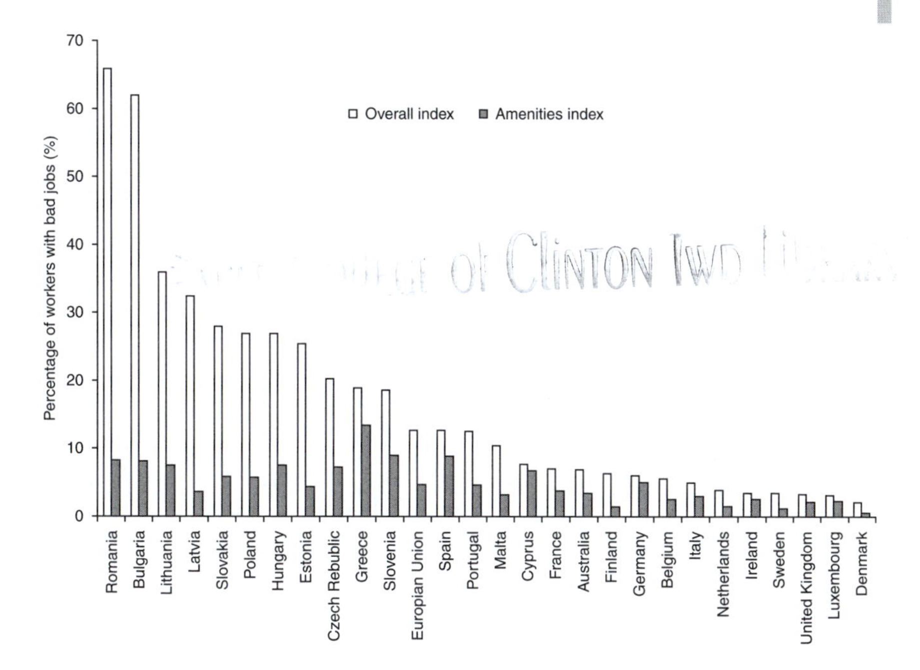

Figure 2.5 Percentage of workers holding bad jobs in the EU using the absolute approach, 2005 (%)

although there is a high correlation between both measures, there are non-negligible differences with the previous ordering. Greece, Slovenia and Spain become the countries with a highest percentage of bad jobs across Europe (19, 19 and 13% of workforces respectively), with most Eastern European countries between 5 and 10 per cent, Continental Europe around five per cent and the Scandinavian and Netherlands with less than two per cent.

A second alternative consists in constructing a truly relative measure, using the same threshold of 60 per cent of the median value of our JQI but in this case defined at the country level (Figure 2.6). The contrast with Figure 2.5 is quite interesting. First, the dispersion of results is much lower because using a national threshold neutralizes the enormous differences in pay levels: the range of values goes from 12–5 per cent (whereas using the absolute measure it went from 65–2%). Second, the countries align less neatly with the usual European institutional clusterings: although Southern and Eastern Europe tend to have higher shares of workers in bad jobs than Northern European countries, there are many exceptions. For example, France is now near the bottom, while Hungary and Slovakia are closer to Denmark than to other Eastern European countries. Lastly, although the amenities index also has less dispersion in this case, the difference is much lower (because as mentioned earlier, using the relative approach neutralizes the cross-country differences in terms of wages).

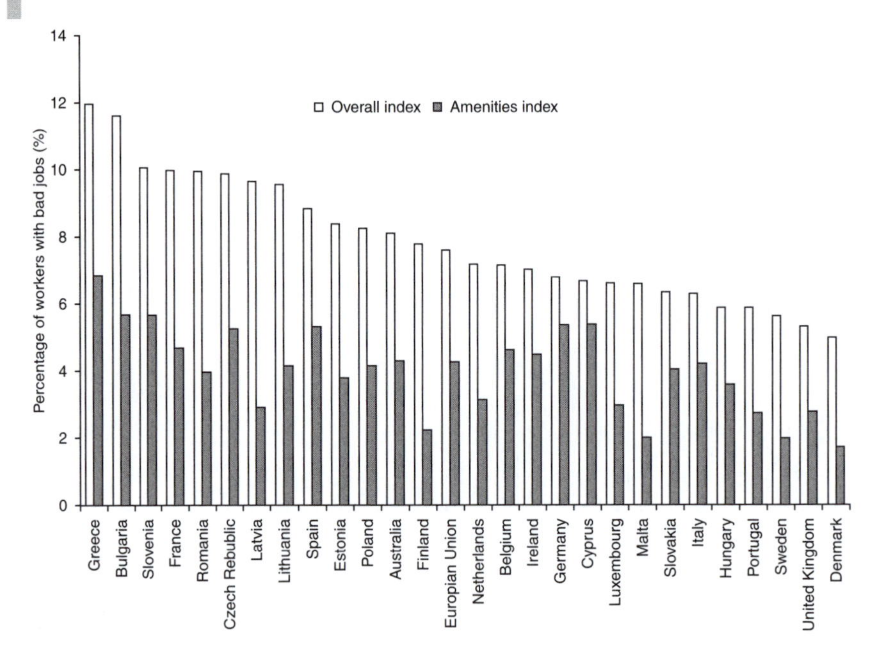

Figure 2.6 Percentage of workers holding bad jobs in the EU using the relative approach, 2005 (%)

It is interesting to assess, even on a preliminary basis, how the proportion of bad jobs according to the JQI compares to the figures obtained using more usual earnings-related indicators and the share of low paid workers. In Figure 2.7 we plot the percentage of employees with bad jobs according to our JQI and the share of low paid employees in 24 EU member states (taken from Eurofound 2010: 32, based on the *EU Statistics on Living Conditions 2007* and defined as those full-time employees with hourly earnings below 60 per cent of the median at national level). As the graph reveals, the association between the percentage of employees with poor-quality jobs according to the JQI is remarkably low (the R^2 is less than 1%). This result also applies when we use the amenities index instead (R^2 is less than 6%). Keeping in mind the discrepancies between both kinds of figures (which correspond to different years and surveys), this confirms that a measure of 'bad jobs' based on a multidimensional indicator of job quality captures a different phenomenon than the usual measures of low pay, which opens the way for a detailed analysis of the discrepancies: the decomposable nature of our index should allow us to identify what components of job quality are behind such a discrepancy. We leave such analysis for further research.

The concept of 'bad jobs' refers to jobs and not to individuals, yet most analyses of this issue are carried out at the individual level. The reason is that normally the data used are gathered at the level of individual workers, not at the level of jobs. However, we can approximate such a job-based analysis

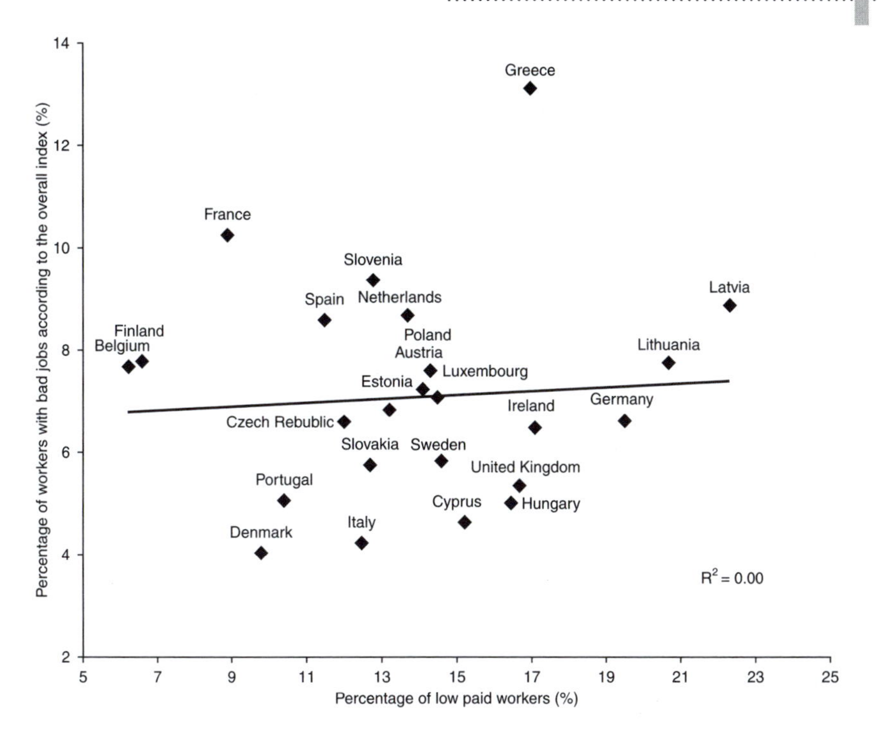

Figure 2.7 Correlation between the percentage of employees with bad jobs in 2005 and the percentage of low paid employees in 2007*
*Both samples only include full-time employees.

of job quality by aggregating the individual-level job quality information for each possible combination of occupation and sector (using the NACE and ISCO classifications at the two-digit level). This combination, which corresponds well with the usual understanding of what a job is (clerks in the construction sector etc.), can then be used as the basic unit of analysis (for more details of this approach see Fernández-Macías 2012). Such an approach is particularly suited to our objectives here since we want to *identify* the bad jobs in Europe and quantify them. That is the basis of our third approach to the identification and quantification of bad jobs in Europe. We computed the weighted average level of job quality according to our index for each job in Europe, defining 'job' as each possible combination of sector and occupation at the two-digit level (defined this way, there would be 1,680 distinct jobs in the EU labour market, although in practice there are fewer because some potential combinations of occupation and activity are too scarce to be captured in the EWCS sample). Then, we ranked all the jobs from high to low job quality, and the jobs that account for the bottom 20 per cent of employment were defined as bad jobs. Table 2.1 shows the ten biggest 'bad jobs' thus defined, which account in total for roughly ten per cent of the EU working population: they include unskilled labourers in agriculture,

Table 2.1 Bad jobs by sector and occupation in the EU, 2005. The ten biggest 'bad jobs' (jobs within the lowest job quality quintile in the EU)

Sector (NACE)	Occupation (ISCO)	Average JQI	Percentage of EU employment (%)	Cumulative percentage of EU employment (%)
Agriculture, hunting and related activities	Skilled agricultural and fishery workers	43.2	3.2	3.2
Hotels and restaurants	Personal and protective services workers	40.2	1.4	4.6
Other service activities	Sales and services elementary occupations	42.8	1.1	5.7
Agriculture, hunting and related activities	Agricultural, fishery and related labourers	39.5	0.7	6.3
Construction	Industrial labourers	39.8	0.6	7.0
Hotels and restaurants	Sales persons and demonstrators	38.2	0.6	7.6
Hotels and restaurants	Sales and services elementary occupations	37.7	0.6	8.2
Manufacture of food and beverages	Other craft and related trades workers	42.5	0.5	8.7
Manufacture of metal, except machinery	Metal trades workers	42.5	0.5	9.2
Health and social work	Services elementary occupations	43.3	0.5	9.7

low-skilled service workers in hotels and restaurants, manual workers in construction and manufacture of food and metals, and low-skilled workers in other services. Tables 2.2 and 2.3 include the distribution of these workers across broadly defined sectors and occupations (one-digit ISCO and NACE). European bad jobs are disproportionately present in agriculture, hotels and restaurants, and other services (these three sectors account for 50% of all

Table 2.2 Distribution by one-digit sectors of 'bad jobs'

	Share in sector (%)	Distribution across sectors (%)
Education	0.4	0.2
Public administration	0.5	0.2
Financial sector	2.0	0.3
Electricity	3.8	0.3
Real estate	4.6	1.5
Retail	5.1	4.0
Health	8.3	2.9
Transport and communication	8.4	2.5
Construction	14.0	5.5
Other services	27.7	12.2
Manufacturing	35.0	33.9
Hotels and restaurants	72.1	13.5
Agriculture and fishing	85.0	22.8
All sectors	20.0	100.0

Table 2.3 Distribution by one-digit occupations of 'bad jobs'

	Share in occupation (%)	Distribution across occupations (%)
Technicians	0.1	0.1
Professionals	0.2	0.1
Managers	0.6	0.3
Clerks	0.8	0.5
Service workers	18.5	11.8
Craft occupations	21.1	14.8
Plant machine and operators and assemblers	49.2	20.1
Elementary occupations	59.0	35.0
Agricultural workers	90.2	17.3
All occupations	20.1	100.0

employment in bad jobs); by occupation, they are most present in elementary occupations, operators and assemblers and agricultural workers (which account for more than 50%).

Figure 2.8 presents the results that can be directly contrasted with Figures 2.6 and 2.7: it quantifies the share of the labour force in each country which works in these EU-defined bad jobs. While the figure for the total EU is 20 per cent, the rest of the information from the graph shows how the employment structure in each European country differs from the overall EU pattern in terms of the share of bad jobs in the labour market. What makes

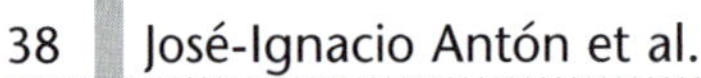

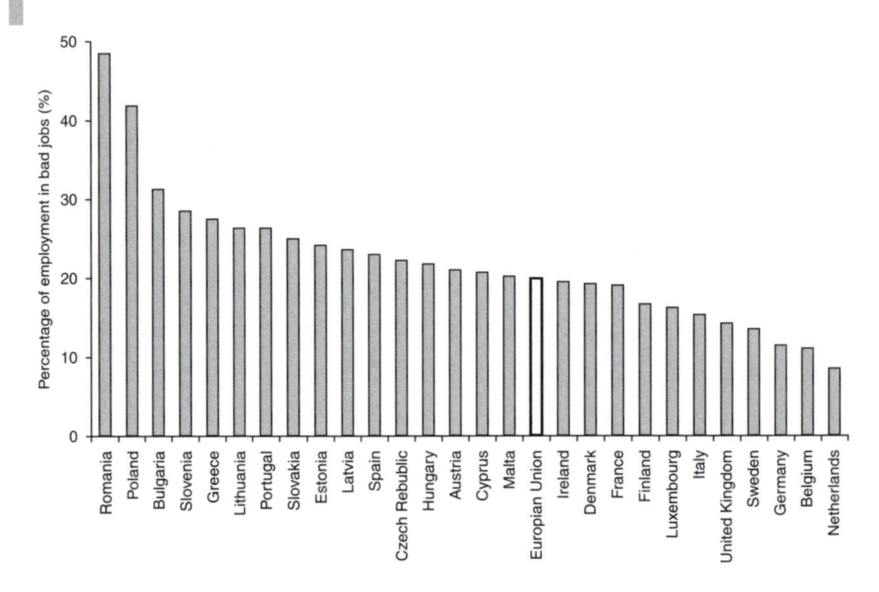

Figure 2.8 Percentage of workers holding bad jobs using the 'jobs' approach in the EU, 2005 (%)

this new approach appealing is that we know that the jobs we are talking about are exactly the same in all countries, so we are really comparing like with like: whereas less than nine per cent of Dutch workers are in those particular jobs, nearly 50 per cent of Romanian workers are in the specific combinations of occupations and sectors that lie at the bottom of the European employment structure.[2] Whereas in the previous analysis two per cent of Danish workers had jobs below a EU-defined threshold of minimum job quality (or five per cent when the threshold was defined within Denmark), in this case nearly 20 per cent of Danish workers (that is, near the EU average) have the jobs that across the EU occupy the lowest fifth of the job quality continuum. While the previous two approaches reveal how many people had jobs that could be defined as low quality, this last approach allows the identification of how many bad jobs exist in each employment structure.

In practice, the picture painted by this last approach is not very different from that of the previous two, but there are interesting discrepancies. First, the amount of variation is somewhere between the two previous approaches: the structural discrepancies across European countries in terms of the amount of bad jobs are quite significant, going from less than nine to nearly 50 per cent. Second, this new approach is similar to the other two in the ranking of countries above but not below the average: as in the two previous cases (and maybe even clearer), Eastern and Southern Europe have the highest proportions of bad jobs; but the countries with fewer bad jobs under this 'structural' definition are not the Scandinavian countries (in particular, Denmark and

Finland are near the middle of the ranking) but the industry-heavy Northern Continental European countries (Netherlands, Belgium and Germany).

The contrast between the results using the usual individual approach and the structural 'jobs' approach has interesting implications. It shows that the differences in the number of bad jobs across countries does not result only, or even mainly, from different conditions of work and employment in the same type of jobs: to a large extent, they result from the fact that the productive structures of the poorest countries are much heavier in jobs that are bad across Europe. In other words, even if we could magically remove all the differences in quality across Europe for the same types of job (so that an agricultural labourer would have the same job quality in Denmark and in Bulgaria), there would be still large differences in the number of bad jobs in the different countries (because poor countries have a larger proportion of employment in jobs which are bad everywhere).

Characterizing bad jobs in Europe

Once we have identified and quantified low-quality jobs across Europe, the next step is to characterize them. For this purpose, we only use the definition of 'bad jobs' on the basis of an absolute European threshold (the first one), as using three different definitions of 'bad jobs' in this section would only result in an excessive multiplication of figures that would unnecessarily complicate the interpretation.[3] Nevertheless, in this section we present all the analysis both for the overall job quality index and for the amenities index in order to take into account the possible distorting effect of the large differences in the pay dimension of our index when using an absolute threshold for defining bad jobs. In practice it makes little difference in most cases.

Figure 2.9 shows a simple descriptive analysis, with the percentage of EU workers with different characteristics that have jobs of bad quality according to our pseudo-absolute definition. There are slightly more women than men with bad jobs, though only for the overall job quality index: if we look at jobs which are bad in terms of amenities (non-pecuniary job attributes such as working hours, autonomy or physical strain) the share of women affected is slightly less than men. This finding is interesting because it is one of the few cases in which the results of the overall JQI and the amenities index are contradictory: what it suggests is that men are slightly more likely to have 'unpleasant' jobs than women (that is, jobs with lower amenities), but that their pay compensation is so much higher that when all job attributes are taken into account they are less likely to have poor quality jobs. By age, there is a clear differentiation between the youngest workers (less than 30 years of age) and the rest, with nearly 18 per cent of the former holding bad jobs

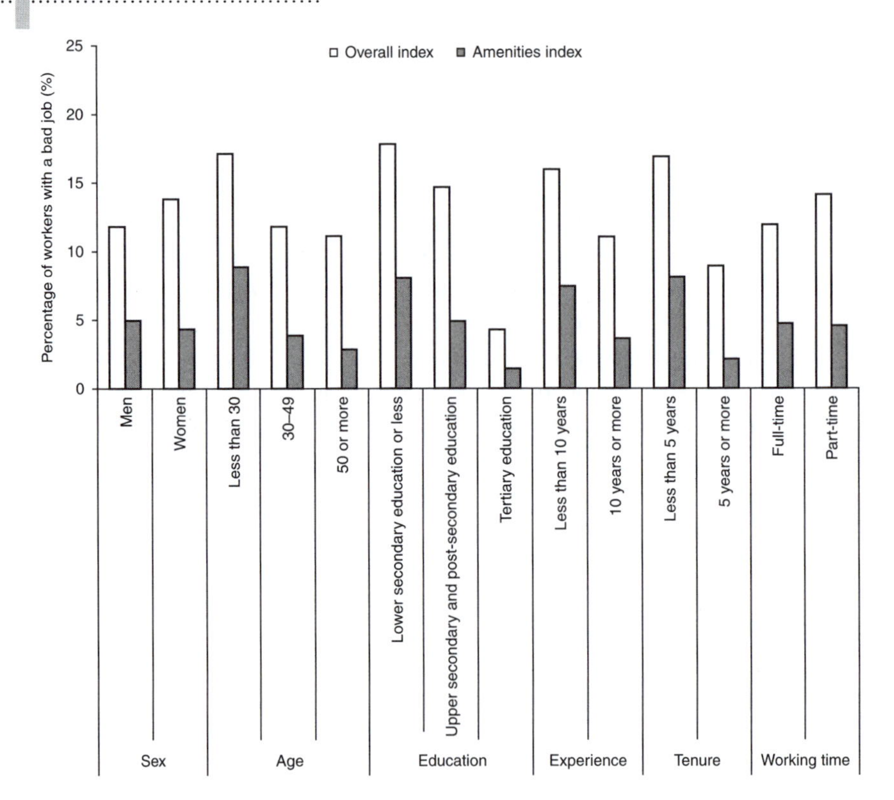

Figure 2.9 Workers holding bad jobs in the EU according to different characteristics, 2005 (%)

compared to 11 per cent of the latter. These results on gender and age are in line with those observed in terms of low pay by Eurofound (2010). The variables related to human capital show the expected results: the percentage of workers holding bad jobs decreases with educational level, experience and tenure. Regarding working time, the share of labourers with low-quality jobs is higher among part-time than among full-time workers. Interestingly, this difference vanishes when the pay dimension is not considered. In relation to the occupational level (not included in the figure), the highest levels of bad jobs correspond to sales and service workers (only in the case of the overall index but not for the amenities index) and blue-collar workers. Finally, those sectors of activity with a larger presence of poor-quality jobs are agriculture and other primary activities (only in terms of the index including earnings), hotels and restaurants and manufacturing, whereas the lowest percentages are found among financial intermediation, real estate, renting and business and electricity, gas and water supply.

Since these figures show only bivariate relations, it could be the case that the differences between categories are the result of their different composition in terms of another variable, which could lead to misinterpretations. For this reason, it is useful to perform a multivariate analysis that determines the influence of each factor, other things being equal. This analysis is performed using a probit regression, where the probability of holding a low-quality job is modelled as a function of sex and human capital variables, that is, sex, age, education, experience and tenure. In addition, in order to control for country-specific effects, we include country dummies in the model. We do not include occupation and sector of activity among the covariates as selection into them is far from being random. Nevertheless, we have repeated the analyses including such variables and the results are basically the same, with the dummies for occupation and sector confirming the findings of the descriptive analysis. The results of the estimation are presented in terms of the average marginal effects of each variable in Table 2.4 and this allows us to depict a more precise profile of low-quality jobs in the EU.[4]

As the table reveals, firstly, women experience a slightly higher probability of holding a bad job (3 percentage points) than men in terms of the overall index. Nevertheless, when only amenities are considered, the effect of sex loses its statistical significance (confirming that the main difference between men and women is pay). Secondly, when controlling for other observable characteristics, age does not affect the probability of having a poor-quality job; although

Table 2.4 Determinants of the probability of holding a bad job across the EU, 2005

	Overall index		Amenities index	
	Marginal effect	Standard error	Marginal effect	Standard error
Female	0.022	0.006***	−0.003	0.005
Less than 30	0.016	0.010	0.017	0.006***
50 or more	0.013	0.009	0.002	0.007
Lower secondary education or less	0.048	0.008***	0.027	0.006***
Tertiary education	−0.088	0.010***	−0.046	0.007***
Work experience	0.000	0.000	0.000	0.000
Tenure	−0.004	0.000***	−0.004	0.000***
Observations	24,404		24,404	
Test of joint significance	F(33, 3,966) = 61.88***		F(53, 3,966) = 13.57***	
Correctly predicted (%)	85.2		82.8	

*** significant at 1% level; ** significant at 5%; * significant at 10% level. 26 country dummy variables are included in the model specification. Average marginal effects of a probit model are reported in table. The reference category is a male worker aged between 30 and 49, with upper secondary or post-secondary education and living in Germany. A bad job is defined as that with an index below 60 per cent of the median value across the EU.

in the case of the amenities index being a young worker (less than 30 years old) slightly increases such risk (by 1.4 percentage points). Thirdly, education has a significant effect, particularly in the case of the overall index, as the probability of having a bad job decreases with the worker's education level. Fourthly, whereas work experience is not significant, once we control for other observable factors, tenure is significantly associated with a lower risk of having a bad job (ten years of tenure reduces the probability by 3 percentage points). If we apply the amenities index, the results are again quite similar.

Conclusion

It is widely known that workers value many job attributes other than monetary rewards (e.g. Clark 2005). Yet little information on job quality, beyond a narrow focus on wage and some aspects of labour contracts, is available for public debate. Methodological difficulties with respect to a more encompassing measure of job quality and a lack of agreement on what job quality actually is have hindered progress in this field. Especially damaging is the lack of more comprehensive information about the nature of jobs at the lower end of the spectrum.

This chapter has tried to identify and quantify bad jobs across EU countries from a more encompassing perspective. We have drawn upon a multidimensional job quality index developed by us elsewhere (Muñoz de Bustillo et al., 2011b), which, we have argued, offers reasonable methodological properties and advantages over previous proposals when applied to the EWCS (2005), which has a questionnaire that allows us to measure most dimensions of job quality in detail.

In so doing, we have explored the issue of bad jobs from three different perspectives: a pseudo-absolute one, using a threshold of 60 per cent of the median job quality at the EU level; a purely relative approach, based on a cut-off line at 60 per cent of the median value at the national level; and a 'jobs'-centred strategy, which looks at the combinations of occupation and sector with the lowest values in terms of job quality.

Overall, the analysis presented in this chapter suggests that deprivation in terms of multidimensional job quality is a concept wider and richer than low pay. From an absolute perspective nearly 13 per cent of European jobs can be considered 'bad' jobs (8% if we use a nationally defined threshold). The dispersion of non-wage job attributes is lower than that observed in earnings, making the distribution of job quality more egalitarian than that of labour income. The percentage of workers with poor quality jobs tends to be lower than that of low paid workers.

Two additional findings are worth emphasizing. Firstly, irrespective of the approach followed, Eastern and Southern European countries tend to exhibit the largest shares of bad jobs (more than half of jobs in Romania and Bulgaria, for example), while Scandinavian states usually show the best scores. Secondly, the 'jobs'-based approach suggests that the incidence of bad jobs responds to both structural differences (that is, the particular jobs present in an economy) and cross-country differences in quality for the same jobs. Bad jobs are concentrated in a handful of sectors and occupations (unskilled labourers in agriculture, low-skilled service workers in hotels and restaurants, manual workers in construction and manufacture of food and metals, and low-skilled workers in other services). Finally, women and workers with low education face a higher risk of holding a 'bad' job, while tenure has the opposite effect.

The approach presented here is far from definitive. On the one hand, the data used impose some important limitations that cannot be solved until more adequate surveys covering the conditions of work and employment are carried out – the sample size of the EWCS is currently too narrow, wages are measured in a very unsatisfactory way and information on the degree of employee involvement and participation at work (what used to be called industrial democracy) is lacking. On the other hand, there is still much to discuss with respect to our understanding of what job quality is and how it is to be measured. But our hope is that our proposal will contribute to advancing in such direction. Ultimately, it has to be remembered that in our data-driven world, as Lord Kelvin once said, often what is not measured does not exist. It is important therefore that we generate a measure for job quality so that policy can be directed to improving it.

Notes

1 It could be argued that low unemployment countries had a different mix of good and bad jobs, making the average job index similar or even higher than high or medium unemployment countries. In order to test that possibility, we have done the same exercise using a distribution-corrected Index of Job Quality, defined as JQI x (1- Gini index). The results remain roughly the same.

2 This approach ignores the fact that job quality varies systematically across countries for the same type of jobs (Gautié and Schmitt 2010), which allows us to focus on the structural differences in employment across countries from a truly European perspective. Of course, the two previous approaches do not ignore such differences and therefore provide a necessary complementary perspective on this issue.

3 To test the robustness of using only the first approach, we carried out the same analysis with the other two alternatives and the results are not substantially different. These analyses are available for interested readers upon request to the authors.

4 We have also estimated a regression of both the overall and amenities indexes on worker's characteristics by Ordinary Least Squares, obtaining remarkably similar results. These calculations are available from the authors upon request.

REFERENCES

Arts W. and J. Gelissen (2002) 'Three Worlds of Welfare Capitalism Or More? A State-of-the-Art Report', *Journal of European Social Policy*, May, 12: 137–158.

Atkinson, A. B. (1998) *Poverty in Europe*, Oxford: Blackwell.

Bazen, S., Gregory, M. and Salverda, W. (1998) *Low-Wage Employment in Europe*, Cheltenham: Edward Elgar.

Clark, A. E. (2005) 'What Makes a Good Job? Evidence from OECD Countries', in S. Bazen, C. Lucifora and W. Salverda (eds) *Job Quality and Employer Behaviour*, London: Palgrave Macmillan.

Esping-Andersen, G (1990) *The Three Worlds of Welfare Capitalism*, Oxford: Polity.

Eurofound (2010) *Working Poor in Europe*, Dublin: Eurofound.

European Commission (EC) (2008) *Employment in Europe 2008*, Brussels: Eurostat.

Fernández-Macías, E. (2012) 'Patterns of Employment Expansion in Europe, 1995–2007', in E. Fernández-Macías, D. Storrie and J. Hurley (eds) *Transformation of the Job Structures* in the EU and USA, London: Palgrave Macmillan.

Gautié, J. and Schmitt, J. (2010) (eds) *Low Wage Work in the Wealthy World*, New York: Russell Sage Foundation.

Grimshaw D. (2011) 'What Do We Know about Low Wage and Low Wage Workers? Analysing the Definitions, Patterns, Causes and Consequences in International Perspective', *Conditions of Work and Employment Series No. 28*, Geneva, International Labour Office.

Lucifora, C. and Salverda, W. (eds) (1998) *Policies for Low Wage Employment and Social Exclusion*, Milan: Franco Angeli.

Lucifora, C., McKnight, A. and Salverda, W. (2005) 'Low-Wage Employment in Europe: A Review of the Evidence', *Socio-Economic Review*, 3:2, 259–292.

Marx, I. and Salverda, W. (eds) (2005) *Low-Wage Employment in Europe: Perspectives for Improvement*, Leuven: Acco.

Muñoz de Bustillo, R. and Antón, J. I. (2007) 'Low-Wage Work in a High Employment Growth Economy: Spain, 1994–2004', *Investigación Económica*, 66, 119–145.

Muñoz de Bustillo, R., Fernández-Macías E., Esteve F. and Antón J. I. (2011a) '*E pluribus unum?* A Critical Survey of Job Quality Indicators', *Socio-Economic Review*, 4:3, 447–476.

Muñoz de Bustillo, R., Fernández-Macías, E., Antón J. I. and Esteve F. (2011b) *Measuring More Than Money: The Social-Economics of Job Quality*, Cheltenham: Edward Elgar.

Parent-Thirion, A., Fernández-Macías, E., Hurley, J. and Vermeylen, G. (2007) *Fourth European Working Conditions Survey*, Dublin: Eurofound.

CHAPTER

3

Job Quality in the US: The Myths That Block Action

Paul Osterman

Introduction

Far too many American adults work in low wage jobs, and a wide range of ideas have been proposed for improving their circumstances. These ideas include enforcing and raising employment standards, strengthening employee voice and working with firms to upgrade work. Many of these interventions are tested and there is good reason to think that taken together they could have a substantial impact. However, there is widespread political reluctance to take these steps, including widespread reluctance among intellectual elites, particularly those in the economics profession. Although some of this reluctance might be ascribed to self-interest by individuals and institutions that benefit from low wages, a fairer reading of the situation is that many good-spirited people are constrained by a set of ideas regarding the supposed negative consequences of intervening in the job market. The goal of this chapter is to examine the myths that constrain action and to show that they are incorrect and that we can move forward with respect to job quality with few negative consequences.

The challenge

What is a decent job and how can we define it? Answers take two tracks. A large literature in sociology and economics asks about the correlates of reported job satisfaction. What job traits – wages, autonomy, prestige, security and so on – are correlated with the degree of contentment people express about their work (Jencks et al., 1988; Clark, 2004; Handel, 2005)? This research is interesting but not really on point for us. We want to know about minimum standards. What baseline should we insist that all jobs provide?

Consideration of this question leads quickly to the conclusion that there is no easy answer and that any measure is bound to be controversial. What aspects of a job should we consider? What level of each such characteristic is required? Neither answer is clear and the uncertainty is compounded by a series of technical issues such as how to account for cost-of-living differences throughout the country and for different kinds of families with varying needs. And, of course, the question is political since different groups have divergent interests in whether the answer indicates that things are going well or badly.

All this said, everyone agrees wages are the most important feature of work, so we will use a measure of relative wages: the fraction of people whose earnings fall below two-thirds of the median. The two-thirds standard is used in many other countries to define low wage work and hence it greatly facilitates international comparisons. Beyond this pragmatic consideration there are more principled reasons for going this route. The core idea is social inclusion: if people's earnings fall too far below the average then in some important sense they are not part of society. They lack the resources to fully participate and they are distanced from the ordinary experience of their fellow citizens. It turns out that many Americans share this view about what it takes to be a full participant in society. A recent review of the job quality literature summarized public opinion poll findings about what Americans think the minimum wage is that enables a family to 'get by'. According to these polls, respondents peg the 'get along' earning at a level between 60 and 70 per cent of the median (Fremstad, 2008).

How many people fall below a reasonable standard for decent work? We limit our calculations to adults aged between 25 and 64 years. Although some young people need to work to support their families, many others are in transitory, casual jobs, so it would confuse the analysis to include youth. Using the best available wage rate data, the 2010 US hourly wage cut-off for the relative standard is $11.61 an hour (since the median wage was $17.60).[1] In 2010, 24 per cent of adults fell below the standard, translating to 27.8 million adults earning less than two thirds of the median. By any measure these are very large and troubling numbers.

It is important to emphasize that we have provided a very conservative estimate of the extent of low-wage work in America. First, our measure does not take into account pensions or health care; when these factors are considered the number of workers in difficulty rises a good deal. Secondly, many observers believe it desirable to construct a 'basic needs budget' or 'living wage' by starting from family consumption requirements rather than starting, as we do, from the distribution of hourly wages. A recent careful effort to do this approach concluded that a family of four, with two working adults and two children, would need each adult to earn $16.10 to meet minimum standards (Wider Opportunities for Women, 2011). This figure is considerably higher than the wage standard that we employ here. The fact that the number of people in low wage jobs is so high while even using a conservative standard makes the case all the more compelling.

The power of ideas

In the years between the Second World War and the late 1970s a strong set of institutions helped create and sustain millions of middle class jobs in the US. These supports have been progressively weakened (Osterman, 1999). Firms once viewed their employees as stakeholders whose welfare had a claim on the firm but this is no longer true. Unions have been battered and are less effective. The government has steadily withdrawn from its role of strengthening the floor and upholding employment standards. All these changes add up to a steady erosion of the quality of employment.

The obvious solution is to upgrade the quality of jobs, but our passivity about intervening in the demand side of the labour market gets in the way. Why? To a surprising extent the obstacles are conceptual, residing a world view that pervades both policy discourse and popular perceptions. The core challenge is a belief in the power and the correctness of the market. In part this belief flows from the central tenets of standard economic theory, one version of which is that market outcomes are optimal and the costs of interfering are substantial. This presumed optimality has been increasingly challenged even within the profession but the subliminal message remains.

As a result of this thinking, the conventional wisdom that dominates most public debate focuses almost entirely on two strategies: improve education so that people can escape the low wage job trap (see Keep and James in this volume) and, for those who cannot, provide some level of support through programmes such as the Earned Income Tax Credit (EITC) which is an income supplement conditioned on work. Education and the EITC are unquestionably worthwhile, but the policy menu that they form is strangely truncated because it takes the nature of the jobs as given. The basic idea is to let the economy generate whatever quality of jobs that firms choose and then, if necessary, compensate by enabling people to avoid the bad ones or by shoring up people who are stuck. This conceptual framework blocks more expansive actions to improve jobs.

To address these conceptual obstacles we take up three myths that stand in the way of serious efforts to address the problem. These are, firstly, that an improvement in the economy and high rates of upward mobility in the normal operation of labour markets will solve the problem; secondly that policy efforts to alter the distribution of economic rewards inevitably lead to slow growth and damage labour market efficiency; and, thirdly, that the key to solving the problem lies in improving low wage workers' skills. We show that none of these myths holds water when confronted with data. This conclusion is good news because these are the myths that have been used politically to block action over the past decades and the fact that they are wrong opens the door to serious consideration of steps to reduce the number of low wage jobs in our labour market.

Myth: as soon as the economy improves the problem will go away

In the 1960s President Kennedy argued that 'a rising tide lifts all boats'. The basic idea was that the problems of low income and bad jobs could be addressed through full employment. If the economy was strong, not only would everyone gain but people would be lifted out of the low wage labour market as better firms, forced by full employment to reach further down in the job queue, hired them and as they gained human capital that improved their productivity. What was attractive about this position from Kennedy's perspective was that it implied that direct intervention in the operation of markets was unnecessary.

When we climb out of the current Great Recession will we also put the problems of the low wage labour market behind us? The experience of the 1990s lets us answer this question with much more certainty than was possible during the debates in the 1960s. As is well understood, the 1990s was a remarkable period of prosperity in the US. Unemployment steadily dropped, from 7.5 per cent in 1992 to 4.0 per cent in 2000. The 1990s add up to a perfect test of a strong overall economy's capacity to solve the challenge of low quality employment.

It stands to reason that when labour markets are tight (i.e. when demand for workers exceeds their supply) wages will rise and employers will adjust hiring strategies and standards in order to meet their needs. Very few jobs require tightly specified credentials or experience (as, for example, the case of doctors or lawyers who cannot work without a degree and license) and even fewer such jobs are at the bottom of the labour market. Much as we would expect, there is evidence that just such a process occurred in the 1990s: wages for the bottom ten per cent did rise.

But just how large were the improvements? Is full employment the silver bullet? As we have seen, in 2010 24 per cent of adults fell below our standard, yet in 1992, at the beginning of the boom, the rate was 22.1 per cent. It is hard to look at these figures and think that the low wage labour market became a much better place in any long-term sense as a result of the 1990s economic growth.

It is important to be clear about the message. Obviously full employment and a strong economy is a good thing. But it is also a limited achievement. Improving the quality of jobs will require more direct policies and interventions.

Related to the (incorrect) expectation regarding overall economic improvement is the view that the American labour market is characterized by high rates of upward mobility and hence people in the low wage labour market stand a good chance of escaping. Despite the popularity and tenacity of this view, the data do not support it.

For instance, there is considerable evidence that US adults remain confined in low wage jobs over the course of their working lives. One study found that among low earners, over six years starting in the early 1990s, a growth period, only 27 per cent raised their incomes enough to rise consistently above the poverty line for a family of four (Holzer, 2004). A more recent study looked at low earners in 1995–2001 and found that six per cent of those working full time and 18 per cent of those working part-time in any year had dropped out of the labour force by the next year. Among those who did stay in the workforce, 40 per cent experienced either a decrease or no change in their earnings (Theodos and Bednarzik, 2006). Using yet a third data source, this time tracking mobility from 2001 to 2003, researchers found that 44 per cent of the employees at poverty wages in 2001 had no better wages in 2003 and an additional 22 per cent were not even employed (Lopreste et al., 2009).

Yet another investigation, this time using Social Security earnings data, found that the correlation of year-to-year earnings was 0.9 (close to a perfect correlation of 1) and that over a ten-year period the correlation was a still very high 0.7. In other words, people stay in the same place in the earnings distribution and moving up is rare. The authors conclude that the data 'show very clearly that mobility has not mitigated the dramatic increase in annual earnings concentration' (Kopczuk et al., 2010: 95).

When it comes to intergenerational mobility, the relationship between a parent's income and the child's subsequent income as an adult, the US is much more rigid than most of us would have expected or thought desirable. Of all children born in the bottom 20 per cent of the income distribution, 41 per cent remain there as adults while only six per cent make it to the top 20 per cent (Hertz, 2006). For children born in the top quintile the storyline is reversed: six per cent end up on the bottom quintile as adults and 42 per cent remain in the top. This rate of intergenerational mobility is lower than in France, Germany, Sweden, Canada, Denmark, Finland and Norway. Reviewing a wide range of evidence the mainstream Brookings

Institution concluded that, 'Compared to the same peer group, Germany is 1.5 times more mobile than the United States, Canada nearly 2.5 times more mobile, and Denmark 3 times more mobile' (Sawhill and Morton, 2008: 5).

Myth: policies to improve job quality hurt economic performance

One critique of any effort to improve job quality and reduce the size of the low wage labour market is that such actions distort incentives and damage overall economic performance. This line of thinking is based on the idea that people will work harder and invest more if they fear the consequences of not doing so. The threat of low wages provides the incentives that will prod people to produce more. In past decades much conservative thought has promoted this view and it has underwritten a critique of social policy. There is, however, an argument on the other side: people respond better to the carrot than to the stick and if working conditions were improved, effort and productivity would rise. Here we ask whether the evidence supports the double-edged critique that inequality improves overall job market performance and that policies that reduce inequality make matters worse.

A good way to test these arguments is to examine the performance of several northern European nations, all at the same level of technological sophistication as the US and all competing in international markets. The UK, France and Germany are the largest continental economies and the UK is most similar to the US in terms of lack of commitment to policies aimed at raising the floor of the job market. Denmark, the Netherlands and Sweden are all considerably smaller but are open economies exposed to the forces of international competition.

How does America compare to these nations in terms of the incidence of earnings inequality? Table 3.1 shows the ratio of the earnings of the top ten per cent of wage earners to the bottom ten per cent as well as the ratio of the median to the top ten per cent. Clearly, the US is the outlier with respect to the gap between the bottom and the top and even between the top and the middle. Given these patterns it is not surprising that the US poverty rate substantially exceeds that of other developed nations.[2]

Do Europeans pay a price for lifting the bottom of the job market? The best measure of the success of an economy in generating jobs for its citizens is the employment-to-population ratio – the fraction of the population that works. Table 3.2 provides 2009 data for so-called prime age workers between

Table 3.1 Earnings dispersion

	Earnings percentile	
Country	90/10	90/50
France	2.91	1.98
Germany	3.32	1.72
Netherlands	2.91	1.76
Denmark	2.73	1.74
UK	3.63	1.98
Sweden	2.28	1.66
US	4.89	2.34

Note: The 90/10 ratio refers to the ratio of earnings at the 90th percentile compared to earnings at the 10th percentile. The 90/50 ratio is analogous.

Source: OECD (2009: Table H). Data refer to full-time workers.

Table 3.2 Employment-to-population ratios, 25–54 year olds, 2009

	Sex	
Country	Men	Women
United States	.81	.70
Germany	.86	.75
France	.87	.76
United Kingdom	.86	.74
Sweden	.86	.81
Denmark	.87	.82
Netherlands	.90	.79

Source: OECD (2009).

25 and 54 years. The focus is prime age workers in order to omit school-age youth, since these countries' educational systems differ greatly in terms of youth work patterns while in school.

It is apparent there is no basis for claiming that a much larger US low wage labour market enables us to deliver more jobs to our citizens; if anything, the US fares worse. Other researchers looking at different measures reach similar conclusions. As Harvard labour economist Richard Freeman (2005: 12) wrote, 'the best summary of the data – what we really know – is that labor institutions reduce earnings inequality but that they have no clear relation to other aggregate outcomes, such as unemployment.'

Myth: do you get what you deserve? The role of education and skill

Why are so many jobs low quality? Why do so many people find themselves trapped in these jobs? Many commentators believe that the answer lies in the education and skills of the workers themselves. In his 2010 State of the Union address US President Obama said that 'the best anti-poverty program is a world class education' (US Office of the President, 2011) and in making this assertion Obama neatly captured the dominant strain of thinking about the challenge of low wage work. Echoing the President's remarks, Alan Greenspan expressed the standard story when he said that inequality is 'a problem caused basically by our skill mix not keeping up with the technology that our capital stock requires' (Weisman and Henderson, 2004).

Scholars and policymakers point to the correlation between education and wages and argue that if people had more human capital then they would not find themselves in bad jobs. Closely related to this view is the argument that the trajectory of technological change has hollowed out the middle, increased the demand for workers with high level skills and, perhaps paradoxically, also increased demand for low skill jobs that by their very nature can only command low pay. This argument adds up to a worldview that the problem is a combination of inevitable market forces and worker skill deficits. The solution lies in education and training, not in shifts in how markets are governed or in how firms do business.

Virtually all US public policy aimed at addressing the problem of low wages has this supply side flavour: improve the skills of the workforce. There is, however, an alternative perspective that points to a different set of considerations. Education and skill are unquestionably important but the pure human capital story is incomplete because it can only explain a limited fraction of the variation in labour market outcomes. To obtain a fuller understanding of what generates and maintains low quality work we need to examine how firms make decisions about how to organize work and what quality of jobs to provide. Penetrating into the firm's decision-making calculus is crucial for developing a more complete and sophisticated view of what drives job quality and what constructive steps forward are possible.

There is no question that the educational attainment of Americans has increased, and that this increase reflects the US economy's demand for more and better skills. In 1950, 9.2 per cent of the labour force had some college education and 7.8 per cent had a college degree; by 2000 these figures stood at 32 per cent and 29.7 per cent respectively (Goldin and Katz, 2008: 96). An extensive scholarly literature confirms that many jobs are more complex today than they were in 1950 and that on average skill demands have grown (see Hilton, 2008).

Likewise, it is common sense to believe that there is a link between a worker's productivity and what he or she can command from the job market and that education is linked to productivity. The most basic evidence supporting these beliefs is the simple relationship between education and wage levels. Table 3.3 shows the average (rounded off) hourly wage in 2010 for employees with different levels of education.

These data do not control for any of the wide range of other personal characteristics (e.g. age, health status etc.) that might be thought to affect wages. In addition, one might worry that educational attainment is simply a proxy for pre-existing abilities. However, an extensive (to put it mildly) literature addressing these questions, and the relationship between education and earnings remains strong after controlling for these other factors. Additional support for the need for improved skills comes from conversations with employers, as well as with advocates for the working poor who manage programmes to help them move up job ladders.

All this said, we need space for another perspective. Although skills are part of the story, they are far from the entire explanation, nor do they provide an adequate intellectual basis for a policy strategy. Policies aimed at shifting the nature of labour demand deserve to loom large in any discussion. In order to do so we need to understand the limits of the skill/education story because it is so commonly accepted that it takes oxygen away from other important ways of thinking about the problem and its solutions.

One clue that a story based solely on education and skill is incomplete comes when we probe more carefully the relationship between education and earnings. It is clear from Table 3.3 that on average there is a relationship between education and earnings but this average masks a great deal of variation. To illustrate this point, Table 3.4 shows the distribution of earnings among men and women with only a high school degree between the ages of 31 and 39 years. Even within these very narrowly defined groups there is much variation in earnings, variation which cannot be explained by education, age or gender since these factors are controlled for in the table. More sophisticated statistical analyses reach the same conclusion.

Table 3.3 US education and wages, 2010

	Hourly wage ($)
Less than high school	10.00
High school degree	14.00
Some college	17.00
College degree or more	26.00

Source: US Census Bureau, 2011. See endnote 1.

Table 3.4 US hourly wages, high school degree or less, 31–39 year olds, 2010

	Sex	
Wage ($)	Men	Women
7.25 or less	3.06%	5.12%
7.62–10.00	19.97%	33.07%
10.01–15.00	30.45%	36.76%
15.01–20.00	20.92%	15.60%
20.01–25.00	12.18%	6.27%
25.01–30.00	6.30%	2.04%
30.01 or more	7.12%	1.14%
	100%	100%

Source: US Census Bureau (2011). See endnote 1.

One response to these complications is to argue that human capital is a multi-dimensional construct and that education is an incomplete measure of the full range of human capabilities rewarded in the job market. Personality and behaviour are also important (Grugulis et al., 2004). It is not hard to come up with a list of traits such as diligence, ability to cooperate with supervisors and fellow workers, and self-confidence. The literature that studies the relationship between these characteristics and earnings is less extensive than that focusing on years of education but nonetheless the evidence seems clear that they do exert an independent impact on labour market success. In fact, a recent review found that personality and behavioural variables were frequently more important than measures of education or cognitive ability in explaining earnings, a finding which is problematic for standard human capital stories (Bowles et al., 2001). Employers often make the same point in conversations, and national surveys of employers confirm this impression, with employers ranking attitudes higher than educational attainment (Cappelli, 1992).

Nonetheless, as was true for the simple years of schooling measure, the question remains how important these traits are in explaining overall wage patterns. If we could control for all of these other personal characteristics would it compress the wage distribution shown in the table? Such a compression would mean that the (augmented) human capital story was successful in explaining most of the variation across people in wages. Few sources of US data provide extensive measures of personality but one of the few is the Panel Survey on Income Dynamics, a nationally representative survey that followed thousands of people over many years. In an analysis of these data, researchers examined the impact of both education and a substantial array of personality measures on earnings (Duncan and Dunifon, 1998). In addition the statistical model included variables measuring the respondents' health status and family background. When all these variables were entered into a model estimating wages, only one third of variance in wages was explained. Another study using two different datasets, each including a range of personality variables, was able to explain only about a quarter of wage variance.[3]

Additional evidence that more is at play than personal characteristics comes from a series of investigations that estimated wage determination models by combining data on individuals with data on the firms in which they work. These researchers consistently find that a very substantial fraction of wage variation is due to firm characteristics and not due to the human capital of the employees (Andersson et al., 2005; Abowd et al., 2008; Groshen, 1991). Related to this pattern are studies that show firms have what might be termed a wage policy. This means that if one occupation is paid above (or below) the average market wage for that job then all occupations in the firm enjoy the same premium (or suffer the same reduction) (Krueger and Summers, 1988). This outcome cannot be explained in human capital terms since both market conditions and skill requirements vary across the different occupations.

The foregoing suggests that the persistence of a low wage labour market cannot be easily explained by a single-minded focus on human capital. Another way of making this point is to ask what would happen if somehow there was a radical increase in the number of people with a college education. Would this eliminate the low skill/low wage labour market problem? The rub here is that all of the evidence commonly cited about the benefits of education focuses on what economists call the margin, that is, what might happen if one additional individual improved his or her education. Telling your nephew to stay in school is clearly good advice. But perform a thought experiment: what if all the employees in low wage jobs suddenly acquired a community college degree or better. Would the jobs they hold disappear? Would the wages of all of them rise? The exact answer to this question differs depending on the time horizon; however over any reasonable period the answer would seem to be no.

For the short or medium run a way to think about the question is to consider what would happen to, say, the jobs chopping lettuce in hotel kitchens. Would the work suddenly become good? Would wages go up? One source of wage increase might occur if the suddenly better-educated employees could work more efficiently, perhaps by planning their work patterns better. But the likely gains from this change, if any, seem very modest. Another source of gain might occur if a more educated workforce permitted employers to install better capital equipment and hence increase productivity but here too the possibilities seem modest at best. Furthermore, given the limit on how much customers are willing to pay for salads the margin for substantial pay increases seem small. In short, over the working life of many of the employees it is hard to see much gain in kitchen jobs.

In the very long run the general increase in education might encourage employers in other sectors to invest in technologies that make use of new skills and this investment could create openings that lead employees to leave kitchen work and move to the better opportunities. This broad idea is behind the belief that education leads to economic growth and there is theoretical basis for believing such an outcome is possible (Acemoglu, 2002). However, this trajectory is of little help for adults working today in low wage jobs and, perhaps, even for their children.

Moving from thought experiments to believable numbers is very difficult because standard economic survey data on individuals is of little use in answering questions that are about non-marginal shifts and the path of economy-wide growth and change. The best hard evidence is the literature on education and economic development. It is thought that in the long run as a society increases its education level it grows richer, although even here the evidence, as one recent review concluded, is surprisingly 'fragile' (Krueger and Lindahl, 2001). The same review concluded that the best guess is that the link is valid but also that the process takes a long time. Drawing on this literature a recent simulation found that if the US could, over a 20-year period, increase its ranking on standardized literacy test scores from the middle of the OECD pack to the top then over the same period our GNP would increase by five per cent from what it would be otherwise (Hanushek and Woessmann, 2008). This uplift would be an important achievement and over a longer time span would compound into a considerable gain. But from the perspective of improving conditions in the low wage labour market over a period that would affect today's generation of workers, the impact is modest.

Conclusion

The myths that block action are just that, myths. Full employment is not adequate and policies that seek to reduce the incidence of bad jobs do not inevitably lead to economic underperformance. Improving the skills of the low wage workforce, while important, is an incomplete response. Public policy can induce some firms to improve their employment practices and reap the benefits from this improvement, and can also compel recalcitrant employers to upgrade work. What this action requires are higher employment standards, more effective enforcement and assistance to firms in training their employees (for a more detailed and fully referenced exposition see Osterman and Shulman 2011).

As matters stand there are two problems with employment standards: they are too low and are poorly enforced. With respect to enforcement there is considerable evidence of widespread violations in US low wage jobs (Bernhardt et al., 2009). That said, enforcement is only part of the story because current US standards are too low. The fall in the value of the minimum wage contributed importantly to the explosion of inequality in the 1980s and early 1990s, and today someone working full time at the minimum wage would not earn enough to put them above the poverty line for a family of four. In addition, standards need to be modernized to account for new employment arrangements, such as contracting out, that create ambiguity regarding who is the responsible employer.

The government itself can lead the way in improving job quality just as it did in the early twentieth century when the Federal government, via Civil Service Reform, created an employment model that was emulated by many private sector firms. States could insist, as some now do, that employment-related tax incentives, such as those used to attract firms to an area, require a decent wage standard. Public reimbursement schemes, particularly in medical care, put downward pressure on wages in industries such as nursing homes and home health care and this acts to the detriment of both patients and employees.

Standard-setting should be complemented by assistance: policy can help firms improve their practices so that upgrading work is not costly. Numerous programmes work effectively with employers to help them train their workforce and create job ladders. These programmes, often termed 'intermediaries', have seen success in health care, hotels and manufacturing, and have been positively evaluated by respected scholars and national research organizations.

The simple but often overlooked fact is that we know how to improve job quality, and we have the tools at hand to make considerable progress. At the end of the day the task of improving low wage work and reducing inequality is a political challenge. Good policy is within our grasp, if we can see past the myths to muster the will to move forward.

Notes

1 These figures are from the Census Current Population Survey Outgoing Rotation Group (ORG) data. For a description of how we arrive at these calculations see Osterman and Shulman (2011).

2 Using standardized measures the US poverty rate was easily the highest, at 17 per cent. By comparison France was 7.2 per cent, Germany 8.3 per cent, the UK 12.4 per cent. The US rate was even higher than the southern nations of Italy and Spain (Burtless and Smeeding, 2007). The data are for the early 2000s and poverty is defined as income below 50 per cent of the median.
3 This research is by Melissa Osborne described in Bowles et al. (2001: 1164–1165).

REFERENCES

Abowd, J., Haltiwanger, J. and Lane, J. (2008) 'Wage Structure and Labor Mobility in the United States', in E. Lazear and K. Shaw (eds) *The Structure of Wages*, Chicago: University of Chicago Press.

Acemoglu, D. (2002) 'Technical Change, Inequality, and the Labor Market', *Journal of Economic Literature*, 40, 1, 7–72.

Andersson, F., Holzer, H. and Lane, J. (2005) *Moving Up or Moving On: Who Advances In the Low Wage Labor Market*, New York: Russell Sage Foundation.

Bernhardt, A., Milkman, R. and Theodore, N. (2009) *Broken Laws, Unprotected Workers: Violations of Employment and Labor Laws in America's Cities*, National Employment Law Project, New York.

Bowles, S., Gintis, H. and Osborne, M. (2001) 'The Determinants of Earnings: A Behavioral Approach', *Journal of Economic Literature*, 39, 1137–1176.

Burtless, G. and Smeeding, T. (2007) 'Poverty, Work, and Policy: The US in Comparative Perspective', testimony given to the US House Subcommittee on Income and Family Support, Committee on Ways and Means, Washington, 13 February.

Cappelli, P. (1992) 'Is the Skills Gap Really About Attitudes?' National Center on the Educational Quality of the Workforce, University of Pennsylvania.

Clark, A. (2004) 'What Makes A Good Job? Evidence From OECD Countries', DELTA Working Paper 2004-28, Centre National de la Recherche Scientifique, Département et Laboratoire d'Économie Théorique et Appliquée, Paris, France.

Duncan, G. and Dunifon, R. (1998) 'Long-Run Effects of Motivation on Economic Success', *Social Psychological Quarterly*, 61, 1, 33–48.

Freeman, R. (2005) 'Labor Market Institutions without Blinders: The Debate over Flexibility and Labour Market Performance', NBER working paper 11286, National Bureau of Economic Research, Cambridge, MA.

Fremstad, S. (2008) 'Measuring Poverty and Economic Inclusion', Center For Economic and Policy Research, Washington, DC.

Goldin, C. and Katz, L. (2008) *The Race Between Education and Technology*, Cambridge: Harvard University Press.

Groshen, E. (1991) 'Sources of Intra-Industry Wage Dispersion: How Much Do Employers Matter?' *Quarterly Journal of Economics*, 3, 869–884.

▶

▶
Grugulis, I., Warhurst, C. and Keep. E. (2004) 'What's Happening to Skill?' in C. Warhurst, E. Keep and I. Grugulis (eds) *The Skills That Matter*, London: Palgrave Macmillan.
Handel, M. (2005) 'Trends in Perceived Job Quality, 1989 to 1998', *Work and Occupations*, 32, 66–94.
Hanushek, E. and Woessmann, L. (2008) 'The Role of Cognitive Skills In Economic Development', *Journal of Economic Literature*, 46, 607–668.
Hilton, M. (ed.) (2008) *Research on Future Skill Demands: A Workshop Summary*, Washington, DC: National Academy Press.
Hertz, T. (2006) 'Understanding Mobility in America', Center for American Progress, Washington, DC.
Holzer, H. (2004) 'Encouraging Job Advancement among Low-Wage Workers: A New Approach', Brookings Institute Policy Brief #30, Washington, DC.
Jencks, C., Perman, L. and Rainwater, L. (1988) 'What Is a Good Job? A New Measure of Labor-Market Success', *American Journal of Sociology*, 93, 1322–1357.
Kain, T. and Rouse, C. (1995) 'Labor Market Returns To Two and Four Year Colleges', *American Economic Review*, 85, 600–614.
Kopczuk, W., Saez, E. and Song, J. (2010) 'Earnings Inequality and Mobility In The United States: Evidence From Social Security Data Since 1937', *Quarterly Journal of Economics*, 91–128.
Krueger, A. and Summers, L. (1988) 'Efficiency Wages and the Inter-Industry Wage Structure', *Econometrica*, 56, 259–293.
Krueger, A. and Lindahl, M. (2001) 'Education For Growth: Why and For Whom', *Journal of Economic Literature*, 39, 1101–1136.
Lopreste, P. Acs, G., Ratcliffe,C. and Vinopal, K. (2009) 'Who Are Low Wage Workers?' ASPE Research Brief, February, Department of Health and Human Services, Washington.
Marcotte, D. E., Bailey, T., Borkoski, C. and Kienzl, G. S. (2005) 'The Returns of a Community College Education: Evidence From the National Education Longitudinal Survey', *Educational Evaluation and Policy Analysis*, 27, 157–175.
Organisation for Economic Co-operation and Development (OECD) (2009) *Employment Outlook*, Paris: OECD.
Osterman, P. (1999) *Securing Prosperity: How The American Labor Market Has Changed and What to Do About It*, Princeton: Princeton University Press.
Osterman, P. and Shluman, B. (2011) *Good Jobs America*, New York: Russell Sage Foundation.
Sawhill, I. and Morton, J. (2008) *Economic Mobility: Is The American Dream Alive and Well?* Economic Mobility Project, Washington, DC.
Theodos, B. and Bednarzik, R. (2006) 'Earnings Mobility and Low-Wage Workers in the United States', *Monthly Labor Review*, 129, 7, 34–45.
US Census Bureau (2011) Current Population Survey, http://www.census.gov/cps/. Consulted, 10 April 2011.
▶

▶
US Office of the President (2011) 'State of the Union Address, 2010', http://www.whitehouse.gov/the-press-office/remarks-president-state-union-address Consulted, 3 August, 2011.

Weisman, J. and N. Henderson (2004) 'Quality of New Jobs Focus of Election-Year Debate', *Washington Post*, June 23.

Wider Opportunities for Women (2011) *The Basic Economic Security Tables For The United States*, Wider Opportunities for Women, Washington, DC.

CHAPTER 4

Good Jobs, Bad Jobs and the Australian Experience

Barbara Pocock and Natalie Skinner

Introduction

Tolstoy began *Anna Karenina* with the remark that happy families are all the same but each unhappy family is 'unhappy in its own way'. The same cannot be said of 'good' jobs and 'bad' jobs. What is good or bad in a worker's job varies according to their circumstances – for example, their health, household situation and life stage. The growing diversity of the labour supply – by gender, care responsibilities, life circumstances, age – means that, unlike Tolstoy's families, good jobs are not all the same, and neither are bad jobs. We need a deeper and more dynamic analysis. These characteristics of the modern labour force have important implications for the regulation of work and the objective of fostering good jobs in a healthy, responsive, flexible labour market. Designing labour law to accommodate diverse workers, care responsibilities, life-cycle changes, a wide array of household types, and multiple career, workplace and job transitions over a working life in which workers enjoy good jobs, is a complex challenge. This is a much tougher ask of labour law than that required for a workforce comprised mostly of men, people without care responsibilities and workers who spend most of their working life in a single job, workplace or occupation.

This challenge matters more and more in a twenty-first century context. Female participation in paid work is increasing in OECD countries. Many countries face an ageing population with rising rates of dependency (that is the ratio of non-working people to the working age population). As a consequence increasing the rate of participation in paid work – especially amongst young, female and mature workers – is a major policy focus. This is a more pressing concern in Australia than in many other countries, given very low official rates of unemployment: 4.9 per cent seasonally adjusted in mid-2011

(ABS 2011). In the face of skill shortages and low unemployment, participation in the paid labour market has achieved a new level of valour as a road to citizenship and dignity. The driving logic of the Australian Government's 2011–12 budget was to 'get more people into work' (Swan 2011: 1). As the Treasurer put it, too many Australians are 'left behind, unwilling or unskilled – and untouched by the dignity of work'. Both major political parties are striving to out-compete each other with 'jobs-first' welfare and economic policy. In this discursive framework, there is less of a focus on 'good jobs' than getting citizens into 'any jobs'.

For many citizens it is true that finding a job increases their well-being, income, skills and effective participation in society. However, crucially these outcomes depend on the quality of the job they encounter. Australia's very stratified regional, occupational and industry labour markets mean that job quality varies widely. While researchers sometimes talk in sweeping ways about national employment and industrial regimes, jobs are very variable within them. That said, comparison of employment regimes is helpful in placing Australia in international perspective.

Gallie's (2007) typology of employment regimes distinguishes three kinds of regimes: inclusive, dualist or market based. Inclusive employment regimes are 'designed to extend both employment and common employment rights as widely as possible through the population of working age' and result in narrow differentials in the quality of jobs and employment conditions (p. 17). In such systems, the work, education and social institutional mix creates positive outcomes for most and is broadly inclusive regardless of age, gender, ethnicity, occupation, industry or form of employment. On the other hand, dualist regimes confer rights on a core workforce while many on the periphery – in lower skilled, lower paid jobs – have inferior conditions. Market-based regimes are characterized by very minimal employment regulation with wide gaps in outcomes reflecting differences in capacity to influence labour market outcomes. Where nations 'sit' in this typology is path dependent: those countries that began with strong inclusive systems tend to retain elements of it even as market influences grow.

Australia lies somewhere between the dualist and market-oriented systems in this typology, having moved away from a more inclusive character over the past 30 years. Some workers are well protected by union-influenced regulation of working conditions with 40 per cent of employees currently covered by union-bargained collective agreements. However, a second-tier of workers exists, covered by minimal conditions comprising ten national employment standards and industry or occupational awards. Beyond these tiers is a third, with workers who do not enjoy many of these quite minimal standards of labour regulation because of their precarious employment status, recent job entry, low unionization, immigrant status or other personal, job or geographical characteristics – or because their employment standards are not actually enforced.

Over the past 30 years, more inclusive aspects of the employment regulatory system have given way to more market influences and the emergence of a sizeable insecure workforce. However, Australians' historic attachment to some form of work-based 'fairness' can be discerned through, for example, a strong minimum wage system. Nonetheless, Australia is increasingly characterized by diversity in employment regulation and outcomes and which fall in predictable ways in relation to age, gender and ethnicity. The hand of the market is increasingly in evidence where strong bargaining power for workers is associated with good jobs, and weak bargaining power – whether because of low unionization, gender or the political economy of an industry – is associated with bad jobs.

The Australian case illustrates the importance of employment regulation and its effective enforcement, of management strategy/choice and behaviour inside the 'black box' of the workplace, as well as the significance of minimum wage campaigns, social norms around decent working conditions and union organization to achieve them. The Australian case also illustrates the importance of action at multiple levels – in the workplace, the sectoral labour market, at the urban/city level and nationally through political engagement around national labour law. While there might be dominant strains of an employment regime in Australia, there is a fracturing of regulatory outcomes, with tendencies associated with all types in Gallie's typology – inclusive, dualist and market based – in evidence at once in different places.

Does the quality of the job matter in Australia?

The effects of unemployment versus employment (whether in good or bad jobs) on health and well-being varies, reflecting differences in national welfare and industrial regimes. For example, limited access to unemployment benefits or to health services when unemployed, makes having a job – any job – a very pressing need in some countries. In these contexts, job quality is less important than being employed. In Australia, a comparatively strong regime of unemployment benefits and universal access to basic health care means that unemployment is less harmful relative to holding a job than in countries such as the US where the 'safety net' around unemployment is weak (Freeman 2010).

Recent research provides some evidence in support of this hypothesis. While, in general, unemployment in Australia is associated with worse health outcomes than employment, when we look at job quality amongst the employed the picture is more complex. Poor quality jobs are associated with similar or poorer health than unemployment. A 2006 cross-sectional study of middle-aged Australians found that poor quality jobs (insecure, low marketability, high demands and low control) were associated with similar or poorer mental health than unemployment (Broom et al. 2006). Each additional job stressor was associated with higher odds of poorer health, 'tempering the notion that any job confers unalloyed health benefits, suggesting instead that the health advantage of work depends on the quality of the job' (p. 585).

More recently, a longitudinal analysis of the relationship between Australians' health and job quality found that while being unemployed was associated with worse mental health than being employed, this association varied with job quality (job demands, complexity, control and perceived job insecurity). Those Australians who were employed had significantly better mental health than the unemployed. However, moving from unemployment into a poor quality job was detrimental to mental health. Workers in poor quality jobs had poorer mental health than those who stayed unemployed, and this increased in a linear way for each additional adverse job quality item (Butterworth et al. 2011). These findings suggest that, in the Australian context at least, job quality matters to workers' health and well-being and that there are good reasons for looking at what makes a job good or a bad, and improving the quality of employment generally.

What makes a job good or bad?

Job quality is a multi-faceted concept, including factors such as job task, skill development, employment stability, contractual status and work–life balance (Gallie 2007), absolute and relative pay rates, benefits, safety, job design, career opportunities and employee voice (Keep 2010).

In our view, on the basis of research amongst Australian workers in many different jobs over the past five years,[1] bad jobs in Australia can be distinguished from good jobs by 11 features: poor pay, job insecurity, poor benefits, poor working time arrangements (long hours, no control, poor fit with preferences, unsocial/shift hours), poor conditions, a poor spatial and/or temporal fit with the rest of life, poor opportunities for learning and progression, little voice, low job control and poor social relations at work. Combinations of these characteristics can result in low job satisfaction; poor integration of work with other life activities, such as caring for family; poor health; low productivity; and high labour turnover.

Some job characteristics, such as pay, working hours and access to paid sick and holiday leave, can be relatively easily objectively measured in

Australia. Others are much more nebulous, for example the quality of social relations at work and job control. The absence of a robust, regular survey of working conditions across Australia makes it difficult to assess job quality and its changes over time and between different categories of workers.

The incidence of bad jobs: pay, security, benefits, working time and work–family

To provide some insight into the quality of jobs in Australia we consider five of the above eleven job quality markers: pay, job security, access to key conditions like holidays and sick leave, working time and work–family arrangements. We have chosen these markers because there is better data on them. And more space would be required for the fuller discussion necessary for all the markers.

In comparison with other OECD countries, Australia has a relatively small proportion of low paid workers amongst its full-time workforce: in 2008, 17.5 per cent of full-time workers met the OECD definition of low paid (i.e. they earned two-thirds or less of median earnings). This figure compares with 24.5 and 21.2 per cent in the US and UK respectively (OECD 2010). Australia was close to the OECD average of 16 per cent and ranked twelfth out of 17 OECD countries. This ranking reflects Australia's relatively robust minimum wage system. However, there are some signs of a widening wages gap between high and low paid and growth in the proportion of low paid: the latter increased by five percentage points over the past 20 years (OECD 2006). In 2006, the after-tax value of the hourly minimum wages of full-timers was 54.0 per cent of the average wage. Australia ranked fifth out of 21 OECD countries on this measure, well above the average of 44 per cent. However, this ratio also suggests some deterioration: it fell four percentage points from 58 per cent in 2000 (OECD 2007).

A relatively high proportion of Australian employees – 30.4 per cent in 2011 – work part-time (i.e. less than 35 hours a week using the Australian Bureau of Statistics definition). Many of these workers are full-time students. Almost half of all working women (45.6 per cent) work part-time, a much larger proportion than in most OECD countries. When part-time workers are also included in the definition of low paid, 24 per cent of the Australian labour force meets the OECD definition of low paid (excluding full-time students).

Australia ranks better in relation to the gender wage gap: in 2008, the gap in median earnings between men and women was 12 percentage points, narrower than the OECD average of 16 per cent, and much narrower than in the US (20 per cent) and the UK (21 per cent). This outcome reflects the effects of equal pay decisions taken nationally in the early 1970s. Unfortunately the gender pay gap has remained stubbornly unchanging in Australia over the past 30 years. The gender pay gap narrowed significantly in the OECD as a whole – from 21 to 16 per cent amongst 26 countries between 1998 and 2008 – but narrowed by only one percentage point in Australia (OECD 2010: 295). The shift to more market-related pay and enterprise-level bargaining has resulted in widening disparities underneath average pay rates with signs that some groups of women are falling well behind. Long standing underpayment of many feminized jobs continues to characterize Australia's employment system and successive attempts at improving gender pay equity have met with resistance, leaving many women in low paid work especially in occupations such as childcare and care of the aged.

Many of Australia's low paid workers experience a second 'bad job' characteristic: insecure employment. The most common form of insecure work in Australia is 'casual' employment. Not common in international comparison, this form of employment is characterized by degraded conditions. Casual workers are employed, effectively, on an hourly basis. They have no ongoing formal employment security; that said, many casuals are actually long-term employees with average tenure of over two years. Casual terms originally applied to seasonal jobs or unexpected peaks in labour demand but are now widespread in Australia. Such terms give employers much greater control over labour deployment. Some employees in pursuit of shorter hours of work find that casual terms are the price of working part-time. While this can help some workers put together a job with caring responsibilities, the price can be high in terms of formal working conditions, job security and access to training and promotion.

Casual workers lack access to many protections and entitlements, including paid sick and holiday leave, and payment for public holidays. While some casual workers receive pay loading to compensate (in part) for the loss of these entitlements, many casual workers do not receive such a loading. Many casual workers do not take holidays or sick leave because of the cost to their income. A wide gap in job quality separates the employment conditions of permanent and casual workers in Australia.

In 2010, 24.3 per cent of all employees were employed as casuals, defined by a lack of access to paid holiday or sick leave. Most were part-time (55.5 per cent; 10.6 per cent for full-timers, ABS 2010: 52). Over a quarter of all working women lacked paid leave (27.6 per cent) compared to 21.2 per cent of men. Access to paid sick and holiday leave is a basic characteristic of a good job, and its absence for so many Australian workers is indicative of serious gaps in the employment regime. Over the past 20 years, the proportion of casual workers has increased rapidly, although the rate of increase has flattened out in recent years, perhaps because the labour market is approaching its 'casualization' saturation point.

Turning to a broader set of employment conditions, it is clear that a large slice of Australian workers are outside the core who have access to the broader range of conditions that might mark a good job. Amongst workers earning around the minimum wage (between $500–600 a week), 30.8 per cent lack access to any paid leave entitlements (sick, holiday, long service leave, maternity/paternity), compared to only 6.9 per cent of workers earning $1,800 or more a week. Thus low paid workers face compounding 'bad job' conditions while more secure, higher paid workers enjoy multiple benefits. The lack of paid leave conditions particularly affects workers in the accommodation and food industries (64.3 per cent) and retail (38.6 per cent).

Turning to the issues of working time and the reconciliation of work and family, many Australian workers are far from a good job. In the 2006 Census, 17.7 per cent of all Australian workers worked 49 hours a week or more, a quarter of all men and nine per cent of women. In the past two decades working hours amongst full-timers have increased and Australia has moved down the OECD ranking towards the long hours' end. Australia's leadership towards a shorter working week – evident in the mid-1860s – has given way to a long hours' culture which unions and labour law have been unable to contain.

Recent surveys of Australian workers show that three-quarters of those working long hours would prefer not to do so, and – not surprisingly – the work–life pressures they face are much higher than amongst those who do not work long hours. Similarly, a large number of Australian workers do not have a good fit between their actual and preferred working hours (52.8 per cent are more than half a day away from their preferred hours, most of them working more than they would prefer, Pocock et al. 2010: 36). This research suggests that a good job is one where hours are reasonable rather than excessive, and where workers have a good match between their preferred and actual hours.

Those working long hours, or more than they would prefer, are not the only Australian workers affected by work–life strains. Our recent annual surveys (2007, 2008, 2009 and 2010) indicate that for the majority of working Australians work negatively affects the rest of life, creating strain and restricting personal, family and community time. Based on these surveys, more than half of all workers find that work interferes with their activities beyond work and they feel often, or almost always, rushed and pressed for time. Mothers are especially negatively affected by time pressures, as are managers and professional workers.

National employment standards

Employment regulation has been the subject of intense political debate in Australia over the past decade. The adoption of anti-collectivist, minimalist employment standards in the form of 'WorkChoices' legislation helped the conservative Howard Government lose office in 2007. In 2010, the new Labor Government implemented labour laws that included renewed support for enterprise bargaining underpinned by a set of 'national employment standards' (the NES) as stipulated in the *Fair Work Act 2009*. The NES set maximum weekly hours of 38 plus 'reasonable additional hours'. They also provide a right to request flexibility for parents of pre-school or disabled children less than 18 years old; unpaid parental leave of a year and the right to ask for an extra year of unpaid leave; four weeks' annual leave (plus an extra week for some shift workers); ten days' personal/carers' leave, two days unpaid carers' leave and two days compassionate leave as required; unpaid community service leave for voluntary emergency activities; long service leave under some circumstances; paid leave on public holidays except when reasonably asked to work; and provision of a 'Fair Work Information' sheet to new employees.

For the first time in Australia the NES provide a directly legislated set of minimal employment conditions. While an advance in some ways, NES does not constitute an 'inclusive' employment regime for three reasons: firstly, the standards are partial (covering a limited range of employment conditions); secondly, some standards are ambiguous or porous (e.g. the 38 hours a week maximum is undermined by the unspecified 'reasonable additional hours' provision); and thirdly, many of the standards do not apply to some classes of workers (e.g. those with less than a year's tenure).

Previously such conditions were set in industry or occupational awards which had limited coverage. The new NES provide a set of lowest common denominator conditions, giving some protection on basic conditions. However, there are many workers who are exempt from these, including many on precarious forms of contracts.

Only some of the NES are available to casual workers, namely two days' unpaid carers' leave and two days' unpaid compassionate leave per occasion, maximum weekly hours, community service leave (except paid jury service), a day off on public holidays unless reasonably asked to work them and provision of the Fair Work Information statement. They are also entitled to an hourly casual loading. Those casuals who have been employed for at least a year on a 'regular and systematic basis and with an expectation of ongoing employment' are also entitled to request flexible working arrangements and to unpaid parental leave. Ongoing, regular casuals also have some rights to protection from unfair dismissal. While a policy move to attach certain rights and conditions to those in regular, ongoing casual work of at least a year's duration is evident, many casuals fall outside this definition and remain poorly paid, with limited job security and poor conditions. Their low rate of unionization leaves them particularly vulnerable (89 per cent do not belong to a trade union compared to 73 per cent of permanent workers, ABS 2010: 5).

In Australia, considering the issues of pay, security, access to basic conditions such as paid leave, nearly a quarter of employees have a job that might reasonably be characterized as 'bad'. Women, part-timers, service sector workers, the unskilled, young employees and those in private sector employment and smaller firms are disproportionately represented in such jobs. A larger proportion of workers are affected by 'bad job' characteristics such as low control over total hours worked and poor work–life interference.

Institutions and social norms matter: employment regulation and enforcement

Three kinds of employment regulation are now at work in Australia: collective bargaining, individual agreements and industry awards. In 2010, 43 per cent of Australian workers' employment conditions were set by a collective agreement (mostly union negotiated), 15 per cent by national awards which set minimum standards (incorporating minimum wages) and 41 per cent by individual agreements – underpinned and related to enterprise agreements or awards in many cases (Fair Work Australia 2011: para 280).

Some workers are outside of this system – working in a cash 'black market' or paid below minimum wage levels because they are in training or have a 'discount' related to a disability. The level of 'cash' employment in Australia is unknown but non-trivial, especially in hospitality and some small business sectors. Estimates of the proportion of workers earning less than the legal minimum wage suggest that around 7–9 per cent of Australian employees earn below the minima (Nelms et al. 2011). These workers are disproportionately women, casual, part-time and young. Healy and Richardson (2007: 6) write that this 'non-trivial' level of underpayment is indicative of 'holes in the safety net [that] undermine its function'.

Proper enforcement machinery is very important. Unions have been the traditional enforcers of labour standards in Australia. However, the low rate of union density – now 14 per cent in the private sector – has neutered this possibility. In this light, in recent years, the role of enforcement machinery through the offices of the Fair Work Ombudsman has achieved greater significance. Fortunately, this state machinery appears to have strengthened in recent years.

One of the main protections against an even greater tail of low quality jobs in Australia has been its relatively robust minimum wage machinery. Under the *Fair Work Act 2009*, a minimum wage panel of six members sets minimum wages annually. The regular adjustment of minimum wages must provide a fair and relevant minimum safety net of terms and conditions taking account of the relative living standards, the needs of the low paid and changing community standards. As the minimum wage panel put it in 2010, there is a strong case to increase the minimum wage 'to provide a fair and relevant safety net to protect the relative living standards of award-reliant [i.e. non-collective bargaining] employees and assist the low paid to meet their needs'. The panel pointed to the 'long provenance' of a minimum wage that allows Australian workers to 'live with dignity' (Fair Work Australia, 2011 para 243). In 2011, the decision was taken to increase minimum wages by 3.4 per cent taking the minimum wage to A$15.51 per hour or A$589.30 for a 38-hour week (Fair Work Australia 2011). This increase applies across the classification scale in industrial awards, affecting not only the lowest rates of award pay but also higher classifications. While the minimum wage-fixing system has faced vigorous opposition from some employers and their peak councils, especially in the latter part of the Howard Government, it has survived, in part reflecting a robust social norm in Australia around fairness at work.

Understanding and improving job quality in Australia: four challenges

Understanding job quality in contemporary Australia raises some interesting analytical challenges which also affect possible policy responses. First, job quality needs to be considered in the context of workplace, industry and the wider labour market. Second, analysis must be located in a larger social context. The third challenge arises from changing employment (and other) needs across life stages. Finally, it is clear that not all bad jobs are at the bottom end of the labour market: many traditionally 'good' jobs now have bad characteristics.

The appropriate unit of analysis?

Our analysis of work in Australia suggests that understanding job quality and the impact of working conditions on workers and their households requires a multi-level analysis that reaches beyond the 'job'. Understanding what makes a job good or bad requires analysis of circumstances and arrangements at the level of the job (e.g. safety, security, supervision), the workplace (e.g.

management cultures, overtime arrangements, job ladders, training), the industry (e.g. profitability and work processes) and the overall labour market (e.g. national regulation and enforcement) (see Table 4.1).

Take the case of work–family conditions: good work will be characterized by a job with a supervisor who implements flexibility to meet workers' family demands, a workplace with policies that enable such flexibility, industry arrangements that set reasonable standards around working hours and labour market regulation that provides paid leave to care for sick children and for parents of new babies. Several factors affect job quality across each of these four levels, including the balance of power between employers and employees and the voice possessed by workers; the nature and effect of the prevailing gender order; how different technologies affect work; the nature of work cultures at job, workplace, industry and labour market levels; regulatory standards; and the rights, characteristics and circumstances of immigrant workers.

Table 4.1 Factors that shape good and bad jobs

Level	What shapes good and bad jobs
Labour market institutions	Labour law Collective agreements Social norms (e.g. norms of 'fairness, work–life, gender (who does what) Education systems: schools, vocational education, university
Industry institutions	Nature of product market (internationalized, profit levels, service/manufacturing, labour intensity) Funding/business model (government, not-for-profit, private profit) High/low skill Industry regulations Industry training arrangements and qualifications frameworks
Workplace	Structure of ownership (private, public, listed) Employer policies on divestment of money and time in training, HR, job design. Management culture and social relations of production Size of firm. Nature of technology. Level of investment in training.
Job	Direct supervisor support. Intensity of work. Social relations of production at job level.

Good jobs/bad jobs and their intersection with household and community circumstances

Our research with Australian workers suggests that the feminization of the labour market, and the growing incidence of dual responsibility for work and care for dependents mean that the ways in which work intersects with household and community life, and the nature of their combined demands the good/bad nature of work. Workers who combine long hours and demanding jobs with a long commute, poor care systems (such as inaccessible childcare) and weak community and family support, have much worse work–life interference, feel stressed, rushed and pressed for time, and struggle to maintain healthy selves, households and strong community connections. In this context, bad jobs are about more than what happens at work: they reflect outcomes of the intersection of work, household and community life. In some cases, workers often trade off job quality (such as job security, higher pay and skill use) in favour of shorter hours to reconcile work and family demands. Women and mothers, especially, often trade good job characteristics for bad. Improving job quality requires attention to job conditions as well as the nature of urban planning, transport systems, care provision and spatial and temporal fit of work with other life activities.

What makes a job 'good' or 'bad' changes over the life course

What makes 'a good or bad job' changes over the life-course. This issue is of increasing significance with changes in household structure and the increasing participation of women in the labour market. A more diverse workforce, with more work-care changes over the life-cycle, means that 'standard' job characteristics do not meet the needs of a growing proportion of workers.

This point is aptly illustrated by the changing circumstances of a worker we interviewed in 2011. 'Jenny' had been working for many years in a highly complex marketing job for a cruise ship firm where she enjoyed good pay and career opportunities. She described it as a 'good' job – despite frequent unpaid overtime and a daily commute of three hours. However, when her first child arrived and her husband lost his management job, she found herself reluctantly 'stuck' in her demanding job and a long commute with an infant in long hours of childcare each day. This situation changed when Jenny's employer started a 'work-from-home' pilot that permits Jenny – now with a second child – to work from home part-time. She 'stepped down' to a non-professional job taking phone bookings. Her husband, who has secured a new management job, starts and ends his city job early, and she works around his hours and their shared care of children. For her, in her new circumstances, a minimum wage part-time job now constitutes a 'good job'. It enables her to spend more time with her children, avoid many hours commuting and have attachment to a workplace that she enjoys. When her children go to school, she will look for more challenging, better-paid work that uses her professional skills, probably within her existing company. Her labour market transitions have been facilitated by her employer's support. Of course her employer has also benefited – from Jenny's unpaid overtime, her work in a part-time job for which she is over qualified and through retention of a highly skilled employee.

For Jenny, what makes a job good has changed over time. Many workers do not enjoy such relatively smooth transitions: their navigations of work around care responsibilities often mean much greater losses of job security and tenure, pay, control, skill utilization and other conditions. The challenge for labour market policy is – as Campbell (2010) and Bosch (2006) put it – to 'preserve the substance' of a good job while redefining its form. Accommodating transitions over the life-course and attaching substantive job-quality characteristics to jobs, rather than setting particular standards, is a major policy challenge.

Are good jobs developing bad diseases?

The fourth 'good/bad job' challenge is to examine how many 'good' jobs are developing 'bad' habits. It is clear from our interviews and surveys in Australia that not all bad jobs are at the bottom end of the labour market, characterized by short hours, and low pay and skill. While many professional and managerial jobs are well paid, with good formal working conditions, their expansive work demands often crowd out skill development, use of leave provisions, job enjoyment, social relations at work and good relationships beyond work. While many professionals and managers enjoy aspects of their jobs, the toxic combination of 'love of the job' with weak or porous temporal or spatial boundaries around it, results in expansive work demands and in some cases 'extreme' jobs: that is, jobs that put personal health and well-being at risk, as well as the stability and temper of household life. New technologies have melted the temporal or spatial boundaries that historically contained work demands exposing many professional and managerial workers in a range of occupations and industries. Measures of work–life interference amongst long hours workers, especially managers and professionals, confirm their poor work–life outcomes relative to those who work reasonable or part-time hours, as well as a poor fit between their preferred and actual working hours (Pocock et al. 2010). Such experiences are often driven by under-staffing, powerful occupational and workplace cultures (for example amongst engineers and lawyers) and – given that they disproportionately afflict workplace managers and leaders – they often set the tone for others in the workplace. Mothers are especially negatively affected, with most working mothers – 70 per cent – feeling almost always rushed and pressed for time. In this context, well-paid, secure, highly skilled jobs with good formal working conditions (such as access to leave, training and development) can be far from good jobs. The growth in occupations afflicted by these 'bad' conditions means that the study of 'good jobs' needs to encompass a broad range of occupations, focusing not on form but on substance: such as having enough resources (including paid time) to meet job demands, opportunity to actually take leave and use flexible working conditions, reasonable working hours and management which actually manages job design and demands.

Conclusion

Over the past three decades the incidence of low pay, insecure employment and long hours of work amongst full-time workers has increased in Australia, making the quality of jobs a significant public policy challenge. As a society with at least a rhetorical attachment to equality and fairness at work, new challenges have arisen. Beyond traditional indicators of 'bad jobs' (such as pay, security and hours), changes in the labour market in recent years are creating new challenges on the job quality front, reshaping what makes a 'good' or 'bad' job. More women are in the labour market, there are more workers with caring responsibilities and more service sector workers who seek, or are offered, jobs with very variable characteristics. Standard employment conditions are no longer dominant, widespread or necessarily sought. Far from an inclusive employment system, various tiers of job quality are in evidence, including a core group of well-protected workers, a sizeable group with minimum conditions, and a further non-trivial number almost entirely outside formal regulation.

Individuals' job aspirations vary over the life-course, and by gender and age. In this context the settings and enforcement of work-related institutions matter a great deal. However, the policy challenge is to create institutional settings that can accommodate difference and labour market transitions without confining 'the different' – or those in transition – to inferiority. Welding onto new forms the substantive conditions of decent pay for a fair effort, job security with some say over the time and place of work is a challenge. Meeting it will require institutional adaption at labour market, industry, workplace and job levels. Doing so relies on action through the conventional industrial institutions that set minimum wages and conditions. But it also relies on changes in social norms and arrangements around care and social reproduction: about who should care and work, and the money, time and gender regimes in which people put together jobs, household and community life.

At present in Australia many individuals navigate personal adaptations to changing work and life circumstances, attempting to craft good quality jobs that allow them to work and live well. However, for many this combination results in 'bad' insecure, low-paid jobs and exclusion from careers and learning, fuelling a circuit of work-care-low pay-bad jobs and making labour market transitions hazardous.

In this context, good jobs are made through policy and action at job, workplace, industry and labour market levels, and good jobs are shaped by intersecting work, home and community contexts. Analysis of good jobs requires a wider life-course lens, and one that extends to jobs traditionally thought of as 'good' that are increasingly affected by expansive and intensive demands.

Note

1 This research includes interviews, focus groups and surveys conducted by the Centre for Work + Life between 2006–10. It covers childcare workers, cleaners and hotel room attendants (Masterman-Smith and Pocock 2008), low paid workers in retail, aged care and food manufacturing (Pocock et al. 2011), workers and residents in ten Australian communities (Williams et al. 2009) and four cross-sectional surveys of Australian workers (Australian Work and Life Index surveys 2007–10 (Pocock et al. 2007; 2008; 2009)). We acknowledge the colleagues, industry partners and funders who assisted with this research. Reports from these studies can be found at http://www.unisa.edu.au/hawkeinstitute/cwl

REFERENCES

Australian Bureau of Statistics (ABS) (2010) *Employee Earnings, Benefits and Trade Union Membership, Australia,* Catalogue number 6310.0, August, Canberra: ABS.

Australian Bureau of Statistics (ABS) (2011) *Labour Force, Australia.* Catalogue number 6202.0, May. Canberra: ABS.

Bosch, G. (2006) 'Working Time and the Standard Employment Relationship', in J. Y. Boulin, M. Lallement, J. Messenger and F. Michon (eds), *Decent Working Time: New Trends, New Issues*, Geneva: ILO, pp. 41–64.

Broom, D. H., D'Souza, R. M. Strazdins, L. Butterworth, P. Parslow, R. Rodgers, B. (2006) The Lesser Evil: Bad Jobs Or Unemployment? A Survey of Mid-Aged Australians, *Social Science and Medicine*, 63: pp. 575–586.

Butterworth, P. Leach, L. S. Strazdins, L. Olesen, S. C. Rodgers, B. Broom, D. H. (2011) The Psychosocial Quality of Work Determines Whether Employment Has Benefits for Mental Health: Results from a Longitudinal National Household Panel Survey, *Occupational and Environmental Medicine* (published online March 2011, accessed 11 July 2011).

▶

▶

Campbell, I. (2010) The Rise in Precarious Employment and Union Responses in Australia, in C. Thornley, S. Jefferys and B. Appay (eds) (2010) *Globalization and Precarious Forms of Production and Employment*, Edward Elgar, Cheltenham, pp. 114–132.

Fair Work Australia Decision (2011) Annual Wage Review 2010–11 http://www.fwa.gov.au/sites/wagereview2011/decisions/2011fwafb3400.htm (accessed 15 June 2011)

Freeman, R. (2010) Good jobs, Bad jobs, Any jobs: Employment in the Aftermath of the Great Recession, presentation to ESRC seminar series Making Bad Jobs Better, University of Strathclyde, http://ewds.strath.ac.uk/Portals/91/pdfs/MBJB1-3-RichardFreeman.pdf (accessed 15 June 2011).

Gallie, D. (2007) (ed.) *Employment Regimes and the Quality of Work*, Oxford: Oxford University Press.

Healy J. and Richardson, S. (2007) *A Strategy for Monitoring the Micro-Economic and Social Impacts of the Australian Fair Pay Commission*, Research report no. 4/07, National Institute of Labour Studies, report for AFPC, Melbourne.

Keep, E. (2010) Note from the first seminar, ESRC seminar series Making Bad Jobs Better, http://ewds.strath.ac.uk/Portals/91/pdfs/MBJB-Note-of-seminar1.pdf (accessed 15 June 2011)

Masterman-Smith, H. and Pocock, B. (2008) *Living Low Paid*, Sydney: Allen & Unwin.

Nelms, L., P. Nicholson and T. Wheatley (2011) *Employees Earning below the Federal Minimum Wage: Review of Data, Characteristics and Potential Explanatory Factors*. Research Report 3/2011, Minimum Wages and Research Branch, Fair Work Australia, Melbourne.

Organisation for Economic Co-operation and Development (OECD) (2006) *Employment Outlook 2006. Boosting Jobs and Incomes*, Paris: OECD.

Organisation for Economic Co-operation and Development (OECD) (2007) *Taxing Wages*, Paris: OECD.

Organisation for Economic Co-operation and Development (OECD) (2010) *Employment Outlook 2010: Moving beyond the Jobs Crisis*, Paris: OECD.

Pocock, B. Skinner, N. and Pisaniello, S. (2010) *How Much Should We Work? Working Hours, Holidays and Working Life: the Participation Challenge: The Australian Work and Life Index 2010*, Centre for Work + Life, University of South Australia.

Pocock, B. Skinner, N. and Ichii, R. (2009) *Work, Life and Workplace Flexibility: The Australian Work and Life Index 2009*, Centre for Work + Life Report, University of South Australia.

Pocock, B., Skinner, N., and Williams, P. (2007) *Work, Life and Time: The Australian Work and Life Index 2007*, Centre for Work + Life, University of South Australia.

Pocock, B., J. Elton, D. Green, C. McMahon, S. Pritchard (2011) *Juggling Work, Home and Learning in Low-Paid Occupations: a Qualitative Study*, National Centre for Vocational Education and Training, Adelaide.

Skinner, N. and Pocock, B. (2008), *Work, Life and Workplace Culture: The Australian Work and Life Index 2008*, Centre for Work + Life Report, University of South Australia.

▶

►
Swan, W. (2011) Budget Speech, Delivered 10 May 2011 on the second reading of the Appropriate Bill (no. 1), 2011/12, Canberra. http://www.budget.gov.au/2011-12/content/speech/html/speech.htm (accessed May 30 2011)
Williams, P. Pocock, B. & Bridge, K. (2009) *Linked Up Lives: Putting Together Work, Home and Community in Ten Australian Suburbs: Overview Report*, Centre for Work + Life, University of South Australia.

CHAPTER 5

A Framework for International Comparative Analysis of the Determinants of Low-Wage Job Quality

Françoise Carré and Chris Tilly

Introduction

Much, indeed most, analysis of job quality is carried out within specific national contexts. However globally, the largest differences in job quality are cross national; these comparisons potentially offer the greatest analytical leverage in understanding the determinants of job quality. They also enable us to consider policy options not otherwise considered when we focus on a single national context.

Analysts have proposed varied frameworks for such cross national comparisons of job characteristics and quality (for example Bamber et al. 2004; Hall and Soskice 2001a; Maurice et al. 1986). However, these frameworks have typically been induced from, and applied to, manufacturing and other higher wage or unionized industries. As contributors to a six-country (US and Europe) comparison of low-wage industries, predominantly in services (see Gautié and Schmitt 2010), we became convinced that existing frameworks must be extended in order to adequately characterize and explain differences in low-wage jobs.

In this chapter, we build on, adapt and extend existing frameworks to understand forces shaping the quality of entry-level, low-wage jobs. We argue that such jobs offer a distinctive and useful vantage point on the sources of cross-national job quality differences. In particular, they spotlight government mandates and supports, and the influence of institutions supporting the reproduction of the workforce. Both macro-level comparative analyses of dominant national institutions and average labour market outcomes, and micro-level comparisons of matched plants or of jobs in the same company, while valuable, leave important analytical gaps.

Meso-level analyses address these gaps; they entail comparing the same *sector* across countries and capturing within-sector, within-country variation as well as cross-country variation. They are useful for understanding variations in job outcomes because they shed particular light on how national-level institutions and organization-level strategies and histories interact. Here we rely on, and build upon, the contributions of meso analysis to develop a flexible framework for cross-national comparisons of job outcomes with broad applicability to low-wage service work – at least in wealthier countries.

A meso-level analytical framework achieves many objectives of comparative analysis but nonetheless encounters three familiar challenges. First, it needs to address the complex interactions between labour supply and demand on the one hand, and institutional and cultural forces on the other. A second challenge is the need to carefully contextualize institutions to avoid unwarranted presumptions of equivalence. A third challenge is presented by the issue of balancing structural influences with employer agency and strategy, as well as considering reactions of other social actors (e.g. worker organizations) to employer strategies.

We use entry-level retail jobs as the illustrative lens through which to apply existing notions as well as elaborate a meso analysis. We draw on our own fieldwork in the US (Carré and Tilly 2007) as well as comparative analysis conducted jointly with others (Carré et al. 2010, Askenazy et al. forthcoming, Esbjerg et al. 2008) and comparative work by other researchers (Baret et al. 2000, Jany-Catrice and Lehndorff 2005). In this earlier comparative research, we and others have wrestled with the problems highlighted in this chapter, and we build very directly on these earlier insights.

Why retail jobs? As a sector, retail generates high volumes of entry-level, low-wage jobs in wealthy countries. In several nations, it has taken the lead in labour deployment practices that tend to erode conventional tools for safeguarding labour standards and sustaining the social safety net. It has also led the push for labour deregulation (Bozkurt and Grugulis 2011). Retail work per se is service work, indeed increasingly so, as is a growing segment of low-wage jobs (and of jobs in general). Furthermore, on the face of it, service producing processes may be more susceptible to national norms and customs regarding work and consumption than manufacturing processes that offer far greater opportunities to implement machine-driven work processes.

In the remainder of this chapter, we start by briefly reviewing macro and micro comparative approaches, and argue for the unique contributions of a meso-level analysis. We continue by elaborating why examining entry-level jobs presents particular vantage points for analysis. We sketch out some of the key elements of a meso-level analysis, using retail jobs as our example. We review what we have learned from conducting such analysis and sketch out areas that require further exploration. We close with brief conclusions. Throughout, we primarily reference the US and the five European countries

(Denmark, France, Germany, Netherlands and the UK) that we studied with other colleagues internationally.[1]

From macro and micro analysis to meso analysis

Most international comparisons of work take the form of macro or micro analyses. Macro analyses take as their unit of analysis the national system as a whole, typically as captured by a small number of indicators. Economic models of trade and development (Samuelson 1948; Solow 1956) predict economic convergence, and early sociological models of industrialization (Kerr et al. 1964) identify sources of cross-national convergence in industrial relations and labour regulations. But stubborn evidence of divergence has directed most macro research energy to explaining differences. Scholars have put forward macro comparisons of the broad mode of economic regulation (Hall and Soskice 2001a), the welfare state (Esping-Andersen 1990), labour relations (Bamber et al. 2004) and many other elements of national political economies (Hall and Soskice 2001b, Whitley 1999). Their typical mode of argument is to identify key institutional differences and then draw out their consequences in terms of national averages or of some set of jobs viewed as typical or archetypical. Much recent work takes the form of construction of a new typology based on some overlooked dimension of work (Dieckhoff 2008, Gash 2008, Hult and Edlund 2008). Some macro analyses examine national systems of stratification, segmentation and inequality (Kalleberg 1988, Kerckhoff 1995). Macro-level analyses provide valuable insights into broad cross-national differences but, because they necessarily focus on a small number of factors and on the average or typical job, they are not well suited to exploring the interaction between varying business strategies and different national institutions.

Micro studies, on the other hand, match a small number of workplaces (often a pair) across different nations, often within the same company, in order to control for as many sources of variation as possible and focus on the impact of differing national contexts (for example Bank Muñoz 2008, Ferner and Almond 2007). Often, this scholarship examines the practices of multinationals abroad to sort out the relative effects of the multinational's home country institutions and those of the host country (Meardi et al. 2009, Royle 2006). Again, these studies have yielded important understandings of how and why jobs differ across national environments. And by construction, they typically omit within-country variation and varied employer strategies.

Meso analyses bring something new to the discussion. Meso analyses examine a single sector across countries, offering a more fine-grained look than macro analyses but capturing intra-industry variation in a way that micro studies do not (e.g. Coiling and Clark 2002, Katz 1997, Katz and Darbishire 2000, Kochan et al. 1997). Such meso analyses are particularly apt at examining the interaction between business strategy and institutions. Much of this work, though not all, looks at unionized sectors, often manufacturing. It is important to extend this level of analysis to less unionized and lower-paid service work. In this regard, the contributions of Baret et al. (2000) and Bosch and Lehndorff (2005a) are significant. Both ground their analyses of institutional effects in multiple domains, building on the seminal work of Maurice et al. (1986) on societal effects. Though the two formulations are distinct, they are closely related. Jean Gadrey (2000) specifies domains of market structure, organizational structure, industrial relations and the domestic sphere (gender roles and social protection). Bosch and Lehndorff (2005b), in their introduction to their edited collection suggest a somewhat different, but related, set of domains: product and consumers, management strategies, labour markets and labour market institutions, and the welfare state and gender relations. The last sphere in each case focuses particular attention on the welfare state and gender relations. In this chapter, we build on these contributions, and most particularly on Gadrey's classification of spheres, seeking to strengthen and more fully operationalize a framework derived from this earlier research.

The particular vantage point of entry-level jobs

Examining interactions of labour supply and demand with institutions as they affect *entry-level, low-wage* jobs in particular – rather than employment systems as a whole – offers particular expectations. First, we expect that national institutions, differing in their role, function and 'bite', will matter more for such jobs. These are jobs that employers have not upgraded – making it difficult to find an important role for organization-level factors and skill/technology factors in job outcomes. To experience job improvement or to make their job 'work' for them, workers in low-wage jobs are likely to rely more than average on standards set in governmental labour regulation, or on aspects of the welfare state.

Gautié and Schmitt (2010) have provided a macro-economy argument for how the volume of low-wage work[2] in a country is affected by the degree of inclusiveness of national labour and social insurance institutions (see also Gallie 2007). A (negative) correlate to inclusiveness is firms' access to exit options from national labour regulations and social insurance standards. But the focus on a particular sector and jobs inherent in meso analysis warrants moving beyond the broad characterization of national institutions to explore how multiple spheres/domains interact with employer strategies.

Second, we also expect an outsized role for institutions and social norms that constitute the reproductive sphere (rather than labour regulation or firm strategies). The performance of low-wage work – particularly *service* work – is less determined by labour-market institutions (e.g. training or labour standards) than other work and more affected by other domains, particularly the reproductive domain (gender roles and responsibilities in the household, welfare state institutions, customary practices).

A meso comparison framework for low-wage work: what we have learned

This section discusses what we have learned about conducting cross national meso analysis of low-wage jobs using retail trade as an example. We also discuss unresolved dilemmas we have encountered and raise questions for future work.

Labor supply and demand ... in context

A typical analytic approach would seek to explain the separate effects of labour supply, labour demand and institutions on job outcomes. However, we argue that labour supply and labour demand are so crucially shaped by institutional context that this exercise would be misleading. Here we briefly lay out an exposition of labour supply and demand *in theory*, then suggest how thoroughly social institutions condition these nominally economic forces.

In a simplified economic model, the demand for any particular type of labour is a derived demand: that is, it channels final demand for goods and services. Thus, it is the outcome of (given) consumer preferences, available technologies of production, workers' potential productivity as a function of their skills and capacities, and the market power of businesses as sellers of goods and as buyers of labour. Similarly simplified, labour supply results from demography (population size, age composition, family structure, immigration) and the preferences of potential workers (in particular, the perceived trade-off between goods and leisure).

However it is not meaningful to describe these factors determining labour supply and demand in some 'pre-institutional' way. Consumer preferences, an element of Gadrey's (2000) market structure sphere, are moulded by norms of prestige and emulation. Technology and the level of worker productivity stem crucially from businesses' choices about the organization of work (Gadrey's organizational structure sphere), choices that involve constant consideration of institutional strictures (the sphere of industrial relations) and 'exit options' from those strictures, such as union avoidance or outsourcing. Thus, although part of the explanation for US retailers' heavy use of short-hour part-time workers is the goal of matching staffing to fluctuating consumer demand, much of the explanation, especially in comparative context, is the lack of restrictions on store opening hours and worker schedule variations, and the low level of worker protection, which allow retailers (and others) to construct part-time work as a second-class status receiving different hourly wages and fringe benefits. Skill development institutions differ greatly across nations. Market power reflects both business structures (corporate governance, systems of finance, nature of business associations) and government regulations (antitrust, but also a variety of other levers: for example, land use practices condition retailers' market clout), thus building on both the market structure and the organizational structure spheres. The availability of workforce groups depends on institutional factors in the domestic sphere such as the availability of childcare, requirements and norms regarding schooling and so on. In short, employers and workers do weigh their tradeoffs but in ways that are thoroughly structured by institutions and norms.

Thinking through the institutional effects

As noted, in the simplest sense, institutions include laws and regulations, and labour relations institutions. They also include institutions regulating the reproduction of the workforce. Finally, social norms and customs, whether encoded in law or recognized practice, play an equivalent role. Here we discuss direct and indirect institutional effects.

Direct institutional effects

The first point of inquiry are the institutions of labour regulation. The comparison of retail jobs in the US and five European countries provides ample examples of direct institutional effects on job quality. For example, the US does not mandate hourly wage and benefit parity between full-time and part-time workers whereas the five European countries do. Descending to the national level, France has set a high relative value for the minimum wage whereas the US has failed to raise the minimum wage over long periods of time. In 2006, the French minimum wage stood at 68 per cent of the median wage. In contrast, by 2007, the US minimum wage had declined to only 30 per cent of the median wage. The minimum wage affects retail workers in two ways: through entry level wages and the reservation wage (the wage level below which workers will not accept an offer of employment). In turn, these differences have much to do with the fact that 42 per cent of retail workers were 'low-wage' in the US as compared to 18 per cent in France for 2002 (Carré et al. 2010).

Strong union representation with active collective bargaining has an impact as well. In Denmark, collective agreements enforce significant wage compression that contributes to the low percentage of low-wage retail employment in that country (Esbjerg et al 2008). Collective bargaining coverage was 69 per cent in 2004–06 (Tijdens et al. 2007). This direct effect has ripple effects as even non-signatory retailers obey the terms of collective agreements. In contrast, US retail collective bargaining coverage is very low (less than 6% in 2007; US Bureau of Labor Statistics 2008); the union threat effect is minimal.

There are also striking US–Europe differences in retail industry scheduling practices, in particular regarding advance notice and the workers' degree of control over their schedule. While retailers in these countries share some practices, such as heavy reliance on part-time hours, workers' day-to-day schedule predictability and control nevertheless varies substantially. For example, in Germany and Denmark, collective bargaining agreements require significant advance notice of schedules (26 and 16 weeks respectively). Though practice falls short of these requirements, retail workers in these countries receive far greater advance notice than US counterparts. The US lacks any mandated notice period; retail workers typically receive three to 14 days' notice of their schedule, and frequently have schedules adjusted on the spot (though with perfunctory request for permission).

Indirect institutional effects

As expected, institutions affect low-wage work outcomes most in indirect ways. By indirect institutional effects we mean those affecting the behaviour of key actors – employers or workers – rather than job outcomes per se. Indirect effects occur primarily as institutions interact with social norms and cultural practices, factors that are less formalized than regulations but are impactful all the same. Through these interactions, institutional effects are mediated, reinforced or weakened.

In short, societal norms have a bearing on *how* labour market institutions affect jobs indirectly. In retail, norms governing shopping hours and shopping frequency have clear impacts on worker schedules and overall staffing patterns. For example, limited UL labour conditions regulation combined with social norms have driven 24/7 operation for supermarkets, which in turn drives the high use of short-hour part-time work, increases pressure on full-time and part-time workers' availability, creates unpredictable schedules and a generalized pressure on compensation. In the European countries, cultural norms encoded in regulations or collective bargaining have so far yielded more circumscribed opening hours (restricted Sunday openings in some countries and no instances of routine 24-hour operation) resulting in less scheduling pressure on workers, less wage depression but, in some countries such as France, concentrated rush shopping hours and thus great workload pressure on cashiers.

In a comparison of cashier jobs in France and US supermarkets, we and our co-authors found that French women's preference for full-time work – reinforced by institutions such as childcare that make it feasible – and the limited supply of teenagers (who face long hours in school) limit retailers' ability to staff with numerous workers on very short schedules. In contrast, short-hour work is an important tool for US grocery stores which face a ready supply of childcare-constrained women and high school students (with lighter class schedules) who seek short work hours.[3]

Moreover, performance of entry-level work invariably relies heavily on skills and behaviours acquired outside the labour market but this pattern is more marked with low-wage *service* work because the work process is less structured through technology. While externally acquired skills and behaviours are also important in the performance of higher skill service work, training credentials matter far more in these jobs. For example, in retail, behavioural requirements entailing social skills, reliability, timeliness and ability to adjust to varying schedules are seen in part as built-in personality characteristics. Employers, however, also recognize that these characteristics are shaped by household or school commitments and by national institutions that affect the reproductive sphere (e.g. access to childcare or maternity leave) (Grugulis and Bozkurt 2011).

Social norms may have more direct effects on job outcomes

Social norms can affect staffing patterns and job outcomes quite directly. We expect that service work settings are particularly susceptible to these effects because 'production' occurs at time of delivery, and is interpersonal in nature. Cashiers are expected to be friendly and chatty in the US, but not in Germany.

Social norms can also trigger institutional changes which in turn have job impacts. For example the strong culture of consumer rights in the US has led to regulatory mandates for individual labelling of products. This requirement results in significantly greater tasks and a strong pressure to generate large numbers of jobs at low hourly wages. This work pattern is in sharp contrast to the shelf-stacking function in France where electronic labelling of shelves has replaced individual labelling.

Employer strategies (and worker responses)

Naturally, employers and workers do not passively observe and react to the institutions that shape labour outcomes. On the one hand, large corporations or employer associations actively seek to alter, evade or game institutions to exert more control over their environment while, on the other hand, unions and worker organizations seek to resist these moves. Both groups are strategists. Differing strategies are particularly important in explaining variation *within* countries, but particular strategies also have varied degrees of success in different institutional environments. Here the focus is employers, who generally dispose of more resources in this contest.

A common channel for strategic action by employers is innovation, both in technology and in management technique. Wal-Mart provides examples of both. Because of its mastery of advanced logistical technology, Wal-Mart was able to dominate retail in the US and Mexico via rapid organic expansion, altering market structure and evading antitrust regulation in both countries (Wrigley 2002, Tilly 2006). On the side of management technique, Wal-Mart developed a low-compensation, paternalistic model incorporating evangelical Christian notions of 'servant leadership' in white rural areas of the US South, which has been highly successful in repelling attempts to unionize in the US, but far less so in some other countries (Moreton 2009, Tilly 2007). Of course, worker organizations also strive to develop more effective organizational models in order to reshape industrial relations; for example, a retail union in New York City has used community-based unionism and global solidarity to win unexpected victories (Gleason 2011).

Sometimes a key innovation simply involves newly expanded use of an industrial relations exit option. Thus, in the US, retailers' tilt towards short-hour part-time employment served to evade both norms associated with full-time work, and unions focused on serving full-time workers. In Germany, likewise, retailers' rapid expansion of short-hour 'mini-jobs' has allowed them to dodge normative and collective bargaining restrictions as well as achieve savings from tax exemptions. In both cases, organizational innovations pioneered in retail have subsequently diffused to other sectors.

Most fundamentally, businesses have a choice among competitive strategies. In US retail, Wal-Mart's 'low road' approach based on low costs and prices is well known. Among Wal-Mart's competitors, we found many attempts to develop some variety of the high road via greater product variety and quality, or better service – though in most cases this was coupled with cost-cutting in ways that often undermined attempts to upgrade. Other, less common strategies included achieving greater operational efficiency through a highly paid, experienced and highly productive workforce, and locating in small rural communities underserved by other major retailers. In France, in contrast, the high minimum wage forecloses low-wage competition, and competition based on efficiency or the exploitation of geographic monopolies is far more common (Askenazy et al. forthcoming). Institutional configurations thus channel competitive strategies but do not fully determine them.

At a certain point, strategy can move from artfully responding to institutions to seeking to shape the institutions themselves. In the US, associations of retailers, fast food restaurants and other businesses fight for a lower minimum wage; unions fight for a higher one. Unions and allies seek to use land-use restrictions and approval processes to set required labour standards for new stores (again, Wal-Mart and other 'big box' chains are major targets).

Furthermore, economic actors can have an impact on *consumer* norms, once more altering the market structure. The late-2000s economic crisis has led retail customers to focus much more on price, but the degree to which this strategy will persist as economies improve will depend significantly on the marketing success of differing business models (*Planet Retail* 2010). Meanwhile, major US unions have sought, with some success, to make worker treatment a criterion in consumers' choice of where to shop.

Conclusion

In this chapter we have reviewed how a cross national meso analysis framework might be applied to understanding the effects of institutions, norms and employer strategies on job outcomes. This conclusion first raises challenging issues for analysis to address, bearing on three areas: how to categorize approaches to job quality, the resilience of social norms and the debate on cross-national convergence of employment patterns. The conclusion then underscores the contribution of meso analysis to understanding low-wage job quality.

The first question is, what are the best ways to use the contrast between high road and low road strategies? Job characteristics and job quality differ within countries as well as across them, and even within local labour markets governed by the same local and national institutions. One reason for this variation is simply ability to pay. But we and other researchers have long noted the importance of a distinction between a 'high road' based on better compensation and more investment in skills as well as greater productivity and a 'low road' (see, for example, Appelbaum et al. 2003; Milkman 1998). Cross-national comparisons should allow added perspective on the degree to which this dichotomy corresponds to workplace reality. What are the circumstances that permit better outcomes? Addressing within-country differences, some researchers (e.g. Batt 2000, Cappelli and Crocker-Hefter 1996) have maintained that distinct market niches are often important in underpinning these differences, and we have argued that this niching is an important element of the oft-cited difference in job quality between Wal-Mart and Costco (Carré et al. 2006). Is it more accurate to characterize job variation as a spectrum or scatter than as a distribution segmented between high road and low road? And how do these patterns differ by sector; is the story different for low-wage service jobs than for higher-wage manufacturing ones?

The second question is, how resilient are social norms? Our discussion of the role of social norms and customers, and particularly our accounts of how they interact with institutions and contribute to the latter's indirect effects on firm behaviour and job outcomes, provide explanations of where things are and how they got to be this way. There remain ambiguities about the predictive capability of this approach. Of course, history matters either through complex influences or simply path dependency. Nevertheless, accounts that give importance to social norms and customs – particularly those not encoded in law – must be held to special scrutiny. Social norms and customs can be eroded, amended or even overthrown at the instigation of employers. While change in social norms is expected progressively over time, sometimes it can occur surprisingly fast, as in the case of German employer defection from tripartite representative bodies (Vanselow 2008).

Important questions then follow. What is the predictive power of analyses that hinge on the interaction of institutions and social norms? Do such analyses help reasonably predict what will happen to jobs? How resilient are norms that safeguard job quality in the face of forces that erode job quality? And when looking across national settings, how can we tell where protective social norms will remain strong in the foreseeable future? What else should be assessed in order to make a reasonable prediction? Do countries fare better where there is a good 'fit' among different areas of regulations and with existing norms?

A third question is how the industrial convergence debate plays out for place-based services. Debates about the likelihood of the convergence of the nature of work in industrial societies date back at least to the eighteenth century and Adam Smith's (1776) *Wealth of Nations*. Despite the appeal of convergence arguments, researchers have consistently found that national institutions do indeed put work on divergent paths. Thus, our emphasis on the importance of institutions is certainly not a new one. However our focus on consumer services and retail in particular – as distinct from manufacturing – adds some new twists to the argument. On the one hand, it is hard to think of anything more culturally embedded than the merchandise offered by retail and consumer services: food, clothing, prepared meals, hair styling and the like. Moreover, such services are predominantly place based: while apparel or food can be manufactured distant from the consumer by workers unfamiliar with local tastes and customs, it continues to mostly (despite the online sales exception) be sold via direct interaction with the customer in ways that assume knowledge of those tastes and customs. This portion of the 'technology' of retail sales is less likely to homogenize than manufacturing production processes (Holmes 2011). On the other hand, the global penetration of giant retailers (starting with Wal-Mart, Carrefour, Metro and Tesco, which between them sell in over 50 countries containing the great bulk of the world's population) and the rapid diffusion of technological innovations in retailing and food preparation (especially in logistics and point-of-sale), suggest powerful forces for convergence. So a question worthy of further exploration is just how the convergence–divergence dialectic differs for place-based consumer services.

In this chapter, we have attempted to extend the argument that national institutions continue to matter to job outcomes when we consider specific jobs in particular sectors. Our contention is that meso-level analysis, comparing particular *sectors* across countries, sheds added light on *how* institutions matter in differing circumstances. We have focused on low-wage service work, using entry-level jobs in retail trade as examples. We have sought to illustrate that low-wage job outcomes are more susceptible to cross national differences in labour market regulations than those involving other kinds of jobs, precisely because workers lack other protections. In general, low-wage workers depend more on national institutions than on employer practices or organizational characteristics for improvements in wages and working conditions. Because low-wage jobs draw heavily on 'non-standard workers' (that is, secondary workers such as students with short-term commitments or parents with limited availability) and reproductive institutions shaping the availability of women and young people weigh particularly heavily on job outcomes. And because service is 'produced' partly in person, characteristics of service work are more prone to be affected by cross national differences in norms, for example those regarding service style and intensity.

In brief, meso analysis can enrich our cross-national understanding of job outcomes and their variation in two ways. First, it introduces sector as an independent determinant of job quality, and a mediator of national and corporate influences. Second, by narrowing the focus within a given country to a particular sector, it makes it more possible to identify sources of variation within country, thus highlighting the role of employer strategies *within* a set of institutions. Meso analysis shifts the research terrain from a model where cross national variations in job outcomes primarily reflect the role of national institutions (and, with globalization, of multinational home country effects) to a model where corporate strategy varies within country by sector, and even within a sector, in ways that are meaningful for job outcomes. It thus opens up a more complex terrain of analysis, facilitating the consideration of interactions between national institutions, sectoral production systems and corporate strategy.

Notes

1 Maarten van Klaveren and Dorothea Voss-Dahm, and Philippe Askenazy Jean-Bapiste Berry and Sophie Prunier-Poulmaire, with publications pending (see references section in the chapter).

2 Defined as receiving pay that is two thirds of the economy-wide hourly median.

3 In 2007, 34 per cent of US retail workers worked less than 20 hours, as compared to 16 per cent in France (Askenazy et al. 2010).

REFERENCES

Appelbaum, E., A. Bernhardt, and R. J. Murnane (2003) 'Low Wage America: An Overview', in E. Appelbaum, A. Bernhardt, and R. J. Murnane (eds) *Low-wage America.* New York, NY: Russell Sage Foundation, pp. 1–29.

Bamber, G. J., R. D. Lansbury, and N. Wailes (eds) (2004) *International and Comparative Employment Relations,* 4th edn. London: Sage.

Bank Muñoz, C. (2008) *Transnational Tortillas.* Ithaca, NY: Cornell University Press.

Baret, C., S. Lehndorff, and L. Sparks (eds) (2000) *Flexible Working in Food Retailing: A Comparison between France, Germany, the UK, and Japan.* London: Routledge.

Batt, R. (2000)'Strategic Segmentation and Frontline Services: Matching Customers, Employees, and Human Resource Systems', *International Journal of Human Resource Management*, 11(3), 540–561.

Bazen, S., C. Lucifora and W. Salverda (eds) (2005) *Job Quality and Employer Behaviour.* Basingstoke: Palgrave Macmillan.

Bosch, G. and S. Lehndorff (eds) (2005a) *Working in the Service Sector.* London: Routledge.

Bosch, G. and S. Lehndorff (2005b) 'Introduction', in G. Bosch and S. Lehndorff (eds) *Working in the Service Sector.* London: Routledge, pp. 1–31.

Bozkurt, Ö. and I. Grugulis (2011) 'Why Retail Work Demands a Closer Look', in I. Grugulis and Ö. Bozkurt (eds) *Retail Work.* Basingstoke: Palgrave Macmillan, pp. 1–21.

Cappelli, P., and A. Crocker-Hefter (1996) 'Distinctive Human Resources Are Firms' Core Competencies', *Organizational Dynamics*, 3: 7–22.

Carré, F., C. Tilly, M. van Klaveren, and D. Voss-Dahm (2010) 'Retail Jobs in Comparative Perspective', In J. Gautié and J. Schmitt (eds) *Low-Wage Work in The Wealthy World.* New York: Russell Sage Foundation, pp. 211–268.

Carré, F., B. Holgate, and C. Tilly (2006) 'What's Happening to Retail Jobs? Wages, Gender, and Corporate Strategy'. Paper to the *Labor and Employment Relations Association Annual Meeting*, Boston, MA, 5–8 January.

Coiling, T. and I. Clark (2002) 'Looking for "Americanness": Home-Country, Sector and Firm Effects on Employment Systems in an Engineering Services Company', *European Journal of Industrial Relations*, 8(3), 301–324.

▶

▶
Dieckhoff, M. (2008) 'Skills and Occupational Attainment: A Comparative Study of Germany, Denmark and the UK', *Work, Employment and Society* 22(1), 89–108.

Esbjerg, L., K. G. Grunert, N. Buck, and A Sonne Andersen (2008) 'Working in Danish Retailing: Transitional Workers Going Elsewhere, Core Employees Going Nowhere and Career Seekers Striving to Go Somewhere', in N. Westergaard-Nielsen (ed.) *Low-Wage Work in Denmark*. New York: Russell Sage Foundation, 140–185.

Esping-Andersen, G. (1990) *The Three Worlds of Welfare Capitalism*. Cambridge: Polity Press.

Ferner, A. and P. Almond (2007) 'Managing People in US-Based Multinationals: the Case of Europe', *Perspectives on Work*, 11(1), 4–7.

Gadrey, J. (2000) 'Working Time Configurations: Theory, Methods, and Assumptions for An International Comparison', in C. Baret, S. Lehndorff, and L. Sparks (eds) *Flexible Working in Food Retailing: A Comparison between France, Germany, the UK, and Japan*. London: Routledge, 21–30.

Gallie, D. (2007) 'Production Regimes, Employment Regimes, and the Quality of Work', in D. Gallie (ed.) *Employment Regimes and the Quality of Work*. New York: Oxford University Press, 1–33.

Gash, V. (2008) 'Preference Or Constraint? Part-Time Workers' Transitions in Denmark, France, and the UK', *Work, Employment and Society*, 22(4), 655–674.

Gleason, C. (2011) 'New Strategies for a Retail Economy', Paper to the Labor and Employment Relations Association Annual Meeting, Denver, CO, 6–9 January.

Grugulis, I. and Ö. Bozkurt (2011) *Retail Work*. Basingstoke: Palgrave Macmillan.

Hall, P. and D. Soskice (2001a) 'An Introduction to Varieties of Capitalism', in P. Hall and D. Soskice (eds) (2001b) *Varieties of Capitalism: The Institutional Foundations of Comparative Advantage*. New York: Oxford University Press, pp. 1–68.

Hall, P. and D. Soskice (eds) (2001b) *Varieties of Capitalism*. New York: Oxford University Press.

Holmes, C. (2011) 'Implications of Polarisation for UK Policymakers', SKOPE Issues Paper 26, Universities of Oxford and Cardiff.

Hult, C. and J. Edlund (2008) 'Age and Labour Market Commitment in Germany, Denmark, Norway, and Sweden', *Work, Employment and Society*, 22(1), 109–128.

Kalleberg, A. (1988) 'Comparative Perspectives on Work Structures and Inequality', *Annual Review of Sociology*, 14, 203–225.

Katz, Harry C. (ed.) (1997) *Telecommunications: Restructuring Work and Employment Relations Worldwide*. Ithaca, NY: Cornell University Press.

Katz, H. C. and O. Darbishire O. (2000) *Converging Divergences: Worldwide Changes in Employment Systems*. Ithaca, NY: Cornell University Press.

Kerckhoff, A. C. (1995) 'Institutional Arrangements and Stratification Processes in Industrial Societies', *Annual Review of Sociology*, 15, 323–347.
▶

▶
Kerr, C., J. T. Dunlop, F. H. Harbison and C. A. Myers (1964 and 1973). *Industrialism and Industrial Man*, 1st and 2nd eds. New York: Oxford University Press.

Kochan, T. A., R. D. Lansbury and J. P. MacDuffie (eds) (1997) *After LEAN Production: Evolving Employment Practices in the World Auto Industry*. Ithaca, NY: Cornell University Press.

Maurice, M., F. Sellier and J-J. Silvestre (1986) *The Social Foundations of Industrial Power*. Cambridge, MA: MIT Press.

Meardi, G., P. Marginson, M. Fichter, M. Frybes, M. Stanojević and A. Tóth (2009) 'Varieties of Multinationals: Adapting Employment Practices in Central Eastern Europe', *Industrial Relations*, 48(3), 489–511.

Milkman, R. (1998) 'The New American Workplace: High Road of Low Road?' in P. Thompson and C. Warhurst (eds) *Workplaces of the Future*, Basingstoke: Palgrave Macmillan.

Moreton, B. (2009) *To Serve God and Wal-Mart*. Cambridge, MA: Harvard University Press.

Planet Retail (2010) 'Winning Strategies for 2010: the New Economic Reality', Webinar, 27 January. http://www.planetretail.net

Royle, T. (2006) 'The Dominance Effect? Multinational Corporations in the Italian Quick Food Service Sector', *British Journal of Industrial Relations*, 44(4), 757–759.

Samuelson, P. (1948) 'International Trade and the Equalization of Factor Prices', *Economic Journal*, 58, 163–184.

Smith, Adam (1977) [1776]. *An Inquiry into the Nature and Causes of the Wealth of Nations*. Chicago: University Of Chicago Press.

Solow, R. (1956) 'A Contribution to the Theory of Economic Growth', *Quarterly Journal of Economics*, 70(1), 65–94.

Tilly, C. (2007) 'Wal-Mart and Its Workers: NOT the Same All Over the World', *Connecticut Law Review*, 39(4), 1–19.

Tilly, C. (2006) 'Wal-Mart Goes South: Sizing Up the Chain's Mexican Success Story', in S. Brunn (ed.) *Wal-Mart World*. New York: Routledge, pp. 357–368.

Whitley, R. (1999) *Divergent Capitalisms*. Oxford: Oxford University Press.

Vanselow, A. (2008) 'Still Lost and Forgotten? the Work of Hotel Room Attendants in Germany', in G. Bosch and C. Weinkopf (eds) *Low-Wage Work in Germany*. New York: Russell Sage Foundation, pp. 214–252.

Wrigley, N. (2002) 'Transforming the Corporate Landscape of US Food Retailing: Market Power, Financial Re-Engineering, and Regulation', *Tijdschrift voor Economische en Sociale Geografie*, 93(1), 62–82.

PART

II

Influences on Job Quality: Sectoral Approaches and Workplace Practices

CHAPTER

6

At the Altar of Shareholder Value? Corporate Governance and Conditions for Better Jobs in Swedish Manufacturing

Tony Huzzard

Introduction

Recent debates on better jobs in Scandinavia have been strongly influenced by union visions of 'good work'.* In Sweden, this vision was initially formulated in manufacturing by the Metalworkers Union (Metall) in 1985 and diffused across the blue collar union movement after 1991 (Huzzard, 2000). Put simply, good work sought better job designs in terms of high job security, fair distribution of rewards, co-determination, teamwork that entailed job rotation and elections of team leaders, competence development, autonomy over working hours, gender equality and a healthy work environment. In general, these components of 'better jobs' are consistent with what many researchers have termed the 'high road to work organization' or 'high performance work systems'. The logic here is that such designs prompt greater employee commitment or discretionary effort and scope for creativity and problem-solving (Becker and Huselid, 1998; Appelbaum et al., 2000), as distinct from low road forms foregrounding cost leadership, leanness, low cycle times and high work intensity.

Job quality has to be understood relative to the employment regime that provides the context for a particular workplace (Gallie, 2007). Sweden's co-ordinated market economy has featured weak markets for corporate control and strongly regulated labour markets (Hall and Soskice, 2001; Aguilera and Jackson, 2003). Swedish industry is relatively egalitarian, collectivistic, has high levels of trust and is based largely on voluntary compliance (Stafsudd, 2009: 68). This has been complemented by a relatively co-operative industrial relations tradition incorporating employee voice mechanisms, participative forms of work organization and active engagement by unions. However, there has been a recent trend in Swedish workplaces towards a tightening of management control, elimination of slack through lean production and in some cases a return to the assembly line (Jonsson et al., 2004; Wallace, 2007; Johansson and Abrahamsson, 2009). The scope for the realization of the vision of good work may thus be receding. But why is this the case?

Thompson (2003), in his 'disconnected capitalism' thesis, has a clear answer to the 'why' question. He recognizes that new forms of work organization have promised a new bargain between stakeholders – in return for employee participation and expanded responsibilities, employers would promote commitment and trust-building measures, through investment in human capital development, enhanced career structures, job stability and performance and skill-based reward measures. However, he argues that these are bargains that employers often cannot keep due to increasingly short-term pressures from financial markets. Yet some nuancing is needed here: not only are there national variations in dominant governance regimes, variations also exist across firms *within* national contexts (Hall and Soskice, 2001; Aguilera and Jackson, 2003).

This chapter explores these issues and argues that as a grand narrative, Thompson's argument rather overstates matters and that local production factors and the exercise of union and managerial agency can interact to make better jobs possible in certain circumstances. The chapter features a comparison between case histories of two firms in the Swedish automotive supply sector. The first of these is characterized by what the corporate governance literature calls patient capital in the form of an enduring governance regime dominated by a traditional capitalist family. The latter in contrast has been partially subject to a regime characterized by the impatient capital of private equity firms. The aim is to explore the implications of these different regimes on work organization and jobs at plant level.

Good work and the high road to better jobs

Union views about what constitute better jobs for members in Sweden have been clearly articulated for some time. In 1985, Metall[1] adopted a 'good work' strategy that promoted semi-autonomous teams, integral job training and the encouragement of job enlargement. Clearly, the approach of good work entailed a rather optimistic scenario about the prospects for better jobs (Gallie, 2007). Union goals included work of a progressively developing nature in healthy, risk-free workplaces as well as distributive justice (Huzzard, 2000). As such, they were consistent with production regime theory that emphasizes managerial choices as shapers of work organization and employment regime theory that emphasizes national regulatory characteristics (Gallie, 2007).

In 2006 Metall merged with the Industrial Workers Union (*Industrifacket*) to form a new union, IFMetall. The new union updated the good work policy under the name 'sustainable work' (IFMetall, 2008). This acknowledged the need for long-term thinking in production design and a more holistic view of developmental work that included planned competency development, payments systems that supported development and the exploration of possibilities for mutual gains. These objectives in many cases echoed the earlier policy. What was new, however, was an apparently more pragmatic stance towards lean production.

Early optimism was prevalent in union circles about the plausibility of the good work project, particularly in the economic context of the late 1980s. Yet progress was patchy by the end of the 1990s (Huzzard, 2000) and even in regression some ten years later (Wallace, 2007; Johansson and Abrahamsson, 2009). Increasingly, it seems that local managers in many firms felt unable or unwilling to take to the high road. In 2003, the union estimated that around 50% of metalworkers were employed at workplaces organized according to the principles of lean production (Metall, 2003). This doctrine yields a different picture of job quality than that of good work: leanness seeks to eliminate any waste in labour processes that does not add value to customers. Moreover, it generally eschews developmental possibilities for workers that do not directly add to the bottom line (Womack et al., 1990).

The trend in manufacturing towards lean production is not restricted to Sweden. Critical scholars have questioned the desirability of the high performance paradigm (Ramsey et al., 2000; Godard, 2004) and its practical possibilities (Durand, 1998; Thompson, 2003). But how might this trend, and consequent implications for job quality, be accounted for by changes in corporate governance regimes? It is to this aspect, in particular the disconnected capitalism thesis, that the chapter now turns.

Disconnected capitalism and corporate governance

Most firms in Swedish manufacturing are apparently on a low road trajectory. For Thompson (2003), this comes as no surprise. Contemporary capitalism is beset by structural tendencies whereby capital markets increasingly require short-term returns on investments. These discriminate against business strategies based on longer term horizons that foreground the role of intangibles such as knowledge, human capital and the capacity to innovate. Some have pointed out that deregulated institutional forms and globalized product markets have had profound implications on capital markets (Streeck and Thelen, 2005; Clark, 2009). Consequently, it is claimed, the neoclassical logic of the capital markets has disconnected with the knowledge and innovation-based logic of the labour market on which the idea of the high road rests. Accordingly, employers are unable to maintain their side of the bargain (Thompson, 2003: 363–367): the relative power of capital obliges managers to bend towards the interests of owners and the logic of shareholder value rather than the interests of employees and the (high road) logic of production.

Nevertheless, it seems over-simplistic to assert that the onset of a 'disconnected capitalism' is a generalizable trend at least in the Swedish context. Corporate governance scholars have detected an increasing role for institutional investors in Swedish capital markets, an increasing marketization of corporate control and an increased attachment to the ideology of shareholder value (Blom, 2007; Tengblad, 2004). Yet many firms in Sweden have been strongly influenced historically by dominant families and remain so through controlling companies that have been the bedrock of corporate power. This ownership form is typified by the Wallenberg family which exerts its power and influence through various foundations. These foundations are the largest shareholder in the family's publicly traded holding company, Investor. Indirectly, the family controls one-third of Sweden's GDP through a banking and industrial empire of more than 12 companies, and has a controlling equity holding in many major companies. Investor owns the vast majority of all multiple voting shares in these which means a disproportionate influence over firms in terms of capital invested. Historically, the Wallenberg Foundation is a paradigm exemplar of what is termed in the corporate governance literature as 'patient capital', that is, capital investors with a relatively long time horizon in terms of assessing returns.

However, the dominance of the Wallenberg family on the Stockholm Stock Exchange has declined somewhat since the 1980s as new financiers and owner groups, especially foreign investors, have increased their ownership share.[2] As elsewhere, a popular choice of alternative ownership is the private-equity model. This presupposes a pool of capital raised and managed for direct investment in a particular company. This may take a number of forms, including limited partnerships whereby the fund has sole control of equity in a portfolio company and eschews being publicly listed (Clark, 2009). The firm is seen as a bundle of assets held together contractually that can be manipulated for short term adding value and disposal, perhaps within a time frame of two to five years. The objective of shareholder value is prioritized, often at the expense of workers and taxpayers (Watt, 2008). The private equity model is thus an obvious example of 'impatient capital'. How, then, might 'patient' and 'impatient' capital impact differentially on production choices at plant level and, in turn, on job quality? Following a brief methods discussion, this question will now be addressed by the presentation and analysis of two case histories.

Method

The automotive supply sector provides a useful site in which to examine the above question. Firms in this sector exhibit various corporate governance and employee participation configurations both within and across countries. Such a range of configurations is not as easily discernible in, for example, final assembly. Moreover, the competitive dynamics of the automotive industry, including suppliers, require firms to exhibit considerable capacity to change and innovate thus presupposing changes in work organization; accordingly, the sector seems particularly suitable for examining the links between corporate governance and choices on work organization.

So how do the contrasting logics of patient and impatient capital play out in terms of job quality at the workplace? The analysis presented here derives from cases of two contrasting firms (here with the pseudonyms Bearings and Plastics) and a focal plant from each. The key differentiating principle behind this selection was that of corporate governance, the former being owned by a family dominated firm and thus relatively sheltered from the capital markets, the latter being a private equity firm thus subject to the short-term financial objectives of the owners. Both firms were, however, subject to the same conjunctural developments in product markets. A critical realist view is adopted whereby choices on work organization and better jobs are seen as outcomes of the dynamics between governance regimes and forms of employee voice. Semi-structured interviews were conducted from identical instruments in the cases concerned with strategic, HR and technical managers and employee representatives with a view to constructing a retrospective case history for each firm that allows for comparative analysis (see Huzzard, 2000, for a similar methodology). Interview data were supplemented where possible with documents for purposes of data triangulation.

Case 1: Bearings

The Bearings group is a world leading global supplier of products, services and solutions in many areas, notably rolling bearings, seals, mechatronics, services and lubrication systems. A traditional emphasis on the manufacturing of bearings has recently given way to 'new solutions' (for the automotive industry). Net turnover and operating profits in 2008 were around 60,000m EUR and 700m EUR respectively. The group employs some 45,000 people at 110 sites in 28 countries.

At Bearings, the current collaborative spirit of co-determination can be traced back to work re-organization in the early 1990s. Previously, employment relations were low-trust and conflictual alongside a traditional, Tayloristic approach to managing the labour process. Prompted by high labour turnover and high absenteeism, the employer, with union support, set out to change the labour process. In the words of the HR Manager,

> So we realised that we needed to do something. [We asked] 'what shall we do in our organization to make people more efficient and keep the people here? How can we keep people healthy enough and not let them stay home sick?' And then we started with our new team-based organization. This was in about 1985. In 1990 the structure was fully implemented.

The new model presaged a period of relative continuity based on co-operation and high trust. This combined human resource management initiatives with a strong union organization and influence at the focal plant. Work organization now entailed autonomous teamwork, multi-skilling, competence development and a concomitantly supportive rewards system.

Bearings' ownership structure has been consistently dominated by one major shareholder, a holding company closely associated with the Wallenberg family. This has provided the basis for much continuity and stability in the company despite a change of strategic focus to diversification and customer orientation. The holding company appears to embody patient capital. According to the union chair at the plant,

> I would absolutely describe the Wallenberg capital as patient capital. They always see the business from a long term perspective. They give the companies quite a good chance to run the business by themselves, a lot of freedom to act... in the 90s we could not see that they became more impatient. They have adopted their style to run the business from the first Wallenberg on and have not changed that style.

Work organization at the plant involved replacing the assembly line with a flexible, team-based organization that still endures. Consistent with the good work strategy, Metall at Bearings sought to establish team-working with responsibility for purchasing orders, materials handling, quality contacts with the departments and planning responsibilities, tasks previously undertaken by supervisors.

The union view was as follows:

> So the biggest change I think was the Congress on good work in 1985 ... we asked: 'how can we extend our members' knowledge?' The company then was only buying their 'hands' not their 'heads'. So we discussed how we could implement the new ideas. Bearings was very willing to discuss this and so we started a new initiative.

Although lean production has become increasingly fashionable in Sweden, albeit with a national twist (Brulin and Nilsson, 1999), the union representatives at Bearings were keen to distance lean production from what was happening at the plant. While more comfortable with the notion of high performance team work, the union perceived that this still fell short of 'good work' because of limitations to staff competence development. The HR Manager was also sceptical about lean production as it was ill-equipped to deal with variability in production levels. Eradicating slack left no scope for rapid production increases; eliminating emergent slack in a downturn also led to competency losses. In the view of the HR Manager,

> Lean production is based on the idea that you use the resources you have to use, nothing more. It is not our main idea that the resources should be reduced as much as possible. We follow the idea of efficient production.
>
> Lean is good if you do the same thing repeatedly. But if you have changing capacities and fluctuations, it will take you down. What will you do if you have an expanding situation? You have no resources available if you have reduced them before to the minimum.

The unions see that greater autonomy in the new labour process has made work less intensive. However, it is admitted that peer-group pressure has become increasingly significant as a mechanism of organizational control (Rennstam, 2007). As the union chair noted,

> Under teamwork the work has not become more intensive in the sense that the team members put pressures on themselves. They are more focused on what is necessary to do. And they do it with their knowledge which has also helped them to limit the pressure. But of course, from time to time the work can become intensive. But in the old days the pressure was higher, because the people had to do what the manager said. Today they have control over their work processes.

In sum, the governance regime at Bearings appeared stable with its owners having a long-term orientation towards return on their investments. Significant here was a single shareholder in the form of a holding company with close links to a dominant capitalist family. This arrangement appears to embody 'patient' capital. However, day-to-day decisions on work organization are made at plant level without direct involvement from the owners. Plant management rejects the low road option of lean production because of its inflexibility in contexts of fluctuating capacities and product markets. Further, at the plant there has been an increasing focus on total customer solutions rather than mass production. This entails both more interaction between the teams and customers and greater knowledgeability in the labour process. The need to meet diverse customer service requirements is not well served by lean production. Accordingly, the plant has been characterized by self-managed autonomous teams, a competency-based rewards system and high cycle times, all of which in the Swedish context are considered as aspects of better jobs.

Case 2: Plastics

The Plastics group is a supplier of engineered plastics to the automotive industry, comprising both interior and exterior components. It claims a strong market position in the premium segment of the car market and the markets for heavy and light trucks. Group turnover in 2008 was EUR 1,300m when it had around 6,000 employees in ten countries and 30 production facilities globally. In March 2009, however, the group's companies went into receivership due to the collapse of the automotive market. Under new owners, a new company was formed in 2009 to resume operations at some of its sites around the world.

All interviewees saw industrial relations as being largely cooperative historically. The union is represented at board level by the chair at the focal plant. At plant level, there is formal reliance on codified agreements and considerable informal dialogue between local union representatives and plant management. Not surprisingly, however, the crisis and bankruptcy of 2008–2009 put industrial relations at the plant under considerable strain.

Plastics, at times in other names, was originally a publicly listed company, then a wholly owned subsidiary until a private equity company purchased most of its stock in 2001. This stock, valued at around €152m, was thereafter bought by another private equity company in 2005. Around 10 per cent of the group was then bought up by a Swedish bank on the reconstruction following the bankruptcy in 2009. The new group had around 600 employees in total. The main objective of the new owners in 2001 was expansion through acquisition, focusing explicitly on plastic components in the automotive sector. A trade union representative saw these periods as follows:

> When we were taken over by the financial investors it was a good thing. The new owners wanted to expand us. The old owner was not really

> focused on the automotive business. It was a diversified corporation with many different products. The main product was aluminium and we are a plastics company. So, when we were sold our business was more focused. This was good...I cannot say they were owners who wanted to enter the company, take money out of the company and then leave us. They really tried to make us grow.

Moreover, the robustness of the co-determination act maintained union influence at board level after the switch to private equity ownership (Bacon et al., 2010). Nevertheless, the private equity firms were driven by short-term financial objectives rather than long-term production objectives. The Technical Manager saw a clear contrast with the period previously:

> When you go back...it was a bit different. Before, you were in less of a hurry. When you have banking people, private equity, you need to deliver on cash. Profit and loss statements, balance sheets, blah blah blah. Core values, human feelings and so on are rather put on hold.

Neither private equity firm had any real interest in production issues, however. They delegated these matters to the management: work organization issues were largely decoupled from the corporate governance system. The new owners were interested only in lowering labour costs. For example, they regarded the old payment system as too expensive, and a new focus was placed on exerting financial controls including greater awareness and transparency in reporting routines and target levels. Increased shareholder value was the explicit aim of the new owners, primarily through higher production volumes and higher profits to present a favourable picture to the stock market after a period of 3 to 5 years. A growth rate of around 5 per cent per year was anticipated.

Plastics saw significant reforms in work organization at the beginning of the 1990s. At the focal plant, management acknowledged that manufacturing jobs were seen as unattractive in a tight labour market, with turnover rates around 30% per year. Although the plant was organized by the then Industrial Workers Union, a similar discussion on good work took place to those at plants organized by Metall. The consensus, as elsewhere, was to leave Taylorism behind by moving towards some form of team-working that afforded employees greater responsibility. This also entailed a concomitant system of work progression through obtaining new competences and a new payment system. This was agreed and implemented in 1992.

Previously, the plant was organized around supervisors on every shift and no team structure. In contrast, the new form of work organization from the early 1990s was strongly influenced by the Japanese ideas of 'kaizen'. The label lean production wasn't used at the plant, but the Technical Manager stated that,

> When I look at lean production today we have all the elements. But we didn't [in the early 1990s] call it lean production. We called it kaizen. If you go through a checklist for lean production we have it all. The substance is the same.

Management retained authority for the direction and pace of work through quality and precision controls, productivity boards and measurement routines. The pace of work was determined by the machines in the plant and the groups that had formed had little discretion over these. Rather more discretion, however, was discernible in the support groups. Overall, however, the teamwork model fell considerably short of the high road ideals of 'good work'. The need for more control on the lines, moreover, saw the early reintroduction of the supervisor with a particular responsibility for overseeing the teams as well as planning and problem solving. However, the impact of work re-organization was seen as patchy in its effectiveness and implementation.

A new impetus for developing the team structure was evident by the end of the 1990s before the private equity buy-out. Discussions focused on reintroducing the teamwork programme across the company: creating groups, with discussions on problem solving and so on within the groups. But this didn't happen largely due to a strong attachment to the old supervisor system within influential circles at corporate headquarters. The union view has been that teamwork should encompass the entire plant, and that everyone in the teams should be able to perform team tasks. This however was not the case at the plant – and following bankruptcy the priority became survival, rather than progressing a work organization agenda.

Although Plastics was, until 2001, owned by a publicly listed company with a reasonably long-term orientation, the union found it difficult to advance the work organization agenda during the 1990s. The switch to a period of ownership by private equity firms from 2001, in other words a transition from patient to impatient capital, did not lead to any discernible changes in the labour process with the exception of a new payments system. Despite active union engagement in the introduction of the (albeit patchy) model of teamwork, what ensued and endured until the late 2000s was essentially a low road variant.

The representatives of the owners, although active at board level in advancing their financial interests, did not actively intervene in decision-making at plant level. Indeed, plant (and notably HR) management were keen to move towards more autonomous forms of teamwork prior to the bankruptcy. There is no evidence in the data of the owners resisting such moves. Unlike Bearings, the labour process has remained that of batch production of fairly standardized components. Bearings' relative move along the value chain to encompass service offerings in the product market was not evident at Plastics. This suggests that the location of productive activity on the value chain influences the scope for higher road production choices (Altmann and Deiss, 1998). At Plastics there is little evidence of the job rotation, team governance and high cycle times sought in union visions of good work.

Discussion

By the end of the 1990s the Metalworkers Union conceded that the objectives of 'good work' had only been realized at around 10 per cent of manufacturing workplaces in Sweden (Huzzard, 2000). The low road doctrines of lean production and downsizing (in some cases inseparable from each other) had become dominant, especially in contexts of standardized work practices. Indeed, by the late 2000s, the ideas of lean production were clearly having a major influence on production designs at Swedish workplaces (Wallace, 2007; Johansson and Abrahamsson, 2009). The exercise of strategic choice was thus not to take to the high road. By the mid-2000s researchers were reporting the reintroduction of assembly lines in the Swedish automobile industry, replacing alternative designs based on semi-autonomous groups and socio-technical principles (Jonsson et al., 2004). However, these latter designs continued to be used in bus and truck production given their lower volumes and more precise customer specifications (Kuipers et al., 2004).

To what extent, then, can linkages be established between the capital markets and job quality? In general, the analysis presented here suggests that it is over-simplistic to draw definite structural linkages between governance regimes and choices on work organization that yield good or bad jobs. In both cases, plant management enjoyed more discretion than that presupposed in the disconnected capitalism thesis. If any causal linkage existed between governance form and work organization outcomes at the workplaces in question, this was of an indirect nature. But governance regimes and ultimately the capital markets do set outer parameters or constraints on work organization outcomes at the firm level. It is, after all, unrealistic to suggest that either plant stood outside of corporate financial controls. In other words, the respective roles of patient and impatient capital would appear to be a key dimension of what has previously been termed 'design space' in the labour process (Bessant, 1983). Clearly this reflects itself in the timescale over which investors pursue their respective objectives and whether these prioritize financial gain (Plastics) or a longer term engagement entailing a production logic that recognizes the roles of employees, knowledge and innovation in adding value (Bearings).

There is evidence in the cases that choices on work organizational forms at plant level are also conditioned by how the actors see the technical nature of the labour process itself. Socio-technical systems theorists have long noted the roles of perceived technological uncertainty and perceived technological independence in shaping design choices (Cummings, 1982). To these factors we can also add the relative position of the work process on the value chain as well as whether production is sequenced or batched as well as the degree of product standardization. In sum, whilst the cases certainly show that there are disconnects in the circuit of capital, such disconnects may not always prevent employers from 'keeping their side of the bargain' (Thompson, 2003).

The accounts by the employer representatives (both strategic and HR) in each case suggest some degree of managerial discretion at plant level. The HR manager at Plastics had a clear plan for developing the model of teamwork along a higher road trajectory in the period from 2006 to 2008 but was ultimately frustrated in this by the bankruptcy of the firm rather than opposition from the owners. The Plastics case does seem to suggest that plant management enjoyed more discretion throughout the period of private equity ownership than that suggested by certain authors (e.g. Watt, 2009), lending support to those who argue that private equity firms adapt to national systems of industrial relations and work organization (Bacon et al., 2010).

Conclusion

This chapter has seen strategic choices on forms of work organization at plant level as outcomes of governance compromises between representatives of capital and labour at both plant and board levels in a context of strong unionism and statutory co-determination rights yet contrasting corporate governance regimes. It has noted a trend in manufacturing away from high road designs which suggests a rather pessimistic take on the prospects for better jobs. Empirically the focus has been on the automotive supply sector in Sweden but the pattern is also apparent elsewhere. The Bearings case, however, does stand out as bucking the trend. Accordingly, contrary to the view of some authors (Ramsey et al., 2000; Godard, 2004; Thompson, 2003), in certain circumstances the high performance paradigm can hold out prospects for better jobs. The two cases show two distinct trajectories in the organization of work at the plants in question. Both shared a similar critical event at the beginning of the 1990s in a governance compromise of introducing some experimentation with teamwork. Yet the forms and fortunes of these experiments diverged quite radically.

The case evidence suggests that not all changes or continuities in work organization can necessarily be traced back to governance issues. Nevertheless, capital markets may play a role as shapers of outcomes in the labour process in terms of work organization. This linkage, however, would appear from the cases to be indirect and best understood as facilitative rather than deterministic. The chapter also suggests that even within the same national system of corporate governance and employee voice, different corporate governance regimes co-exist. The chapter has elaborated on the differences in governance compromises between a family-controlled business and a private equity model and the different philosophies of each. Further research would be fruitful on the governance compromises in a third regime type, namely firms where institutional investors have a dominant position.

Thompson's disconnected capitalism thesis is ultimately an example of what Gallie (2007) characterizes as a pessimistic universalistic theory of job quality. The Plastics case endorses the thesis to some extent in that better jobs have not been on offer. But it is by no means evident that events in the capital markets have been the main determinant in the unfolding of events at the plant. The Bearings case, on the other hand, clearly offers a more optimistic story. However, the relationship between corporate governance and job quality is a complex one. The evidence here suggests that a number of mediating factors might facilitate a more positive take on the prospects for better jobs. These include the contingent nature of the conditions in product markets, the technical characteristics of the labour process, a well organized trade union that proactively pursues a good work agenda at both board and plant levels, co-determination (and/or high union influence) as well as plant level managers authentically committed to what Watson (2001) has called an empowerment, skills and growth discourse rather than a discourse of control, jobs and costs.

To be fair to Thompson, his argument is intended as painting a big picture and certainly concedes that actors at the workplace, both managers and union representatives, may play a mediating role in certain contexts. But the evidence from this chapter indicates rather more scope for agency than his thesis would seem to allow. This suggests that future analyses require serious investigations of the power resources, interpretive frames and motivations of key actors. In other words, the prospects for better jobs through high road work organization – and whether employers are able to keep their side of the bargain – cannot solely be accounted for in relation to capital markets. Further research is needed on how the structural dynamics of these markets interact with the technical characteristics of the labour processes in and with the agency of unions and managers at the workplace.

Notes

*I would like to thank the Hans Böckler Foundation and the Swedish Council for Work Life Research (FAS) for their support for this study as well as Inge Lippert for her help with the fieldwork and conceptual work in connection with the broader study of which this chapter is a part.

1 The Metalworkers Union merged with the Industrial Workers Union on 1st January 2006 to form IFMetall.
2 For example, foreign holdings of equity amounted to around 10 per cent up to 1990 and increased thereafter to around 40 per cent by 2000 and remaining around that level since then (Jansson and Larsson-Olaison, 2010).

REFERENCES

Aguilera, R. V. and Jackson, G. (2003) 'The Cross-National Diversity of Corporate Governance: Dimensions and Determinants', *Academy of Management Review*, 28(3): 447–465.

Altmann, N. and Deiss, M (1998) 'Productivity by Systemic Rationalisation: Good Work – Bad Work – No Work?' *Economic and Industrial Democracy*, 19(1): 137–159.

Appelbaum, E., Bailey, T., Berg, P. and Kalleberg, A. L. (2000) *Manufacturing Advantage: Why High-Performance Work Systems Pay Off.* Ithaca, NY: ILR Press.

Bacon, N., Wright, M., Scholes, L. and Meuleman, M. (2010) 'Assessing the Impact of Private Equity on Industrial Relations in Europe', *Human Relations*, 63(9): 1343–1370.

Becker, B. E. and Huselid, M. (1998) 'High Performance Work Systems and Firm Performance: A Synthesis of Research and Managerial Implications', *Research in Personnel and Human Resources Management*, 16: 53–101.

Bessant, J. (1983) 'Management and Manufacturing Innovation: The Case of Information Technology', in Winch. G. (ed.), *Information Technology in Manufacturing Process: Case Studies in Technological Change*. London: Rossendale.

Blom, M (2007) *Aktiemarknadsorienteringens Ideology*. Lund: Lund Business Press.

Clark, I. (2009) 'Owners and Managers: Disconnecting Managerial Capitalism? Understanding the Private-Equity Business Model', *Work, Employment and Society*, 23(4): 775–786.

Cummings, T. (1982) 'Designing Work for Productivity and Quality of Work Life', *Outlook*, 6: 35–39.

Durand, J-P. (1998) 'Is the "Better Job" Still Possible Today?' *Economic and Industrial Democracy*, 19: 185–198.

Gallie, D. (2007) 'Production Regimes, Employment Regimes and the Quality of Work', in Gallie, D. (ed.) *Employment Regimes and the Quality of Work*. Oxford: Oxford University Press.

Godard, J. (2004) 'A Critical Assessment of the High-Performance Paradigm', *British Journal of Industrial Relations*, 42(2): 349–378.

Hall, P. A. and Soskice, D. (eds) (2001) *Varieties of Capitalism: The Institutional Foundations of Comparative Advantage*. Oxford: Oxford University Press.

▶

▶
Huzzard, T. (2000) *Labouring to Learn: Union Renewal in Swedish Manufacturing.* Umeå; Boréa.

IFMetall (2008) *Hållbart arbete. En plattform för utveckling av arbetsorganisation.* Stockholm: IFMetall.

Jansson, A. and Larsson-Olaison, U. (2010) 'The Effect of Corporate Governance on Stock Repurchase: Evidence from Sweden', *Corporate Governance: An International Review*, 18(5): 457–472.

Johansson, J. and Abrahamsson, L. (2009) 'The Good Work – a Swedish Trade Union Vision in the Shadow of Lean Production'. *Applied Ergonomics*, 40: 775–780.

Jonsson, D., Medbo, L. and Engström, T. (2004) 'Some Considerations Relating to the Reintroduction of Assembly Lines in the Swedish Automobile Industry', *International Journal of Production & Operations Management*, 24(8): 754–772.

Kuipers, B. S., De Witte, M. C. and van der Zwaan, A. H. (2004) 'Design or development? Beyond the LP-STS debate; inputs from a Volvo Truck case', *International Journal of Production & Operations Management*, 24(8): 840–854.

Metall (2003) *Metallarbetarna och Lean Production.* Stockholm: Metall.

Ramsey, H., Scholarios, D., and Harley, B. (2000) 'Employees and High Performance Work Systems: Testing inside the Black Box', *British Journal of Industrial Relations*, 41(2), 501–531.

Rennstam, J. (2007) *Engineering Work: On Peer Reviewing as a Method of Horizontal Control.* Lund: Lund Business Press.

Stafsudd, A. (2009) 'Corporate Networks as Informal Governance Mechanisms: A Small Worlds Approach to Sweden', *Corporate Governance: An International Review*, 17(1): 62–76.

Streeck, W. and Thelen, K. (eds) (2005) *Beyond Continuity: Institutional Change in Advanced Political Economies.* Oxford: Oxford University Press.

Tengblad, S. (2004) 'Expectations of Alignment: Examining the Link Between Financial Markets and Managerial Work', *Organization Studies*, 25(4): 583–606.

Thompson, P. (2003) 'Disconnected Capitalism: Or Why Employers Can't Keep Their Side of the Bargain', *Work, Employment and Society*, 17(2): 359–378.

Wallace, T (2007) 'Is That Something We Used to Do in the 70s?: the Demise of 'Good Work' in the Volvo Corporation', in Bolton, S. (ed.) *Dimensions of Dignity at Work.* Amsterdam: Elsevier.

Watson, T. (2001) *In Search of Management* (revised edn). London: Thomson.

Watt, A. (2008) 'The Impact of Private Equity on European Companies and Workers: Key Issues and a Review of the Evidence', *Industrial Relations Journal*, 39(6): 548–568.

CHAPTER 7

Making Bad Jobs Better: The Case of Frontline Health Care Workers

Janette S. Dill, Jennifer Craft Morgan and Arne L. Kalleberg

Introduction

Frontline health care occupations play an essential role in the quality of life experienced by workers and clients as well as the health of nations.* Yet in the United States, these occupations are often poorly paid and provide few opportunities for advancement. The frontline workforce currently constitutes half of the total US health care workforce, with more than six million workers. It consists of a diverse set of occupations within various health services and health care delivery roles, including nursing assistants, respiratory therapy technicians, social and human service assistants, home health aides, mental health counsellors and medical transcriptionists (Schindel et al. 2006). Many frontline health care occupations are projected to be among the fastest growing occupations as the US population ages. Workforce development in the health care sector in this country has traditionally focused on medical professionals and highly skilled health care workers, while frontline workers have largely been ignored, because it is presumed that these workers can easily be replaced due to the low skill levels required for these jobs. However, the increasing demand for frontline workers and concerns about quality of care have led to a growing interest in improving the skills and retention of this large group of workers.

In this chapter, we examine how 35 health care organizations in the US are attempting to address these challenges by making 'bad jobs' into 'better jobs' through the development of career ladders for frontline health care workers. We identify strategies employers are using to develop career ladders and discuss the impact of these strategies on job quality and career mobility. Career ladders are characterized by employees moving up from the bottom ranks of the organization and working their way through a succession of job titles associated with the progressive development of skill and knowledge (Althauser and Kalleberg 1981; Fitzgerald 2006). Career ladders can provide advantages to both employers (who benefit from having a supply of workers with firm-specific knowledge and skills to fill vacant positions) and employees (who receive opportunities for upward career mobility).

US frontline health care workers and job quality

Frontline health care workers (FLWs) are those who offer a high level of direct patient care or care delivery support services. These occupations often have relatively low thresholds of entry (typically a high school degree with little extra training) and low levels of compensation. Thus, these occupations have many 'bad job' characteristics, including low wages and few opportunities for advancement (Kalleberg 2011). Some health care employers, particularly acute care hospitals, provide frontline health care workers with high quality, affordable employment benefits, though this certainly is not the case across all health care organizations: benefits are not always offered, and when they are, workers often cannot afford to pay the high premiums. Frontline health care jobs can also have heavy workloads and be very physically and emotionally demanding. Not surprisingly, there is high turnover in frontline positions for many health care employers.

Career ladders and the US health care context

Some employers have simply accepted high turnover among frontline workers as a fact of business in the health care industry. However, as the labour market tightened for the workers in the early 2000s, some health care organizations began to invest in frontline health care workers by developing career ladders for these low-wage workers (Fitzgerald 2006). This tightening of the labour market is due in large part to the intersection of the growing demand for workers and quality of care as well as cost concerns influenced largely by government-driven (e.g. Medicare and Medicaid) requirements. Health care organizations are consistently short on staff as a result of turnover, causing middle-class patients and their families to be increasingly dissatisfied with the quality of care being provided. Furthermore, a growing percentage of overstressed frontline workers join unions. All these groups – patients, families, payers and workers – are placing greater pressure on organizations to improve quality of care through the improvement of frontline health care jobs (Fitzgerald 2006).

Health care organizations also face shortages of mid-level health care workers (i.e., nurses and allied health professionals), most notably in nursing. While shortages in the United States have temporarily lessened with the economic recession and rising wages for nurses, this reprieve may be short lived (Rother and Lavizzo-Mourey 2009). The nursing workforce is much older than the average age of labour force members, and though many nurses on the cusp of retirement have delayed retirement, it is likely that retirement will increase once the economic situation has improved and there is less economic uncertainty. There has also been a decline in younger women choosing nursing as career. Consequently, in the future, nursing shortages are likely to become much more severe unless there is a rapid increase in foreign-born Registered Nurses (RNs) or in younger cohorts' interest in nursing as a career, which would likely need to be induced by wage increases (Buerhaus et al. 2003). Filling mid-level positions by training and promoting frontline health care workers offers the promise of addressing this shortage. Such strategies may also have other benefits, including raising cultural competences within health care organizations with high racial/ethnic minority populations, increasing the quality of language translation to improve communication and enhancing economic development for underserved and vulnerable communities through creating better jobs for community members.

The role of organizations in enhancing frontline worker career mobility

As in the broader economy, there has been a move towards the use of low-wage labour in the health care sector. The US health care sector has a higher rate of low-wage workers with lower levels of training relative to other developed countries. For example, to control costs, US hospitals have made greater use of nursing assistants and other low-skill workers to replace Registered Nurses, a practice that is less common in European hospitals (Appelbaum and Schmitt 2009). Examples from other developed countries suggest that frontline health care jobs are not inevitably 'bad jobs'. The fact that these jobs are 'bad' – low compensation, low skill – in the US thus reflects both the labour market institutions that influence the ways these jobs have been designed (e.g. to minimize the skills involved, thereby keeping wages low) and the availability of economically vulnerable populations who are compelled to take these kinds of job for lack of more suitable options (such as women, minorities and immigrants).

The problems of worker retention and skills have led some employers to adopt policies and practices in which they assume more risk for worker training and advancement. While such career development efforts are not widespread in health care today (Méhaut et al. 2010), organizational policies and practices play an important role in who advances out of low-wage work, above and beyond the impact of national policies and norms. Health care is one of the few industries in the US that successfully transitions workers out of low-wage work (Andersson et al. 2005). However, there is broad variation among health care organizations in frontline worker advancement. Indeed, Andersson et al. (2005) found that only a small fraction of firms account for a significant amount of low-wage worker mobility in the health care sector. Although many health care organizations have the capacity to facilitate upward mobility for frontline workers, it appears most do not.

US health care organizations have the potential to be a source of 'good jobs' for low-wage, low-skill workers (Wolf-Powers and Nelson 2010), though this promise is as yet unrealized. The multi-layered nature of many health care organizations, hospitals in particular, may make them especially well-suited to the development of career ladders and advancement for low-wage workers. For example, clearly identified job demarcations and credential-based promotion make is possible to build pathways that workers can follow, with appropriate training. The heavy emphasis on sector-specific and firm-specific credentials in health care organizations means that there are frequent opportunities for frontline workers to move up within the organization without significant investment in college-level education. Another feature of hospitals is their 24-hour operation, which provides more opportunity for entry-level employees to advance into supervisory roles than is the case in industries with an eight-hour day. In addition, unlike many economic sectors in the global economy, health care is not easily outsourced off-shore. This geographic stability means that health care organizations are often a major source of employment for community members in underserved and vulnerable communities from which other employers have disinvested. Consequently, health care employers in economically depressed areas are often the largest employer in the region and a strong partner in community economic development.

In summary, the anticipated growth in demand for health care services and concerns about quality of care, the multi-layered structure of many health care organizations, and the precedents set in other countries and a handful of progressive US firms all contribute to singling health care as an industry where 'bad jobs' have the potential to get 'better'. In this chapter, we seek to learn from innovative health care organizations what policies and practices are related to the creation of better jobs for workers. We argue that employers have a choice as to how they organize work and that 'bad jobs' are not inevitable in the health care industry.

Methods

We studied 35 US health care organizations, including acute care providers, community health centres, behavioural health centres and long-term care organizations. Health care organizations included in our sample have received funding as part of the *Jobs to Careers: Transforming the Front Lines of Health Care* initiative to build partnerships with educational institutions to help them to implement educational and training programmes aimed at frontline worker career advancement. Types of frontline workers that participated in *Jobs to Careers* programmes included direct care (e.g. nursing assistants), entry level (e.g. dietary, housekeeping) or administrative workers (e.g. unit clerks). A few programmes trained frontline workers for mid-level positions, such as nursing, during the grant period. However, most programmes trained workers in the lower rungs of frontline health care jobs to move up into frontline jobs with greater skill requirements and higher compensation. Organizations viewed these upper-level frontline jobs as 'next steps' in the career ladder for frontline workers. Table 7.1 summarizes the kinds of organization included in the sample, the educational and career outcomes, and the types of worker targeted.

For the content analysis, we draw on 287 semi-structured key informant interviews (e.g. administrators, middle managers and HR personnel), 33 frontline worker focus groups and 31 frontline supervisor focus groups. In interviews with administrators and managers, we gathered information about their motivations for implementing career ladders, the challenges they faced during the implementation process and details about the programmes developed. We also heard from frontline supervisors and workers about working and staffing conditions, challenges that frontline workers face in moving up within the organization and how they had experienced the *Jobs to Careers* programme that had been implemented at their place of employment. We conducted interviews with every grantee site during each year of funding (for a total of three visits per grantee), and conducted focus groups in the first and last year of funding.

We coded interview and focus group transcripts for themes using NVivo 8.0. Each transcript was coded twice; discrepancies between codes were discussed until consensus was achieved. Primary level thematic coding was completed to understand the breadth of policy and practice changes implemented to support frontline worker career advancement.

We also use data from a web-based survey administered to key informants at health care organizations and educational institutions that applied for funding through the *Jobs to Careers* initiative to better understand employer motivations for investing in career ladders for frontline health care workers. Because organizations applied for the grant as a partnership (i.e. an employer and an educational institution applied for a joint grant), we calculated a partnership response rate. A total of 147 partnerships out of the 204 who applied for a grant were represented in the sample, resulting in a response rate of 72 per cent. Of the 147 organizations that responded to the survey, 66 were health care organizations (the other organizations were educational institutions or workforce intermediaries). The web-based survey instrument inquired about the opportunity for and specific types of training for frontline workers, employer motivations for investing in frontline workforce development, and past initiatives targeted to this group. We use the survey data to quantify the extent to which health care organizations are adopting career ladder policies and practices and their motivations for doing so.

The health care organizations included in our sample may differ in some ways from the 'typical' health care organization. In applying for a *Jobs to Careers* grant, organizations had to demonstrate that they had a commitment to utilizing policies and practices to promote frontline worker advancement. Many proposals included examples of policies and programmes already in place to support frontline workers and evidence that they had conducted a needs assessment of frontline workers. Thus, frontline health care workers included in our focus group sample work in health care settings that have shown an interest in 'high-road' job redesign. This selection does not detract from our research goals, however. When identifying strategies to make 'bad jobs' better, it makes sense to look at the practices of organizations that are developing innovative and novel programmes and practices related to the development of career ladders. An examination of these types of organization allows us to better understand what is possible rather than what is typical.

Organizations' motivations to create 'better' frontline health care jobs

Quality improvement

Health care administrators are primarily motivated to improve frontline workers' jobs in order to enhance the quality of care, although *how* such programmes would improve quality of care varied between organizations. Indeed, 95 per cent of the respondents to the web survey of proposal applicants (hereafter referred to as survey respondents) cited improvement in quality of care as the major motivation for doing so, and this was also a major theme in interviews with health care administrators. In general, strategies for improving quality of care focused on two areas: first, worker skills and, second, worker recruitment and retention.

Table 7.1 Overview of organizations, programmes and workers

	Type of health care organization	Job title(s) of participants	Targeted educational outcomes	Targeted job position outcomes	Rewards for completion
1	Behavioural health	Resident Assistants, Mental Health Technicians, Mental Health Tech Supervisor, Therapist Assistant, Shift Supervisor, Facility Manager	• Behaviour Health Technician Certificate • 21 Credits towards Behaviour Health Tech Certification at four-year university	Behavioural Health Technician	$100 gift card, job enrichment
2	Health care system	Frontline workers from Nursing, Lab, and Imaging departments	Certificate in Health care Informatics	Health care Informatics Position	Salary Increase
3	Health care systems	Clinical Assistant/Patient Care Technicians	• Continuing Education Credit • 2 hours of college credit	Clinical Technician	Job enrichment
4	Health care systems	Dietary Aides, Transportation workers, Environmental Services workers	Certified Nursing Assistant training, Patient Care Technician certification	CNA, Patient Care Technicians	Promotion into CNA and Patient Care Technician jobs
5	Community health centres	Health Technician	One non-degree elective credit	Health Technician, Community Health/ Health Promotion Worker	Promotion -Integrated into performance review system
6	Health care system	Hospital-wide involvement	Associate Degree Nurse	Registered Nurse	Promotion to nurse
7	Long-term care	Resident Assistant, Service partner	Industry recognized credential	–	Job enrichment
8	Community health centre	Medical Assistants, Receptionists	3 Credit hours for each course completed	–	Salary increase

9	Behavioural health	Human Service Workers, Substance Abuse Specialists	• 15 hours college credit for training through technical programme • 4 hours college credit through community college	Certified Addictions Counsellor	Job enrichment, Salary Increase
10	Long-term care	Certified Nurse Assistants	CNA Clinical Specialty Certificate	CNA (Progress through tiers I,II, and II)	Salary increase tied to tier advancement
11	Community health centre	Resident Care Assistant, Medical Assistants, Clerical Associates	• Internal certification • 3 college credits	Certified Auxiliary Interpreters	Job enrichment, Stipend
12	Health care system	Environmental Services, Nutrition	Certified Health Unit Coordinator	Health care Associate Unit Clerk	Promotion
13	Health care system	Nursing Assistants, Dietary Aides, Transporters, Housekeepers	Internal certification	Unit Clerk	Promotion 5-6% Raise
14	Behavioural health	FLWs in the community health department	Community Health Worker Certificate	Community Health Worker	Job enrichment
15	Behavioural health	Village Based Counsellors	Behavioural Health Aide Level I, College credits	Behavioural Health Aide	Job enrichment, salary increase
16	Health system	Clinical Service Representatives, Non-clinical entry level positions	Medical Assistant Certification	Certified Medical Assistant	Promotion
17	Community health centre	Medical Assistants, Patient Service Representatives	Medical Administrative Assistant in the Health Field Certificate	–	Job Enrichment, $1,000 Raise

Source: Jobs to Careers National Evaluation (2011) *Organizational Profile Survey and HR Checklist*. Chapel Hill, NC.

Three-quarters of the survey respondents were motivated to develop career ladders for frontline workers in order to improve their employees' skills. Health care administrators were focused on improving a range of skills, from medical terminology and clinical skills to translation and customer service skills. One behavioural health organization had focused their frontline worker training on teaching workers to de-escalate situations of conflict and prevent adverse events between workers and patients. The development of career ladders improved workers' skills so that they can move into new, more skilled positions, a fact that was not lost on many supervisors who were reluctant to lose their best workers. However, administrators recognized that, while frontline workers were undergoing training to move up within the organization, they would bring their new skills back to their current jobs, thus improving the overall skill set of the frontline workforce.

Administrators were also eager to improve worker retention and address staff shortages. They hoped that the development of a career ladder would offset costs currently incurred in recruiting for higher-level health care professionals, while reducing turnover and improving recruitment for lower level positions, because career opportunities would then exist for frontline workers to reach higher level positions. This policy approach reflected two concerns: first, an understanding that some upcoming needs would not be adequately addressed by current recruitment strategies, particularly in rural and underserved areas of the US; and, second, in some organizations, a commitment to increasing diversity in higher-level positions by promoting frontline staff. Administrators also hoped that workers who advanced within the company would have a higher degree of cultural competence because they would be more familiar with the organization and clientele. In many cases, frontline workers were of the same minority population served by the organization, while mid-level and upper-level staff was not. Consequently, helping frontline workers move up within the organization would also increase the representation of minority groups in higher job levels.

Increasing revenue

Most administrators discussed how generally improving employee morale and quality of care is 'good for business'. However, some organizations had explicit goals to increase revenue through the development of career ladders for frontline workers (35% of survey respondents). For example, one organization's outpatient counselling department was losing money due to a lack of certified clinical workers. This organization developed a career ladder for frontline workers to become certified clinical workers that enable it to bill directly for these workers' time, making their services more profitable.

Concern for workers

Some health care administrators were motivated to improve frontline jobs because they felt that it was the 'right thing to do' for workers in these positions (41% of survey respondents). Several administrators mentioned that, given that their organizations had development programmes for mid- and upper-level employees, training the frontline workforce seemed like a logical extension of other efforts. Community health and behavioural health centres were particularly concerned about the well-being of their workers and saw helping their frontline workers achieve upward mobility as part of service to their communities.

Innovative practices to promote frontline health care workers' career advancement

Developing career ladders for frontline workers within health care organizations is a complex process that involves the cooperation and effort of many actors. Organizations in our sample of 35 health care employers used a variety of strategies to build career ladders; many of these practices presented a variety of challenges. We begin by focusing on partnerships between health care organizations and educational institutions, followed by strategies used at the organizational level.

Partnering with an educational institution

Educational institutions, usually community colleges, or training organizations such as union-based or independent training providers, can provide essential services for low-wage workers' career advancement, particularly in the health care sector. These services include the provision of standardized credentials, credit for prior learning and the delivery of remedial education. Consequently, partnering with an educational or training institution is an important component in building career ladders for frontline workers.

Standardized credentials

The standardization of positions within the health care industry often requires that employees earn industry-approved credentials to practice within a health care setting (e.g. a state-wide nurse aide certification). Most mid-level positions require specific training and certification, including patient care technicians, respiratory therapy technicians and pharmacy aides. Because of the strict educational requirements for positions, many of which are mandated by state and federal regulations, health care organizations cannot, or chose not to, promote workers without the necessary training and certification. For example, a supervisor often cannot promote frontline workers because they do not have the necessary certification to move to the next level, despite demonstrated hard work and job skills.

Consequently, the development of a strong career ladder for frontline workers within the health care sector requires that organizations partner with an education institution – typically a community college – that can provide workers with meaningful credentials. Unlike firm internal labour markets of the past, which primarily provide workers with firm-specific training (Althauser and Kalleberg ,1981), career ladders within health care organizations often necessitate training in both firm-specific *and* industry-specific skills.

Credit for prior learning

Credit for prior learning policies are designed to give college credit for activities or classes taken outside the normal college routine. This may include classes taken outside of traditional educational institutions, on-the-job training or simply experience at work. Credit for prior learning policies translate these experiences into academic credit, which can apply towards a college degree and cut down significantly on the time and cost of getting a degree. Because the next meaningful promotion for many of the frontline workers in the organization would require additional education, employers included in our sample attempted to partner with community colleges that would grant college credit for prior learning as a means of advancing workers into these positions more quickly.

Remedial education

Organizations became keenly aware of the lack of educational readiness among many frontline workers when they sought to implement career ladders and engaged in practices that facilitated the success of their programmes in the face of these obstacles. For example, most sites offered a range of remediation assessment and education including standardized assessment tools (e.g. WorkKeys, COMPASS, Key Train), tutoring, remedial continuing education through the employer organization and full-scale remedial coursework with the educational partner. Job/career coaches who help frontline workers navigate the educational system and develop career goals and paths were also a feature of many partnerships. A few sites went beyond testing and remedial coursework to address students' fears and inexperience surrounding formal education and the learning process by providing individualized coaching aimed at reducing anxiety and increasing/maintaining motivation. A few partnerships have formalized this process by designating a person on staff who teaches workers how to be students, engages them and advocates for them as they navigate the requirements of the educational institution and the employer.

Changes in organizational policies and practices

While a strong partnership with an educational institution is needed to build career ladders, organizational changes are also needed to support low-wage workers. Organizations support career advancement and 'better jobs' for frontline workers through changes in three key areas: human resource policies, organizational culture and management practices, and work processes.

Human Resource (HR) policies

HR policies enabled systemic changes within organizations by formalizing components of the *Jobs to Careers* programme and relationships with educational institutions. Policies outlining tuition assistance, competency-based raises and promotions, educational release time, and formal mentor positions were often revised to support career advancement for frontline workers. Approximately three quarters of employers in our sample offer some tuition reimbursement policies, but most of these policies are either not accessible or not taken up by frontline workers. Working directly with educational institutions to cover the costs of tuition so that frontline workers do not incur initial out-of-pocket tuition costs can effectively remove the financial barrier for frontline workers. For most organizations, tuition policies were originally designed to cover coursework that leads to an Associate's or Bachelor's degree. Employers found that low-wage workers were in need of tuition support for non-degree or continuing education coursework that addresses basic skills, college readiness or certificate programmes.

Employers in our sample also developed career maps outlining specific competencies for jobs across the organization. These maps provided not only clarity for workers trying to get ahead but clear rubrics for assessing workers as they gain skills to qualify them for better jobs. While there often are opportunities for workers to move up within health care organizations, promotion paths may not be clear or transparent to frontline workers, particularly in large health systems. HR personnel in our sample worked with supervisors and frontline workers to develop demarcated competency-based job descriptions attached to career ladders, or lattices, so that skills needed to obtain to qualify for a particular position are clear to workers. Job descriptions for positions within a career ladder were also often developed in partnership with a community college, which would be providing the training necessary.

Organizations in the sample also created educational release time policies to allow frontline workers to attend classes, work with preceptors and do homework on work time. While these practices are common among mid- and upper-level health care workers, they are not common for frontline workers. One organization took educational release time to the next level by creating formal training positions that allowed frontline workers to train and receive mentorship on-the-job. Table 7.2 includes a list of HR policies utilized by these organizations to support frontline worker development and advancement.

The extent to which organizations had utilized many of these HR policies and practices varied. About two-thirds of survey respondents reported that the health care organization in which they worked had provided career coaching, on-site classes and tuition reimbursement or remission for frontline workers. Much smaller shares of organizations had adopted clear career ladders for frontline workers that specified skill and educational requirements for positions with the organizations (32%) or college credit for prior experience or work-related training (14%).

Organizational culture and management practices

Organizational culture refers to a collection of values and norms that are shared by people and groups within an organization. Management practices influence organizational cultures by setting the tone and instituting practices that reflect the values and shared norms in an organization. A strong record of developing workers in upper- and mid-level positions appears to facilitate organizational support for expanding the development of opportunities down the hierarchy. For example, one organization had a history of career development programmes and a culture of advancement and promotion, which was exemplified by a CEO who was very proud of the fact that he worked his way up through the ranks from frontline staff to his current position. The hospital had implemented a series of pipeline programmes (including part-time, largely on-site Licensed Practical Nurse (LPN) programmes, LPN-RN bridge programmes, Associates and RN to Bachelor of Science Nurse (BSN, which entails a four-year college degree) programmes for incumbent workers) and frontline workers were a logical next group to target for these development programmes.

Supervisor practices and relationships with frontline staff are important components of organizational culture. In one organization, frontline supervisors were keenly aware of the barriers facing their subordinates and were supportive of career ladders for their frontline workers. Many supervisors and

Table 7.2 Selected HR policies that support career developing and training for frontline workers

Policy	Description
Case management services for FLWs	Providing FLWs with access to a case manager that can help them with access to resources, such as childcare, transportation, or health care.
Competency-based pay raise	Pay raises upon documentation of having learned a competency or set of competencies.
Competency-based promotion	Promotion upon documentation of having learned a competency or set of competencies.
Educational release time	Providing paid time-off for workers to attend classes, participate in WBL activities, or study.
Formalized mentoring positions	Designating mentoring as a job responsibility and formally including it in a job description; sometimes includes additional compensation for increased responsibility.
In-house credentialing	On-site training that leads to additional credentials for participants.
Promotion from within	Hiring current employees for jobs that advance their careers; often includes specific policies regarding how long a job will be posted within the organization before it is posted outside the organization.
Replacement staff for educational release time	Providing either a 1) pool of workers or 2) additional funds to hire temporary or agency workers to cover scheduling gaps that result from educational release time.
Skills assessment for new FLWs	Administering tests of basic skills to all FLWs to determine their training and remediation needs.
Tuition advancement	Providing FLWs with funds for tuition at the beginning of a course (rather than the end) so that FLWs do not have to pay tuition costs up-front.
Tuition reimbursement on a sliding scale	Providing additional funds for FLWs for higher education as compared to other job categories with higher wages.
Tuition remission	Arranging for educational institutions to bill employer organizations directly so that FLWs do not have to pay tuition costs up-front.

Source: *Jobs to Careers National* Evaluation.

administrators had climbed career ladders themselves, and they had empathy for employees who are trying to advance their careers. They actively encouraged their employees to pursue additional education and allowed them to take time off the floor to attend classes; workers affirmed that they felt that their supervisors were trying to help them advance their careers. However, in many organizations, supervisors said that they wanted to be helpful but had not really been educated in how they could support frontline workers or they faced time constraints limiting their ability to advise frontline workers.

Work process

Organizations in our sample adapted frontline workers' activities to accommodate their education, training and career advancement at work. For example, many organizations arranged job tasks and responsibilities in ways that enabled workers to make a steady progression up a career ladder as they obtained additional skills. This sometimes involved setting aside time to allow on-the-job training by supervisors or encouraging workers to share information in a way that reinforced the learning for the entire group. Another example of a change in work process was a more explicit inclusion of the frontline worker into the work team. This often meant including frontline workers in the care planning team so as to improve their access to learning opportunities and minimize separateness between supervisors and frontline workers.

Organizations in our sample have developed concrete ways in which to support education and training programmes and frontline worker career advancement. These policies and practices serve both to tangibly support these initiatives but also contribute to improving 'bad jobs' by addressing key areas of low job quality.

Conclusions

The introduction of career ladders is a departure for many US health care organizations, where frontline workers have long held jobs characterized by low wages, limited benefits, heavy workloads and few possibilities of career advancement. While career ladders benefit workers by increasing their chances of upward mobility, they may also offer health care employers a way to increase commitment and retention of frontline workers and solve mid-level worker shortages. An important benefit of career ladders may also be improvement in job performance (and therefore quality of care) that results from increased acquisition of education and training, strengthening of organizational learning culture and greater engagement or commitment of the workers.

This concluding section discusses the organizational conditions that promote successful implementation of career ladders. It then closes with a reminder of the compelling need for better quality jobs in health care in the future.

Developing career ladders for low-wage workers is not without challenges. Communication and coordination between educational institutions and employers are vital for programme development, but these organizations have different cultures, norms, and bureaucracies that can make negotiation difficult. For example, educational administrators frequently complained that the bureaucracy within health care organizations and the rigid schedules of workers made timely and efficient implementation of classes and training difficult. Many key informants in health care organizations also reported difficulties in negotiating alternative training methods, such as work-based methods, with educational partners. College administrators and faculty were often reluctant to approve alternative training methods because of a lack of staff resources, concerns about academic rigour, or lack of protocol. Health care organizations also struggled to comply with state Board of Nursing requirements or other licensing bodies while also trying to incorporate less traditional teaching methods, such as using online courses or on-site training. These challenges point to the changes that need to take place within the educational sector for career ladders to be successful within health care organizations.

Health care organizations and educational institution partnerships in our sample were most successful in overcoming these obstacles when they built mutually beneficial relationships. An example of such an arrangement is sharing employees as faculty. Community colleges are often in need of nursing faculty (due, in part, to lower levels of pay as compared to clinical work), while health care organizations benefit from having on-site clinical faculty for their students. Sharing space is also a mutually beneficial arrangement. One community health centre in our sample allowed its on-site training centre to be used as a satellite campus for a community college. The community college benefited from being able to offer classes in an underserved community, and the community health centre benefited from being able to offer its employees on-site for-credit instruction through the community college.

Another key component in creating successful career ladders is educating frontline worker supervisors about their roles in helping low-wage workers advance their careers. In health care organizations, supervisors typically have training in their clinical area but not necessarily in supervisory skills. However, many mid-level clinicians have significant supervisory responsibility. For example, in assisted living it is common for one RN to have supervisory responsibility for all the nursing staff in the entire building. RNs also make up a large proportion of the managers in hospitals, community health centres and behavioural health clinics. Despite this fact, RNs, and other health care managers, are infrequently provided education (in school or in continuing education) in supervisory skills such as coaching, performance review, career counselling or providing constructive feedback for workers.

Finally, health care employers in our sample were most successful when adequate support was provided for low-wage workers. Strategies included case management, coaching, basic skills training, technology training, and addressing time, logistical and financial constraints. The availability of on-site training at least partially during work time was critical to overcoming real and perceived barriers to educational advancement. Workers reported being more comfortable with classes taught on-site, particularly when they knew their instructors through work. The arrangements also eased logistical burdens such as transportation and childcare arrangements.

Population ageing in combination with the US health care reform (Affordable Care Act 2010), which may add 34 million insured patients, will strain the capacity and resources of health care organizations. Using low-wage workers is a very common tactic used by US health care organizations to reduce health care costs (Appelbaum et al. 2003; Méhaut et al. 2010). However, as we have argued in this chapter, bad jobs are not inevitable in the frontline health care workforce, and the health care sector has the potential to turn many low-wage 'bad jobs' into better jobs by making them a stepping stone to jobs with better compensation and prestige (see also Pindus et al. 1995). US health care employers are likely to be increasingly motivated to develop their frontline workforce because it comprises half of the sector's workforce and it has a high level of interaction with patients. They have become increasingly aware of how important their frontline workforce is for client satisfaction and productivity. Career ladders have the potential to address the skill and staffing needs of employers, improve quality of care and create better jobs for frontline health care workers.

Note

*We acknowledge the remainder of the study team, including Dr Thomas (Bob) Konrad, Melissa Mann, Ashley Rice, Emmeline Chuang, Brandy Farrar and Kendra Jason for their contributions to the large scale data collection and analytic effort. We also thank the many key informants and participants who took time to discuss the benefits and challenges of career development for frontline workers. This research was funded by Grant 59245 from the Robert Wood Johnson Foundation to evaluate the 'Jobs to Careers: Transforming the Front Lines of Health Care' programme with supplementary funds from The Hitachi Foundation. Data collection protocols were approved by the University of North Carolina at Chapel Hill Institutional Review Board.

REFERENCES

Althauser, R. and A. L. Kalleberg (1981) *Firms, Occupations, and the Structure of Labor Markets: A Conceptual Analysis*. New York: Academic Press.

Andersson, F., H. Holzer and J. Lane (2005) *Moving Up or Moving On: Who Advances in the Low-wage Labor Market*. New York: Russell Sage Foundation.

Appelbaum, E., P. Berg, A. Frost and G. Preuss (2003) 'The Effects of Work Re-Structuring on Low-Wage,Low-Skilled Workers in U.S. Hospitals', in E. Appelbaum, A. Bernhardt, and R. Murnane (eds) *Low-Wage America: How Employers are Reshaping Opportunity in the Workplace*. New York: Russell Sage Foundation, pp. 33–76.

Appelbaum, E. and J. Schmitt (2009) 'Review Article: Low-Wage Work in High-Income Countries: Labor-Market Institutions and Business Strategy in the US and Europe', *Human Relations*, 62, 1907–1934.

Buerhaus, P. I., D. O. Staiger, and D. I. Auerbach (2003) 'Is the Current Shortage of Hospital Nurses Ending?' *Health Affairs*, 22, 191–198.

Fitzgerald, J. (2006) *Moving Up in the New Economy: Career Ladders for U.S. Workers*. Ithaca, NY: Cornell University Press.

Kalleberg, A. L. (2011) *Good Jobs, Bad Jobs: The Rise of Polarized and Precarious Employment Systems in the United States, 1970s–2000s*. New York: Russell Sage Foundation.

Méhaut, P., P. Berg, D. Grimshaw, and K. Jaehrling (2010) 'Cleaning and Nursing in Hospitals: Institutional Variety and the Reshaping of Low-Wage Jobs', in J. Gautie and J. Schmitt (eds) *Low-Wage Work in the Wealthy World*. New York: Russell Sage Foundation, pp. 269–318.

Pindus, N. M., P. Flynn, and D. M. Smith (1995) *Improving the Upward Mobility of Low-Skill Workers: the Case of the Health Industry*, The Urban Institute, Washington, DC

Rother, J. and R.Lavizzo-Mourey (2009) 'Addressing the Nursing Workforce: A Critical Element for Health Reform', *Health Affairs*, 28, w620–w624.

Schindel, J., E. O'Neal, B. Iammartino, K. Solomon, D. Cherner, and J. Santimauro (2006) *Workers Who Care: A Graphical Profile of the Frontline Health and Healthcare Workforce*. Princeton, NJ: The Robert Wood Johnson Foundation.

Wolf-Powers, L. and M. Nelson (2010) 'Chains and Ladders: Exploring the Opportunities for Workforce Development and Poverty Reduction in the Hospital Sector', *Economic Development Quarterly*, 24, 33–44.

CHAPTER

8

When Good Jobs Go Bad: The Declining Quality of Auto Work in the Global Economy

Jeffrey S. Rothstein

Introduction

Concerns about 'bad jobs' tend to focus on poorly paid employment in the service sector or sweatshops. In countries like the US, the decline in manufacturing and growth of service industries has led to lower incomes, fewer benefits and less job security for unskilled, semi-skilled and even some skilled workers. The accompanying shift of manufacturing to low wage countries has renewed concerns over sweatshops that tend to dominate the discourse around labour standards in the global economy.

By contrast, auto work has long been a 'good job' offering stable employment, high pay and an array of benefits. During the Fordist era, auto work was widely associated with the rise of a blue-collar middle class in industrialized countries. Likewise, regardless of their industrializing strategy, developing countries nurtured domestic auto industries as key to economic growth offering broad prosperity. This perception persists. Governments continue to promote auto industries (e.g. the US government's intervention to save General Motors) while local policymakers compete to offer incentives intended to lure automakers' 'good jobs' to their regions or keep those already present. When these efforts are successful, prospective employees flood the automakers with applications. Whether in Michigan, Alabama or Guanajuato, Mexico, an auto plant offers some of the best jobs around.

However, those policymakers may not be getting quite what they expect. True, auto work remains among the best jobs available. However, the quality of those jobs has been steadily eroding. The pace of work has intensified while remuneration has declined. So, while labour conditions in the auto industry may not compete for 'bad job' status against those in sweatshops and the unskilled service sector, the degradation of auto work – even as those jobs remain among the most coveted of blue-collar employment – may serve as a valuable barometer for the impact of globalization on workers.

These conclusions are based on ethnographic fieldwork at three General Motors assembly plants producing similar SUVs (Sport Utility Vehicles) in the US and Mexico, as well as a comparative-historical analysis of the impact of globalization on industrial and labour relations in the US and Mexico. The chapter first compares the three plants to refute the claims of lean production enthusiasts that the manufacturing system hinges on teamwork and employee participation, or is beneficial to workers. Instead, by exposing standardized work routines to be the only common feature among the plants, I highlight intensified labour to be the primary goal and impact of lean production in the auto industry. Borrowing from the tradition of the extended case method (Burawoy 1998), I continue by arguing that the variation in the plants' operations reflects the two countries' different historical trajectories and the manner in which traditional labour relations institutions have been undermined in each, resulting in lower pay and benefits. These findings lead to a conclusion that, though the degradation of work may not be inevitable, stemming the trend of declining labour standards will require more than a promotion of 'core' labour standards in the global economy. Instead, it will require more broadly regulating international labour standards to shape globalization in a manner that shores up, rather than undermines, labour relations institutions that facilitate collective bargaining and rising standards of living. Otherwise, we face the continued degradation of even the best jobs the global economy has to offer.

Lean production and the intensification of work

Among the supposed benefits to workers of globalization has been the spread of post-Fordist philosophies that reject Taylorist prescriptions for separating the conception and execution of work. Across industries and continents, firms have reorganized in ways credited with enhancing the work experience by reengaging workers intellectually and even empowering them – all the while improving efficiency and quality. In the auto industry, lean production has become the predominant manufacturing system. Enthusiasts of lean production claim teamwork and an expanded role for assembly workers in ensuring quality and improving the manufacturing system makes work more challenging and enjoyable (Kenney and Florida 1993; Womack, Jones, and Roos 1990). Critics (Babson 1995; Dassbach 1996; Graham 1995; Milkman 1997; Parker and Slaughter 1995) warn, however, that lean production is not 'a radical break with Fordism but merely a more advanced form' in which 'labour control occurs through a set of far more subtle and carefully contrived strategies than in Fordist factories' (Dassbach 1996: 21). Fundamentally, this debate is over what lies at the heart of lean production – harder work or smarter work.

This debate remains unsettled at least in part because the diversity of firms, plants, products and work processes in the current literature allows only for broad comparisons. This study controls for many of these variables. The three plants were all owned and operated by GM. They assembled similar and identical vehicles built on the same platform, and were under orders to implement a common Global Manufacturing System (GMS). However, the implementations of the GMS varied in all aspects but one, the meticulous standardization of work routines. The result was an intensification of work as industrial engineers choreographed workers' every movement with the goal of keeping each assembly line worker busy for 55 seconds of each minute.

As explained by GM executives, the GMS was 'basically the old Toyota production system' that GM learned from Toyota at NUMMI, the two automakers' joint venture in Fremont, California. As such, the GMS incorporated all the key shop floor components of lean production found in the various descriptions of Toyota's manufacturing system (Adler 1995; Adler 1999; Fujimoto 1999; Mishina 1998; Womack et al. 1990): standardization of work, the organization of workers into teams with team leaders, Andon systems to allow workers to summon help and halt production and employee participation programs to solicit ideas for continuously improving the system – what the Japanese call 'kaizen'.

However, aside from the universal standardization of work, sharp differences existed between the implementations of all the other aspects of the GMS. For instance, the organization of workers into teams often seen as key to lean production was thoroughly incorporated in Silao, but completely superficial in Janesville. In Silao, teams of six workers rotated through a series of jobs each day and performed administrative tasks to chart important performance metrics under the guidance of quasi-supervisory team leaders responsible for managing and coordinating all the team's work. By contrast, in Janesville and Arlington workers were technically organized into teams, including a 'team coordinator'. However, these were mostly groupings of consecutively placed workers on the assembly line, each of whom performed a single job. Team coordinators in Janesville did little more than spell workers who needed a break, while in Arlington they had an expanded role, but not one that approached the supervisory tasks of their counterparts in Silao.

The degree and style of implementation of the Andon system mirrored the extent and type of teamwork practiced in the three plants. If a line operator in Silao had a problem on the line and pulled the cord triggering the Andon system, the entire team converged on that worker to problem-solve as a group and, in most cases, quickly resolve the issue. However, in Janesville workers mostly ignored the Andon system to avoid upsetting supervisors who might scold them for slowing production. In Arlington, workers used the Andon system to alert their team coordinators, who helped resolve the issue and alerted a supervisor if they could not.

A similar dynamic was found in the manner and degree to which workers contributed their ideas for improving the production system or their plant, which GM encouraged by offering bonuses for cost-saving ideas. According to the plant's Personnel Relations Manager, 85 per cent of line operators in Silao made at least one recommendation annually, based on the data they maintained through their own record keeping and their experiences on the assembly line. Systemically, line operators' suggestions were useful in working out the kinks associated with annual model changes that required engineers to re-choreograph each job on the line. But in Janesville, workers complained that management ignored their ideas. Supervisors confirmed this, asserting that workers' ideas were frequently demands that had nothing to do with production. Again, Arlington showed greater functionality than Janesville, if less complete implementation than in Silao. Both management and union officials reported widespread participation that focused on money-saving ideas that would earn bonuses. Like in Silao, the number of recommendations increased with annual model year changes.

Overall, the GMS was implemented wholesale in Silao from the plant's inception in 1994. By contrast, in Janesville implementation was piecemeal, with some components completely ignored, while Arlington offered an approach somewhere in between. If, as post-Fordist theorists contend, teamwork and employee participation are integral to lean production, the facility in Silao should have been producing higher quality vehicles more productively than the US plants, and certainly the factory in Janesville.

However, this pattern appears not to be the case. According to J.D. Power & Associates, whose annual report on product quality is the industry standard, consumers of vehicles assembled in Janesville, Silao and Arlington reported nearly identical rates of quality defects in the first three months of ownership. In its 2005 analysis, J.D. Power claimed that purchasers of the sport utility vehicles reported 108 problems per 100 vehicles assembled in Janesville, and 109 problems per 100 vehicles made in Silao and Arlington (Leute 2005). Therefore, it seems that overall quality was not influenced by teamwork, Andon systems or other forms of employee participation.

Direct comparisons of productivity are not possible, because the industry standard of Hours Per Vehicle (HPV) does not adequately control for differences in product mix, levels of automation and outsourcing, all of which varied between locations. However, we should still be able to compare the plants' rates of productivity improvement over time to determine whether the version of the GMS in Silao was outperforming that in Janesville and Arlington. Again, this expectation appears not to be the case. Between 1998 and 2004, when the three plants were all assembling the vehicles studied, each made impressive improvements to their HPV. Arlington improved its productivity 38 per cent over the period, from 33.78 to 22.39 HPV. Janesville cut its HPV 33 per cent, from 36.17 to 24.28. Silao improved 29 per cent, cutting HPV from 38.13 to 27.02 (Harbour Report North America 1999, 2000, 2001, 2002, 2003, 2004, 2005).

Certainly, if post-Fordist theories espousing the importance of teamwork and employee participation are accurate, then the plant in Silao should have been outperforming its counterparts in the US in terms of quality or productivity, if not both. Instead, these finding point to the Taylorist standardization of work found in each plant as key, a factor which was overwhelmingly emphasized by both management and labour at each of the plants. In addition, the systematic scaling back of work rules on the shop floor has allowed the pace of the standardized routines workers perform to be intensified, with GM's goal to keep workers moving for 55 seconds of each minute.

Herein lies the bitter irony for workers. Theoretically, according to lean enthusiasts, teamwork and participation are supposed to enhance job satisfaction in auto plants, just as they are credited with doing in other industries. Instead, the elimination of work rules and loss of union control over the shop floor that has been pitched as necessary to implement teamwork and participation has led to the intensification of traditional work routines. Workers with new jobs in Silao may be oblivious to this intensification, but workers at GM's plants in the US are painfully aware of it. An examination of changing labour relations under globalization provides explanation as to how workers have been forced to concede work rules, while simultaneously documenting a decline in their wages and benefits, even as work intensifies.

Globalization, de-unionization and declining labour standards

The decline in auto industry labour standards is best understood through an examination of the manner in which the globalization of the North American auto industry has undermined the unions and labour relations institutions through which workers in both the US and Mexico negotiated themselves into the middle class. For roughly 30 years in the post-Second World War period, the growth and consolidation of domestic auto industries in the US and Mexico, relatively free from foreign competition, created an environment in which unions flourished. Despite very different industrial relations systems, autoworkers in the US and Mexico negotiated ever increasing wages and benefits. Likewise, within the factories, unions negotiated work rules limiting managerial prerogative on the shop floor and protecting workers from arbitrary and capricious treatment. But in both countries, unions' negotiating capacity has been steadily eroded, as an examination of the strengthening and weakening of these unions reveals.

US pattern bargaining and the growth of good jobs

For decades in the United States, auto industry-wide pattern bargaining removed workers' wages as a source of competition among the automakers. By ensuring that wage scales remained comparable between the Big Three automakers (GM, Ford & Chrysler), and that similar work was compensated equally within and between the factories of all the companies, the United Auto Workers (UAW) union could bargain up wages and benefits without risking the competitive stature of any of the firms. In addition, the UAW negotiated an ever expanding array of benefits, including generous health insurance, pensions and a supplemental unemployment benefit (SUB) to protect workers during layoffs. Between 1948 and 1980, the cost of these benefits rose 1,177 per cent, considerably faster than real wages which increased 313 per cent (Katz 1985).

Within guidelines established at the national level, local union representatives and plant management negotiated over the specifics of job classifications used in their plant, the local seniority system and local work rules. Local contracts detailed job descriptions and the plant seniority system by which jobs were assigned or chosen, safety and health standards, and any other issues concerning conditions of work, which might include everything from payment schedules to establishing cleanliness standards for the bathrooms, employee entitlement to lockers and parking regulations at the plant (Tolliday and Zeitlin 1992). While technically, local agreements maintained management's sole discretion to organize production, this was qualified by the local union's right and obligation to protect their members' safety and health, as well as their responsibility for ensuring decent working conditions.

Each factory was therefore governed by a pair of lengthy, detailed collective bargaining agreements laying out all the responsibilities of management and labour, and establishing a process for adjudicating disputes. Under this system, autoworkers in the post-Second World War US became a privileged group of blue-collar workers, even in comparison to other unionized industrial workers – a status that was only accentuated by their seeming immunity to the economic erosion and decline impacting most workers. While other private sector workers saw their real wages stagnate or decline as consumer prices rose in the late 1960s and 1970s, autoworkers saw their standard of living continue to improve as their wages kept pace with inflation. By 1980, the average hourly earnings of autoworkers were 50 per cent higher than other private sector production workers (Katz 1985).

Mexican corporatism and the growth of good jobs

During this same period, Mexican autoworkers became a privileged group within their own country, owing to an entirely different industrial relations system. For most of the twentieth century, and ending with the election of Vincente Fox in 2000, Mexico's Institutional Revolutionary Party (PRI) governed the country as a tripartite corporatist system in which business and labour were officially represented so that the state became '... a privileged arena for resolving disputes between capital and labour' (de la Garza 1994: 196). Until the early 1980s, auto workers were beneficiaries of both this system and the government's import substitution industrialization (ISI) development strategy to promote the growth of targeted domestic industries, including auto, steel and oil, through subsidies and strict limitations on imports. Under ISI policies, auto imports were banned while a limited number of manufacturers (including the US Big Three) were encouraged to manufacture for the Mexican market. Within the corporatist system, the ruling party maintained a tenuous national compromise. In selected industries that the government targeted for industrialization, manufacturers enjoyed a captive market and other government protections. In exchange, these firms were expected to pass a portion of their profits onto their employees through wages and benefits. Mexico's 'official' labour unions were then responsible for rallying workers in support of the party. As a result, like their counterparts in the United States, autoworkers in Mexico became a blue-collar elite.

Globalization and the undermining of traditional labour relations

The process of globalization that ultimately integrated the auto industries of the US and Mexico, along with Canada, into a single North American automotive sector undermined the foundations of the industrial and labour relations systems through which unions in each country had benefitted. In the United States, beginning in the 1980s, the UAW found its bargaining power steadily eroded by a combination of the union's inability to organize any of the factories opened by foreign automakers, the Big Three's declining market share and the widespread adoption of lean production techniques. In Mexico, the government quickly shifted its development strategy to promote exports and, in a drive to become suddenly internationally competitive, pressured the official unions to disavow the wages, benefits and working conditions gained during the import substitution era. This undermining of labour has compromised wages and benefits, and facilitated the intensification of work found in Silao, Janesville and Arlington.

The UAW in decline

Beginning in the late 1970s, the Big Three's US market share declined steadily. As foreign nameplates gained an ever bigger foothold in the United States, Japanese, German and later Korean automakers opened their own assembly plants, mostly in the traditionally non-union southern states. The inability of the UAW to organize any of those 'transplant' factories has struck at the heart of the pattern bargaining through which the union once took labour costs out of competition. By 2006, transplant factories employed over 60,000 workers, with perhaps another 40,000 having been created at suppliers and contractors (Center for Automotive Research 2005).

Over the same period, the Big Three shed nearly half a million jobs as they repeatedly downsized, restructured and reorganized in an effort to regain their traction, competitiveness and profitability. In 1978, the Big Three had 667,000 hourly employees (Barlett and Steele 1996). By 2003, that number had fallen to 275,000 (McCracken 2003). It would fall another 100,000 over the next five years as a result of these changes and further loss of market share.

Initially, despite decreasing union density, wages and benefits at the Big Three, and in auto assembly more broadly, continued to rise. In part, this was due to the early union avoidance strategies of foreign automakers opening factories in the United States, which included matching the wages, and to a lesser degree the benefits, earned by unionized workers. Over time, however, a wage and benefit gap did develop between union and non-union assembly plants. As a result, the UAW found themselves making concessions. These were small at first, but the collective bargaining agreement negotiated between the UAW and the Big Three at the end of 2007 included deep labour concessions. For a supposedly one-time cost of approximately $52 billion, the UAW relieved the automakers of their $90 billion, long-term obligation to provide retirees health insurance for life, by transferring that responsibility to a union run Voluntary Employees Beneficiary Association (VEBA). This left the UAW responsible for their members' retiree health insurance and any cuts in benefits that might be forthcoming. In the wake of the industry crisis that saw GM and Chrysler declare bankruptcy, much of the $52 billion was paid in the new companies' stock, leaving retirees dependent on the success of the restructured firms for their benefits.

Furthermore, to bring wages more in line with non-union assembly plants, the UAW agreed to establish a two-tier wage system that sacrificed the wages of future workers to preserve those of current ones. New hires would earn half the rate of workers already employed, with the automakers permitted to pay up to 20 per cent of their workforces the lower rate. In making the deal, the UAW conceded not only wages, but two fundamental principles of industrial unionism – that all workers be paid equally and that seniority systems be used to determine job assignments so that older workers could select the most attractive and least physically challenging work in the plant.

However, well before these wage concessions, the UAW had been under real pressure from the automakers for concessions at the local level, as the automakers came to see work rules as the biggest obstacle to their implementing the lean production practised at newer, non-union factories. For decades, the bifurcated system of collective bargaining in the auto industry afforded local union leaders a modicum of power to tailor working conditions to suit local concerns. As long as the companies were growing and profitable, local unions could negotiate greater control over the shop floor in exchange for their commitment to keep the assembly lines moving. But as the Big Three's market share dropped and they began consolidating rather than expanding, this dynamic reversed. The automakers realized they could gain concessions by forcing local unions to compete against one another to keep their plants open and their jobs in place. Under the pressure of this practice known as 'whipsawing', local unions steadily relinquished many of the work rules governing the shop floor to allow the automakers to reorganize production (Rubenstein 1992) and intensify the pace of work.

In Janesville, the whipsawing began in 1985 and continued until 1991, when GM announced it would retool the plant to introduce the Chevy Suburban product line. It continued as the plant's age (it dated to 1915) made it increasingly vulnerable to closure, which ultimately occurred at the end of 2008. The Arlington plant survived perhaps the most famous case[1] of whipsawing in the auto industry in 1992, after GM pitted it against the automaker's iconic Willow Run assembly plant in Ypsilanti, Michigan. Both Janesville and Arlington became home to many 'GM Gypsies' – workers who uprooted their families to take jobs in GM plants after their own factories closed. The plant closings, whipsawing and union concessions left many workers bitter, a factor that influenced the degree to which they were willing to embrace teamwork and employee participation. But they begrudgingly accepted the intensified standardized routines at the heart of the GMS because they understood that resistance might provoke GM to close their plant.

Role reversal in Mexican unionism

Unlike the steady and gradual decline of the UAW's bargaining strength in the US, union capitulation in Mexico happened almost overnight as the government sought to deal with the economic crisis of the early 1980s. As the government reversed course, abandoning import substitution strategies to instead promote economic development through export growth, the automakers argued that the industry's high pay and stringent work rules were incompatible with efforts to become internationally competitive. In response, the government exploited the same corporatist industrial relations system through which it had supported higher wages and benefits to pressure union officials into signing national 'pacts' limiting pay increases and returning control of the shop floor to management (Bensusán 2000; de la Garza 1998; Grayson 1989).

Perhaps not surprisingly, the use of corporatist mechanisms that once benefited auto workers to weaken labour contracts faced a backlash. Their status as blue-collar elites fading, and their unions no longer providing the economic security they once had, activists at some auto plants attempted to democratize their unions, organizing numerous strikes to challenge the concessions, and the process by which they were handed down as well as to demand reform of the labour movement. For the most part, each of these movements were thwarted through various governmental, union and firm maneuvering, as well as occasional violence. Ford responded to a 1987 strike protesting changes in working conditions by shutting the plant and reopening it with a drastically reduced workforce under a collective bargaining agreement ceding the company full control over the production process. By 1993, a new democratic movement surfaced, but was again put down in a violent clash on the factory shop floor, during which a union democracy activist was killed (Carrillo 1995; Garcia and Hills 1998; von Bülow 1998). Workers at GM's plant in Mexico City struggled for nearly a decade to democratize their union before the company finally closed the plant in 1995 (Micheli 1994), just a year after initiating its new one in Silao.

In fact, though the automakers began opening plants in the northern part of Mexico in part to reduce the distance cars would have to be shipped as the market shifted to the US, the move was also intended to allow them to start afresh with new workers and unions, to escape the union activism in and around the traditional industrial heartland (Micheli 1994). In opening their new plants, the automakers increasingly recognized unions affiliated with the Confederation of Mexican Workers (CTM), the 'official' union that espoused the greatest support for the government's economic policies and which helped protect the automakers from union militancy. Many of these unions were hand-picked by the firms for their willingness to engage in a 'new union discourse' (Bayón and Bensusán 1998: 128) that eschewed labour militancy in favour of cooperation and embraced experimentations with new forms of work organization (Carrillo 1995; Shaiken

1990; Shaiken 1994). In fact, collective bargaining was reformed to focus nearly exclusively on remuneration, ceding to management full control over the shop floor.

In Silao, GM handpicked just such a regional industrial union to represent their employees before any workers had even been hired. While not a sham 'sindicato blanco' or 'white union', SITIMM (as it was known by its Spanish acronym) was also not militant. Rather, the union espoused a 'new labour culture' of management–labour cooperation summed up by one union official at the GM plant who said 'I love my wife. I love my daughter. I love General Motors. And I love my union. And I see no contradiction in any of that.'

Bi-annually, SITIMM negotiated wages and benefits, though union officials acknowledged having little bargaining leverage. On a day-to-day basis, the union provided services to help workers acclimate to factory work and take advantage of their steady incomes, a function carefully aligned with GM's own goal of maintaining low labour turnover. The union helped the workers open checking accounts and apply for a government programme to get low rate mortgages. Union officials kept track of workers with sick relatives and made hospital visits. They took the lead in organizing funerals when a worker's relative passed away.

However, SITIMM did not interfere with the day-to-day running of the shop floor, or in any way interfere with the organization of work. The union staffed an office off the shop floor, but did not have representatives available to workers in the production area. In fact, there was no grievance procedure. Moreover, the union did not challenge GM's broader labour relations strategy which extended beyond the plant's gates to involve the entire supply chain growing up around them. These firms divided up the local labour market according to sex and education level and maintained a wage hierarchy with GM at the top paying roughly $200 a week to men with a ninth grade education. Down the road, GM's former subsidiary Delphi paid women with a sixth grade education $42 a week to assemble wire harnesses (Rothstein 2004).

So, just as the limitations on the implementation of the GMS at the plants in Janesville and Arlington reflected the manner in which workers and their supervisors at those facilities experienced the steady decline in union bargaining power that accompanied the globalization of the industry, the wholesale adoption of the GMS in Silao was manifest of the abandonment of traditional labour relations in Mexico and its replacement with a more compliant form of unionization. In all three locations, GM line operators had among the best jobs in the area. However, in both the US and Mexico, as union bargaining power declined, work on the assembly line intensified, while wages and benefits slipped.

Conclusion: are declining labour standards inevitable?

While there is nothing inevitable about the decline in pay, benefits and working conditions in the North American auto industry, reversing this trend in the gradual hollowing out of what are still considered 'good jobs' presents a far greater challenge than is commonly posed by labour scholars and activists concerned with labour standards in the global economy. Oftentimes, the concern over the most blatant forms of exploitation and ways to stop the spread of sweatshops dominates. Even the International Labour Organization has declared that among its myriad of conventions there are a set of four 'fundamental principles and rights at work': (1) the abolition of forced or compulsory labour; (2) the abolition of child labour; (3) the elimination of discrimination in employment and occupation; and (4) freedom of association and the right to collective bargaining. This focus is intended to provide remedy for the greatest abuses found in what are acknowledged to be 'bad jobs' in the global economy.

Instead, this research points to a more fundamental problem with globalization, and a greater challenge for labour advocates. Globalization enables the undermining of national labour relations institutions; for decades these institutions shaped labour markets in ways that facilitated the mobilization of workers to claim a standard of living that fostered the growth of a blue-collar middle class. For globalization to be, instead, an overall benefit to workers, policies that shape globalization must shore up rather than undermine these institutions. This goal requires a reversal of current policy from one that welcomes nations into the global economy regardless of their record on labour rights and standards to one that holds the protection of workers' rights to achieve good, and improving, wages, benefits and working conditions as a prerequisite to trade.

Building such a regime would logically begin with the ILO, which has been establishing labour standards since its inception in 1919. In addition to the 'core' labour standards, ILO conventions address an array of topics including, but not limited to, minimum wages, work hours and paid time off, unemployment insurance and social security, and job security. The ILO has regulations dealing with radiation, asbestos, chemicals, industrial accidents and even potential cancer risks. The organization has even dealt with labour challenges in specific industries known to have their own unique problems, including construction, mining, agriculture, seafaring, dock work and fishing. As a body of work, the ILO conventions offer an expansive guide to promoting worker rights and labour standards.

No doubt, converting ILO conventions from voluntary recommendations to enforceable international law, and thereby transforming the ILO into a regulatory body with the authority to enforce international law, would be a monumental task. It would require the amassing of political power by labour movements even as unions have been weakened by the absence of just such protections. However, to view the current decline in wages, benefits and working conditions in the global economy as simply inevitable would be to deny that the trend could be, and should be reversed, if only there were the political will to do so.

Note

1 See, for example chapter 4 in Martin (2004).

REFERENCES

Adler, P. (1995) '"Democratic Taylorism": The Toyota Production System at NUMMI', in S. Babson (ed.) *Lean Work: Empowerment and Exploitation in the Global Auto Industry* (Detroit: Wayne State University Press).

Adler, P. (1999) 'Hybridization: Human Resource Management at Two Toyota Transplants', in J. K. Liker, W. M. Fruin, and P. Adler (eds) *Remade in America: Transplanting and Transforming Japanese Management Systems* (New York: Oxford University Press).

Babson, S. (1995) 'Lean Production and Labor: Empowerment and Exploitation', in S. Babson (ed.) *Lean Work: Empowerment and Exploitation in the Global Auto Industry* (Detroit: Wayne State University Press).

Barlett, D. L. and Steele, J. B. (1996) 'America: Who Stole the Dream?' in *Philadephia Inquirer* (Philadelphia).

Bayón, C. and Bensusán, G. (1998) 'Trabajadores y Sindicatos ante la Globalización: El Caso del Sector Automotriz Mexicano', in H. Juarez Núñez and S. Babson (eds) *Confronting Change: Auto labor and lean production in North America* (Puebla: Benemérita Universidad Autónoma de Puebla).

G. Bensusán (2000) *El Modelo Mexicano de Regulación Laboral* (Mexico City: Plaza y Valdés).

Burawoy, M. (1998) 'The Extended Case Method', *Sociological Theory*, 16, 4–33.

Carrillo, J. (1995) 'Flexible Production in the Auto Sector: Industrial Reorganization at Ford-Mexico', *World Development*, 23, 87–101.

Center for Automotive Research (2005) 'The Contribution of the International Auto Sector to the US Economy: An Update', Ann Arbor, MI, Center for Automotive Research.

Dassbach, C.H.A. (1996) 'Lean Production, Labor Control, and Post-Fordism in the Japanese Automobile Industry', in W. C. Green and E. J. Yanarella (eds) *North American Auto Unions in Crisis* (Albany, NY: State University of New York Press).

de la Garza, E. (1994) 'The Restructuring of State-Labor Relations in Mexico', in M. L Cook, K. J. Middlebrook, and J. M. Horcasitas (eds) *The Politics of*

▶

▶
Economic Restructuring: State-Society Relations and Regime Change in Mexico (San Diego: Center for US-Mexican Studies).
de la Garza, E. (1998) 'Modelos de producción, estratégias empresariales y relaciones laborales', in E. de la Garza (ed.) *Estrategias de modernización empresarial en México, flexibilidad y control sobre el proceso de trabajo* (Mexico City: Rayuela Editores).
Harbour and Associates (1999) 'The Harbour Report North America 1999', Harbour and Associates, Inc., Troy.
Harbour and Associates (2000) 'The Harbour Report North America 2000', Harbour and Associates, Inc., Troy.
Harbour and Associates (2001) 'The Harbour Report North America 2001', Harbour and Associates, Inc., Troy.
Harbour and Associates (2002) 'The Harbour Report North America 2002', Harbour and Associates, Inc., Troy.
Harbour and Associates (2003) 'The Harbour Report North America 2003', Harbour and Associates, Inc., Troy.
Harbour and Associates (2004) 'The Harbour Report North America 2004', Harbour and Associates, Inc., Troy.
Harbour and Associates (2005) 'The Harbour Report North America 2005', Harbour and Associates, Inc., Troy.
T. Fujimoto (1999) *The Evolution of a Manufacturing System at Toyota* (New York: Oxford University Press).
Garcia, P. R. and Hills S. (1998) 'Meeting Lean Competitors: Ford de México's Industrial Relations Strategy', in H. Juarez Núñez and S. Babson (eds) *Confronting Change: Auto Labor and Lean Production in North America* (Puebla: Benemérita Universidad Autónoma de Puebla).
L. Graham (1995) *On the Line at Subaru-Isuzu: The Japanese Model and the American Worker* (Ithaca, NY: Cornell University Press).
G. Grayson (1989) *The Mexican Labor Machine: Power, Politics, and Patronage* (Washington, DC: The Center for Strategic and International Studies).
H. C. Katz (1985) *Shifting Gears: Changing Labor Relations in the US Automobile Industry* (Cambridge: MIT Press).
M. Kenney and R. Florida (1993) *Beyond Mass Production: The Japanese System and Its Transfer to the US* (New York: Oxford University Press).
Leute, J. (2005) 'Rankings Give GM Good News', *Janesville Gazette*, 19 May.
C.R. Martin (2004) *Framed!: Labor and the Corporate Media* (Ithaca, NY: Cornell University Press).
McCracken, J. (2003) 'UAW May Consider Plant Closings', *Detroit Free Press*. 16 May.
J. Micheli (1994) *Nueva Manufactura Globalización y Producción de Automóviles en México* (Mexico City: Universidad Nacional Autónoma de México).
R. Milkman (1997) *Farewell to the Factory: Auto Workers in the Late Twentieth Century* (Berkeley: University of California Press).
Mishina, K. (1998) 'Making Toyota in America: Evidence from the Kentucky Transplant, 1986–1994', in R. Boyer, E. Charron, U. Jurgens and S. Tolliday (eds) *Between Imitation and Innovation: The Transfer and Hypbridization of*
▶

►
Productive Models in the International Automobile Industry (New York: Oxford University Press).

Parker, M. and Slaughter, J. (1995) 'Unions and Management by Stress', in S. Babson (ed.) *Lean Work: Empowerment and Exploitation in the Global Auto Industry* (Detroit: Wayne State University Press).

Rothstein, J. S. (2004) 'Creating Lean Industrial Relations: General Motors in Silao, Mexico', *Competition & Change*, 8, 203–222.

Rubenstein, J. M. (1992) *The Changing US Auto Industry: A Geographical Analysis* (New York: Routledge).

Shaiken, H. (1990) *Mexico in the Global Economy: High Technology and Work Organization in Export Industries* (San Diego: Center for US-Mexican Studies Monograph Series).

Shaiken, H. (1994) 'Advanced Manufacturing and Mexico: A New International Division of Labor?' *Latin American Research Review*, 29, 39–71.

Tolliday, S. and Zeitlin, J. (1992) 'Shop-Floor Bargaining, Contract Unionism and Job Control: An Anglo-American Comparison', in S. Tolliday and J. Zeitlin (eds) *Between Fordism and Flexibility: The Automobile Industry and Its Workers* (Oxford: Berg Publishers).

von Bülow, M. (1998) 'Restructuración Productiva y Estrategias Sindicales: El Caso de Ford-Cuautitlán (1987–1994)', in F. Zapata (ed.) *Flexibles y Productivos? Estudios Sobre Flexibilidad Laboral en Mexico* (Mexico City: El Colegio de México).

J. P. Womack, D. T. Jones and D. Roos (1990) *The Machine That Changed The World* (New York: Rawson Associates).

CHAPTER 9

Frontline Managers Matter: Labour Flexibility Practices and Sustained Employment in US Retail Jobs

Susan J. Lambert and Julia R. Henly

Introduction

The continued gloomy economy is drawing needed attention to employer practices that contribute to the growing precariousness of employment (Gottschalk and Moffitt, 2009; Kalleberg, 2009).[1] Even before the current economic downturn, however, many employers had adopted labour flexibility practices intended to minimize expenditures for labour by enabling ready adjustments to staff size and work hours in response to variations in consumer demand (Bernhardt et al., 2008; Carré and Tilly, 2009; Lambert, 2008). Both reason and research suggest such practices may give firms a competitive edge in the face of intensified global competition. Not surprisingly then, cost-saving labour flexibility practices can be found at the lower levels of firms across a wide range of industries, in countries with diverse policy contexts and among firms espousing both 'high road' and 'cost leader' business strategies (Appelbaum et al., 2009; Carré et al., 2009; Grugulis and Bozkurt 2011; Haley-Lock and Ewert, 2011; Lambert and Waxman, 2005).

Yet labour flexibility practices have not completely penetrated all sectors of the labour market, and firms vary in the extent to which they engage in practices that transfer undue risk onto workers. As a result, the quality of jobs, even low-level jobs, varies across firms within the same industry (Appelbaum et al., 2009; Bozkurt and Grugulis 2011; Haley-Lock and Ewert, 2011; Lambert, 2008). In this chapter, we consider the further possibility that even within the same firm, labour flexibility practices may be unevenly implemented by managers, resulting in variation in job quality across stores in the same company. Specifically, we examine within-firm variation in store managers' hiring and scheduling practices in a national women's apparel retail firm in the US. Our primary goal is to identify opportunities for manager agency within a cost-containment context by examining how variations in hiring and scheduling practices contribute to employees' prospects for sustained employment. Analysing corporate administrative data and manager surveys from a sample of 139 stores, we elaborate the accountability pressures facing frontline managers in this firm, describe the extent of variation in managers' hiring and scheduling practices and examine the relationship between these practices and store-level rates of employee turnover and retention. The chapter concludes with some thoughts on the possibilities and limits of frontline management practices in shaping job quality at the lower end of the labour market.

Background

Like all decisions, management decisions represent the interplay of environmental constraints and individual agency. At every level of the organization, managers' decisions are constrained by broader political and economic conditions, institutionalized conventions and idiosyncratic firm-level routines (Andersson et al., 2011; Appelbaum et al., 2009). The strategic management literature explicates how broader economic and political forces combine with firms' business strategies to determine frontline procedures that guide (and constrain) decisions concerning employee hiring, placement and promotion (c.f. Eisenhardt and Zbaracki, 1992). This literature makes clear, however, that even when strategic direction is unambiguous and procedures are codified, frontline managers may vary in their approach to everyday management tasks, sometimes in ways consistent with and other times at odds with strategic directives (Bourgeois, 1984; Wright and McMahan, 1992). For example, in their study of two large British supermarket chains, Grugulis et al. (2011) detail how managers carved out 'discretionary spaces' amid intense regulation and standardization of almost all business processes. Managers took great pride in these 'small freedoms', which the researchers report 'made a great deal of difference to the individual managers' (p. 209).

Manager agency may also make a great deal of difference to employees. In the Grugulis et al. study, many of the 'small freedoms' managers secured helped pave the way towards work intensification. Manager discretion need not always be detrimental to workers, however. For example, the work and family literature provides ample evidence that some supervisors find ways to create flexibility for workers whereas others obstruct it (Ryan and Kossek, 2008). Understanding where discretionary spaces lie amid pressures for cost containment and how frontline managers exploit those spaces may reveal both the possibility of and limits to frontline manager actions in shaping job quality.

To examine manager agency in the face of cost containment pressures, in this chapter, we attempt to balance a focus on constraints and agency by examining the cost containment pressures store managers face and their responses to these pressures as revealed through store hiring and scheduling practices. Across industries, firms attempt to contain labour costs by constraining the actions of frontline managers around these practices (Appelbaum et al., 2009; Carré and Tilly, 2009; Lambert, 2008). For example, firms often hold frontline managers accountable for maintaining a tight link between variations in consumer demand and outlays for wages, reprimanding them for exceeding weekly or monthly labour hours provided for scheduling purposes (Carré et al., 2008; Grugulis et al., 2011; Lambert, 2008). Firms may also limit managers' ability to hire staff with high fixed costs, resulting in a staff comprised primarily of part-time or contingent workers rather than benefit-eligible full-time employees (Tilly and Carré 2011; Jordan 2011; Lambert et al. in press). Nevertheless, store managers may have some discretion in *how* they meet pressures for cost containment, shaping the quality of jobs in their stores and in turn, employees' prospects for sustained employment.

In this chapter, we address four research questions. First, what are the cost containment pressures on frontline store managers? Second, how much do managers vary in terms of the hiring strategies they use to contain labour costs? Third, how much do managers vary in terms of the scheduling practices they use to contain labour costs? Fourth, to what extent do managers' hiring and scheduling practices explain variation in store-level turnover and retention?

The case of retail

Retail provides a useful setting to address these questions for at least two reasons. First, cost containment pressures are particularly strong in retail (Carré and Tilly, 2009; Grugulis and Bozkurt, 2011). Demand for labour is tightly linked to the broader economic climate and to predictable seasonal sales fluctuations and thus, is likely to provide a conservative estimate of the scope of manager agency (Andersson et al., 2011).

Second, the retail industry, including retail and food service and drinking establishments, employs one-fifth of the US workforce (National Retail Federation) and retail sales positions are forecasted to be a top-ten growth occupation from 2008 to 2018 (BLS Occupational Handbook). The expansion of this sector is not necessarily good news for American workers though. Wages average less than $10 per hour and a disproportionate and growing proportion of positions are part-time (US Department of Labor, 2010–2011; Jordan, 2011; van Klaveren and Voss-Dahm, 2011). Thus, the sheer size of the retail industry and its concentration of low-wage jobs, suggests its importance for any broad-based initiative to improve job quality (Bozkurt and Grugulis, 2011).

The current study

The site for the *Work Scheduling Study* (WSS) is a national women's apparel retailer with stores concentrated in Midwestern and Eastern states. Stores have an average staff size of ten employees (range: 5–17) and are located mostly in suburban strip malls. Data analysed in this chapter come from two sources: a survey of store managers and corporate administrative data. The broader study includes organizational data at the store level and a telephone survey of employees (see Lambert, 2009, for an overview).

The telephone survey of store managers was conducted in 2006 and 2007. All stores (N=151) within a 50-mile radius of urban centres in the Midwest and Northeast were selected for inclusion and 139 store managers voluntarily participated (92 per cent response rate). Monthly personnel data from corporate administrative records provide basic demographic and job information on each employee and are used to calculate store turnover and retention.

Women make up the vast majority (98.6%) of sales staff, which is otherwise quite diverse. Sixty per cent of sales staff is non-Hispanic White, 26.8 per cent African American and 9.3 per cent Hispanic. While one-fifth (19.4%) is between the ages of 18 and 24, the average age is 42 years, with over one-third (37.2%) 50 or older. Like the sales staff, store managers are also predominantly women (one respondent is male) and racially diverse (65.8% non-Hispanic White, 21.6% African American and 8% Hispanic). Although store managers range in age from 24 to 69 years, the majority (68%) is between ages 35 and 54 (average 45 years). The limited social distance between store managers and sales staff may heighten the probability that managers use their discretion to protect job quality and promote retention.

For this study, annual employee turnover and retention refer to the 12-month period following the date the store manager completed the survey. Both are calculated from corporate administrative records. Monthly employee turnover – number of employee separations during the month divided by number of employees at the beginning of the month – is added across the 12-month period; turnover can exceed 100 per cent because employees can be replaced multiple times. The 12-month turnover rate was 106 per cent among part-time sales staff and 77.7 per cent among full-time staff (excluding store managers). These turnover rates are substantially higher than those reported by government sources and private industry. For example, the *Job*

Openings and Labor Turnover Survey (JOLTS) conducted by the Bureau of Labor Statistics reports that employee separations in the US retail sector overall averaged around 4 per cent each month throughout 2007 and 2008, yielding a 12-month turnover rate of approximately 48 per cent (*JOLTS*, 2008). It is hard to discern, however, whether turnover is unusually high in this firm or whether other reports underestimate turnover. Notably, *JOLTS* does not break down employee separations by occupation or job status and is based on employer estimates which generally exclude employee separations occurring within 'probationary' periods when turnover is especially high. The turnover rate we calculate includes all separations that occurred during the 12-month period, regardless of employee tenure.

The over-100 per cent average turnover rate in part-time jobs suggests that part-time employees' prospects of sustained employment beyond one year were nil. This would be true were turnover equally distributed among staff, but rates of retention indicate otherwise. About half (50.4%) of part-time employees were still working at the store 12 months after the survey; 57.5 per cent of full-time workers still held their position. The data reveal a core group of employees who stay longer and a group that leaves quickly – a dynamic that is partially obscured when early employment separations are excluded from calculations of turnover or retention.

Both employee turnover and retention rates vary across stores. The top quartile of stores averaged a turnover rate of 140 per cent among part-time staff and 115 per cent among full-time staff and the bottom quartile averaged 66 per cent turnover among part-time workers and 33 per cent among full-time staff. In terms of retention, the top quartile retained 100 per cent of full-time employees and 66.7 per cent of part-time associates, while the bottom quartile retained only one-third of both full-time and part-time employees.

Findings

What are the cost containment pressures on frontline store managers?

As is common practice across industries, the retail firm studied maintains significant control over labour costs by closely monitoring the number of work hours managers assign to their staff. Each month, store managers receive an allotment of hours broken out by week. The ration of hours is derived from a formula that factors in the past year's sales and current retail trends. In addition to monthly hour allotments, district managers monitor store sales throughout the workday, instructing managers to reduce and occasionally, to add hours to a particular day or week.

Managers take seriously the company's expectations to 'stay within hours'. When setting schedules, 83 per cent of managers report that staying within the hour limits set by the corporation is 'very important' in scheduling their store, contrasted by 32 per cent who say that employees' preferences for work hours and days is 'very important' and 60 per cent who say having the right mix of skills is 'very important'.

Managers do not find it easy to follow this corporate directive. Notably, a larger proportion of managers (46.7%) rated 'staying within hours' as extremely challenging than meeting sales targets (32.1%). One reason managers find hour rations so challenging is that they complicate managers' ability to achieve other business objectives. Managers report that hour limits make it difficult to meet sales goals either weekly (22.4%) or a few times a month (19.8%). Managers also report that hour limits regularly make it hard to provide sales associates with enough hours (27% weekly; 22.6% a few times a month) and to comply with the company's guidelines for minimum store staffing levels (27.6 % weekly; 16.4% a few times a month). Approximately half of the managers report that hour limits regularly make it difficult to provide good customer service (28.4% weekly; 20.7% a few times a month). As one store manager observed, 'Our Company believes strongly in good customer service and you can't offer good service when there is not enough coverage.'

Even though staying within hours makes it difficult to meet core business objectives, the majority of managers (69.3%) report that, in the past year, they have rarely exceeded the hour limits assigned to their store (14.9% never; 20.1% once or twice; 34.3% a few times), attesting to the power of this accountability requirement in constraining their behaviour.

How much do managers vary in terms of the hiring strategies they use to contain labour costs?

Our data suggest three related hiring strategies that managers use to meet pressures for cost containment: maintaining a relatively large staff on payroll, hiring a disproportionate number of part-time staff and emphasizing open availability as a key job qualification. Managers vary more on their implementation of the first two strategies than the latter.

Keep headcount high. Managers were asked whether they pursue a staffing strategy that gives priority to providing workers with enough hours or one that is intended to maintain a highly flexible staff. Although the majority (67%) chose the statement 'I like to keep my sales associate staff on the large side so that I have several associates I can tap to work when needed,' one-third chose the statement 'I like to keep my sales associate staff on the small side to help ensure that workers get hours.' Responses are related to the actual number of employees managers maintain on payroll, with those preferring a large staff averaging 10.3 employees and those preferring a small staff averaging 9.1 employees ($p<.01$).

Managers' choice to favour a small rather than large staffing strategy has implications for the number of hours employees receive. That is, because managers are responsible for staying within the allocated hours no matter how many workers on their payroll, the more sales associates on the payroll, the fewer hours available, on average, for each. Because the stores are small, a reduction of even one employee on the payroll may make a real difference in the number of hours available to store employees.

Although not all employees want the same number of hours, census data indicate that, across industries, 35 per cent of women who work part-time in hourly jobs would prefer additional work hours (Lambert, in press). In a companion survey that we conducted with a sub-sample of employees in the current study, we find that more than 50 per cent of part-time employees would prefer additional hours at this company and report that they are not working more because 'their manager does not have additional hours to assign' (Lambert et al. in press). The manager strategy of maintaining a large headcount in order to respond flexibly to changing scheduling needs may be one reason for this scarcity of hours.

Hire part-time staff. Another related strategy used to contain labour costs is to hire part-time staff. Part-timers can be slotted for short shifts of work and present few fixed costs in the form of employee benefits or minimum hours (see also Jordan 2011; Lambert et al. in press). On average, 62 per cent of the staff hold part-time positions. Full-time hourly workers are primarily assistant managers, with only eight per cent of sales associates holding a full-time job.

Although this firm does not cap the proportion of full-time jobs in a store as other firms sometimes do, store managers must still receive approval from their district manager before moving someone from part-time to full-time or adding a full-time worker to the payroll. Nevertheless, managers can determine within limits the mix of part- and full-time staff. Some stores have one full-time assistant manager while other comparably sized stores have three and the proportion of part-time sales staff varies across the 139 stores, albeit modestly: the lowest quartile of stores averages 57 per cent part-time and the highest quartile averages 70 per cent part-time.

Managers' strategies around the mix of part-time and full-time staff are related to their preference for keeping relatively high or low headcount. Managers reporting a preference for keeping headcount low have a staff composed of 58.9 per cent part-timers on average as compared to 63.9 per cent part-timers in stores in which the manager reports preferring a larger headcount ($p<.05$).

Hire employees with wide availability. The vast majority of managers reports wanting to hire employees with 'open availability', that is, the ability to work varying work hours across a wide range of shifts. As one store manager put it, 'The sales associates have to be flexible. They signed on for "whatever" – they agreed to this when they were hired.' There is little variability across managers on this preference: 94 per cent of those surveyed agree that 'they try to hire workers with maximum availability' and almost half (47.5%) agree that they are reluctant to hire an associate with limited availability, regardless of her other qualifications. If managers have agency to hire workers with limited availability, few seem to put it to use.

How much do managers vary in terms of the scheduling practices they use to contain labour costs?

Store managers are held accountable for staffing their store within the hour limits assigned by the corporation. More so than the managers of supermarkets in the Grugulis et al. (2011) study mentioned earlier, managers in this firm have significant latitude in divvying up hours among staff. For example, managers largely decide who to schedule for what shifts and how far in advance to post schedules. Managers often described similar approaches to the scheduling process, but they also evinced variation on practices that may portend differences in job quality across the stores.

Who gets what hours? When assigning work hours, managers are intensely focused on meeting the dual business objectives of cost containment and strong sales performance. In particular, when asked what employee qualities they consider when assigning hours, most report giving more hours to associates who are good at sales (51.1 % strongly agree; 40.3% agree), who are reliable (40.3% strongly agree; 48.2% agree) and who are available to work a variety of times and days (31.7% strongly agree; 47.5% agree). Moreover, managers report that when scheduling their store it is important (55.9 % very important; 31.6% important) to give their best sales associates the best shifts. The importance of employee performance is further reflected in the fact that managers report reducing hours for associates with performance problems such as low sales or poor attendance (39.1% strongly agree; 44.9% agree). As one manager observed, 'If they [sales associates] aren't doing what they are supposed to do – making sales – why would I give them the hours?' Another commented, 'There is not a minimum hour guarantee [for sales associates]. They have to earn their hours.'

Few managers report taking individual employee qualities beyond those related to business objectives into account when scheduling their store; for example, only 10.8 per cent agree or strongly agree that they give more hours to associates who seem to 'really need the money'. Still, the majority of managers report that, beyond performance and availability, they do their best to accommodate associates' scheduling requests, regardless of the reason (48.2 per cent strongly agree; 55.9 per cent agree) or the person (24 per cent strongly agree; 55.9 per cent agree).

Hour limits challenge managers' ability to respond to employees' scheduling requests. About 40 per cent report that limits on staffing hours regularly make it difficult to provide associates with preferred days and shifts (14.9% weekly; 24.6% a few times a month) and about half (49.6%) indicate that limits on staffing hours regularly make it difficult to provide associates with enough hours (27% weekly; 22.6% a few times a month.)

Overall, these findings on how managers assign hours suggest that cost containment pressures curtail, but do not derail, managers' ability to respond positively to employees' scheduling needs. Most managers report using the agency they have to schedule in ways that support both business goals and employee preferences, while privileging the former over the latter.

Advance notice of work hours. Previous research indicates that many retail employees receive work schedules with limited advance notice (Henly et al., 2006). A short lead time in posting schedules is a strategy that can help managers stay within assigned hours as it gives managers flexibility in 'real time' to adjust to changing sales levels and last-minute employee requests. For employees, however, short lead times can make planning other activities difficult, interfering, for example, with child care arrangements and the coordination of a second job or a spouse's job.

Although store managers in our study receive hour allotments from their district managers for a full month at a time, the majority (64%) report that they typically post a single week's schedule, usually the Tuesday or Wednesday before the workweek begins on Sunday. Almost one-third of managers (30%) report that they post two weeks of schedules at a time and an additional six per cent post three weeks or more, indicating that some managers find it feasible to provide employees with more than one week of advance notice. Although this variation is limited, the difference between planning for one week versus two or three weeks may be significant from the point of view of an employee who is managing the near term, for example scheduling a doctor's appointment or arranging a carpool for a child's after-school activities.

Challenging hour limits. Overall, our findings provide strong evidence that hour allotments set by the corporation tightly structure the scheduling parameters within which all managers act. Nevertheless, approximately one-fifth of managers report that they regularly (6.7% weekly; another 15.8% at least once a month) schedule their staff for more hours than allotted, suggesting at least some agency on their part in determining the overall number of hours to distribute among store staff.

In sum, the data suggest that pressures to contain labour costs shape the scheduling practices that store managers adopt. Almost all managers report giving the best schedules to workers with a record of strong performance and wide availability because these attributes are perceived as critical to achieving business objectives. Managers also report trying to accommodate employee preferences for particular shifts or hours, though some place greater priority on this than others. Finally, managers vary in how far in advance they post work schedules and some managers, albeit a minority, schedule workers for more hours than their allotments allow.

To what extent do managers' hiring and scheduling practices explain variation in store-level turnover and retention?

In keeping with our goal of identifying 'discretionary spaces' that managers might exploit to foster job quality, we assess whether particular manager practices shape employees' prospects for job stability, as measured by store-level rates of turnover and retention. Our choice to focus on turnover and retention as a marker of job quality follows from our belief that employment stability is likely to be responsive to manager practices and turnover and retention are 'hard' indicators of employee experience that are exogenous to the manager practice measures themselves.

To assess the contributions of manager practices to turnover and retention, we estimate four multiple regression models for each dependent variable. Rates of turnover (98.6% overall) and retention (53.7% overall) are calculated at the store level and are based on the 12-month period following the month the manager survey was conducted. The models regress each dependent variable on four key management practices: preferred staffing strategy (keeping head count relatively large or small), taking employee preferences into account, the length of advance schedule notice and inclination to exceed hour allotments. We home in on these four practices for both conceptual and practical reasons. Conceptually, we hypothesize that, firstly, smaller staff sizes will be related to lower turnover and higher retention because fewer employees will be competing for limited hours; secondly, managers who take employee scheduling preferences into account and who post schedules with greater lead time will enjoy lower turnover and higher retention because employees will be better able to orchestrate their work and non-work activities; and, thirdly, exceeding the hour allotments provided by the company may provide workers with more hours and reduce on-the-job stress, both of which could reasonably reduce turnover and promote retention. From a practical standpoint, there is sufficient variability on these four practices within our data to assess their contribution to turnover and retention. Because the part-time/full-time mix variable is related to managers' preferences for maintaining a large or small staff, we do not include it in these regressions.

The relationship between these four practices and turnover and retention is considered net of six control variables that may be related to turnover and retention as well as to the management practices of interest. Specifically, all regressions control for the composition of stores' workforces, including mean age and the percentage of employees who are Hispanic or African American. Mean tenure of store employees at the time of the manager interview is entered to control for the fact that most employment separations occur early in workers' tenure; stores with a more seasoned staff may have relatively low rates of turnover in the subsequent 12 months regardless of manager practices.[2] Local area unemployment rates, based on store zip code, are entered to control for the vigour of the local labour market.[3] Finally, the minimum number of weekly hours the store was allotted in the past year is included to control for the tightness of accountability pressures that managers had to work within.

Tables 9.1 (turnover) and 9.2 (retention) report the results of the regression models. Models 1 through 4 consider the independent association of each management practice under study, net of controls. In models that included

Table 9.1 Dependent variable: store-level turnover[1]

	Model 1	Model 2	Model 3	Model 4
Variables[2]	Keeps headcount down	Exceeds hour limits	Takes employee preferences into account	Greater advance notice
Headcount (1 = large; 2 = small)	–19.51* (9.12)			
Exceeds hour limits		–5.17 (3.33)		
Takes employee preferences into account			–22.90** (6.06)	
More advance notice				–13.93 (8.67)
Observations	139	139	139	139
R-squared (adjusted)	0.15	0.13	0.20	0.13

[1]Turnover is reported as a percentage. Monthly employee turnover – number of employee separations during the month divided by number of employees at the beginning of the month – is added across the 12-month period. Turnover can exceed 100 per cent because employees can be replaced multiple times.

[2]Control variables are not included in the table. Beta coefficients are unstandardized; standard errors in parentheses. **$p < 0.01$, *$p < 0.05$, +$p < 0.1$.

Table 9.2 Dependent variable: store-level retention[1]

Variables[2]	Model 2 Keeping headcount down	Model 3 Exceeds hour limits	Model 4 Taking employee preferences into account	Model 5 Greater advance notice
Headcount (1 = large; 2 = small)	7.12+ (3.97)			
Exceeds hour limits		3.55** (1.42)		
Takes employee preferences into account			6.63* (2.69)	
More advance notice				5.63 (3.76)
Observations	139	139	139	139
R-squared (adjusted)	0.19	0.21	0.21	0.18

[1]Retention is the percentage of employees still employed at the store 12 months after the manager survey was conducted. It can range from 0 per cent, no employees still on payroll, to 100 per cent, all employees still employed.
[2]Control variables are not included in the table. Beta coefficients are unstandardized; standard errors in parentheses. $^{**}p < 0.01$, $^{*}p < 0.05$, $^{+}p < 0.1$.

only the control variables (not shown), stores with relatively younger employees and employees with lower mean tenure at the time of the manager survey had statistically significantly higher turnover and lower retention, and stores with relatively fewer hours had lower retention in the 12 months after the survey. These associations generally hold across all model specifications.

Model 1 indicates that stores in which managers report preferring a smaller staff size enjoys 19.5 per cent lower turnover and 7.1 per cent greater retention. Model 2 shows that stores in which managers more often exceed hour allotments have somewhat lower turnover (5.2%) and slightly higher retention (3.6%), although the association is only statistically significant for retention. Model 3 indicates that stores in which managers report attending more closely to employee schedule preferences have 22.9 per cent lower turnover and 6.6 per cent greater retention. Finally, Model 4 demonstrates that stores in which managers post more than one week's schedule do not have statistically significantly different levels of turnover or retention, although the associations are in the hypothesized directions. All these findings reflect associations net of the six control variables.

Not shown in Tables 9.1 and 9.2, a hierarchical model that considers the overall contribution of the control variables entered as a block and the four manager practices entered as a block suggests that the four management practices contribute an additional ten per cent of the variance in turnover and an additional six per cent of variance in retention after accounting for the effects of the control variables. Overall, the full hierarchical model explains 22 per cent of turnover and 24 per cent of retention.

Conclusion

Our primary goal has been to identify opportunities for manager agency within a context of cost containment. Our results uncovered two practices – keeping headcount relatively low and exceeding hour limits set by the company – that may contribute to job quality by affecting the stability and adequacy of employees' work hours. Two additional practices – taking employees' preferences into account and posting schedules with greater advance notice – may improve job quality by facilitating a better fit between employees' work and non-work schedules. Although in this chapter we did not examine pathways through which these manager practices shape employees' experiences, we did establish their potential for improving prospects of sustained employment, as evidenced by store-level turnover and retention.

On one hand, the results presented in this chapter are encouraging. They suggest that frontline managers can carve out 'discretionary spaces' within pressures for cost containment, allowing them to adopt practices that enhance employees' chances for sustained employment. On the other hand, the results are sobering. Most all managers report that staying within hours was their top priority when scheduling staff and sought employees who could work the fluctuating schedules characteristic of many retail jobs in the US (Carré et al., 2008; Lambert, 2008). The weak relationship found between advance schedule notice and turnover and retention might be explained by the limited variation in management practice. Moving from one week to two weeks' advance notice (where most of the variance in our sample was) may indeed ease everyday work–family management, but our data suggest that it may not be sufficiently powerful to sustain employment.

Manager actions alone cannot change the fact that staffing hours are tight and accountability pressures significant. If individual managers varied enough in their practices to radically alter employees' prospects for sustained employment, then we should find that the longer the manager is in a store, the stronger the relationship between manager practices and sustained employment. Yet we tested this possibility in supplemental regression analyses that included a measure of length of 'exposure' to the managers' practices and interaction terms to assess whether the strength of the relationship among the four manager practices and turnover or retention depends on length of exposure.[4] None of these variables was significant. It could be that there was not sufficient variation on 'manager exposure' during the

18-month observation period (mean=14.89 months, sd=4.08) to gauge how 'exposure' might condition the effects of particular management practices on store-level outcomes. Or it could be that the real culprit, or hero, is a factor not captured in our models, such as store norms, worker qualities or local economic conditions beyond unemployment rates.

Our findings are consistent with those of Grugulis et al. (2011) that suggest that although frontline managers may find 'discretionary spaces' in the face of tight accountability practices, their discretion is limited in scope and impact. In our study, although key manager practices significantly increased employees' chances for sustained employment, the effect sizes are modest. For example, turnover was 19 per cent lower in stores in which managers said they try to keep headcount down, which one might consider remarkable except for the fact that turnover exceeded 100 per cent among part-time employees and was almost 80 per cent among full-time employees. Employees' prospects for sustained employment appear slim regardless of the 'small freedoms' exploited by their manager.

This bleak outlook should not be interpreted as an argument against efforts to improve the quality of lower-level jobs through changes to manager behaviour. Indeed, we suspect that the managers in this firm have more capacity than they realize to improve jobs. By way of example, despite a widely held belief that demand fluctuations make advance scheduling infeasible, our calculations of the difference between the minimum and maximum weekly staffing hours assigned stores across a year indicate that, for the majority of stores, 80 per cent of store hours remain stable week-in, week-out (Lambert and Henly, 2010). By developing scheduling practices that capitalize on that stability, managers could improve the stability or at least the predictability of workers' schedules (Lambert and Henly, 2009). There are undoubtedly other possibilities for manager agency that would reveal themselves if our study had incorporated employees' perspectives on the manager practices that make a difference to them.

Notes

1 The authors are grateful for generous support from the Ford, Russell Sage and Annie E. Casey Foundations. Thanks to Eric Hedberg, Lauren Gaudino, Jacob Lesniewski and Lindsey Whitlock for excellent research assistance and the full Work Scheduling Study research group for significant contributions to the broader study. Thanks also to Chris Tilly for providing helpful suggestions on an earlier draft of the chapter.
2 The findings remain substantively the same when employee tenure is excluded from the analyses.
3 Unemployment rates are *local area unemployment statistics*, provided by the Bureau of Labor Statistics, accessed at http://www.bls.gov/lau/home.htm.

4 Specifically, supplemental regression analyses included an 'exposure' variable, measured as the total number of months the manager had been in the store for the 6 months prior to the survey plus the 12 months after the survey and the interaction of this variable with the four manager practices examined in Models 1 through 4 respectively. All other variables in previous models were also included, and we centered the manager practice and manager tenure variables in order to reduce multicollinearity (Aiken and West, 1991). These analyses produce no significant associations between manager exposure and turnover and retention, nor are the interactions significant. The manager practice coefficients remain relatively unchanged across the models.

REFERENCES

Aiken, L. and West, S. (1991). *Multiple Regression: Testing and Interpreting Interactions.* Sage Publications, Newbury Park.

Appelbaum, E., Bosch, G., Gautie, J., Mason, G. Mayhew, K., Salverda, W. Schmitt, J. and Westergaard-Nielsen, N. (2009). Introduction and Overview. In J. Gautie and J. Schmitt (eds) *Low Wage Work in the Wealthy World* (pp. 1–32). New York: Russell Sage Foundation.

Bernhardt, A., Boushey, H., Dresser, L. and Tilly, C. (2008). *The Gloves-Off Economy: Workplace Standards at the Bottom of America's Labour Market.* Champaign, IL: Labour and Employment Labour Relations.

Bourgeois, L. J. (1984). Strategic Management and Determinism. *Academy of Management Review,* 9(4), 586–596.

Bozkurt, O. and Grugulis, I. (2011). Why Retail Work Demands a Closer Look. In I. Grugulis, I. and O. Bozkurt O. (eds) *Retail Work* (pp. 1–21). Hampshire, England: Palgrave Macmillan.

Carré, F. and Tilly, C. (2009). *America's Biggest Low-Wage Industry: Continuity and Change in Retail Jobs.* Center for Social Policy, University of Massachusetts – Boston. Working paper: 2009-6, http://www.mccormack.umb.edu/centers/csp/documents/working_papers/2009_6_Carre_and_Tilly.pdf

Carré, F., Tilly, C. and Holgate, B. (2008). *Continuity and Change in Low-Wage Work in U.S. Retail Trade.* Unpublished working paper, University of Massachusetts Lowell Center for Industrial Competitiveness and University of Massachusetts Boston Center for Social Policy. http://129.63.176.200/centers/CIC/Research/Tilly_Research/Carre%20Tilly%20Holgate%20Release%20April%2008-05.01.08.pdf

Carré, F., Tilly, C., van Klaveren, M. and Voss-Dahm, D. (2009). Retail Jobs in Comparative Perspective. In J. Gautie and J. Schmitt (eds), *Low Wage Work in the Wealthy World* (pp. 211–267). New York: Russell Sage Foundation.

Eisenhardt, K. M. and Zbaracki, M. J. (1992). Strategic Decision Making. *Strategic Management Journal, 13,* 17–37. doi:10.1002/smj.4250130904

Gottschalk, P. and Moffitt, R. (2009). The rising instability of U.S. earnings. *Journal of Economic Perspectives,* 23(4), 3–24.

Grugulis, I. and Bozkurt, O. (eds) (2011). *Retail Work.* Basingstoke: Palgrave Macmillan.

►

▶
Grugulis, I., Bozkurt, O. and Clegg, J. (2011). 'No Place to Hide'? the Realities of Leadership in UK Supermarkets. In I. Grugulis, I. and O. Bozkurt (eds) *Retail Work* (pp. 193–212). Basingstoke: Palgrave Macmillan.

Haley-Lock, A. and Ewert, S. (2011). Waiting for the Minimum: U.S. State Wage Laws, Firm Strategy and Chain Restaurant Job Quality. *Journal of Industrial Relations*, 53(1), 31–48.

Henly, J. R., Shaefer, H. L., and Waxman, R. E. (2006). Nonstandard Work Schedules: Employer- and Employee-Driven Flexibility in Retail Jobs. *Social Service Review*, 80, 609–634.

Job Openings and Labor Turnover Survey (2008). Bureau of Labor Statistics, Department of Labor. http://www.bls.gov/news.release/archives/jolts_11132008.pdf

Jordan, L. (2011). Avoiding the 'Trap': Discursive Framing as a Means of Coping with Working Poverty. In I. Grugulis, I. and O. Bozkurt (eds) *Retail Work* (pp. 149–171). Basingstoke: Palgrave Macmillan.

Kalleberg, A. L. (2009). Precarious Work, Insecure Workers: Employment Relations in Transition. *American Sociological Review*, 74, 1–22.

Lambert, S. J. (2008). Passing the Buck: Labour Flexibility Practices That Transfer Risk onto Hourly Workers. *Human Relations*, 61(9), 1203–1227.

Lambert, S. J. (2009). Making a Difference for Hourly Employees. In A. Booth and A. Crouter (eds), *Work-Life Policies That Make a Real Difference for Individuals, Families, and Organizations* (pp. 169–195). Washington, DC: Urban Institute Press.

Lambert, S. J. (2012). 'Opting In' to Full Labour Force Participation in Hourly Jobs. In B. D. Jones (ed.), *Confronting the 'Opt-Out Revolution': Women in Today's Workforce*. New York: New York University Press, pp. 87–102.

Lambert, S. J. and Henly, J. R. (2009). Work Schedules in Hourly Jobs. Series on *The Low-Wage Labor Market for the Twenty-First Century Economy*. Washington, DC: The Mobility Agenda.

Lambert, S. J. and Henly, J. R. (2010). *Managers' Strategies for Balancing Business Requirements with Employee Needs*. Report of the University of Chicago Work Scheduling Study, http://www.ssa.uchicago.edu/faculty/Univ_of_Chicago_Work_Scheduling_Manager_ Report_6_25.pdf

Lambert, S. and Waxman, E. (2005). Organizational Stratification: Distributing Opportunities for Work-Life Balance. In E. Kossek and S. Lambert (eds) *Work and Life Integration: Organizational, Cultural, and Individual Perspectives* (pp. 99–122). Mahwah, NJ: Lawrence Erlbaum Associates.

Lambert, S. J., Haley-Lock, A., and Henly, J. R. (in press) Schedule Flexibility in Jobs with Scarce and Fluctuating Work Hours: Unanticipated Consequences and Promising Directions. *Community, Work & Family*.

National Retail Federation. U.S. Non-Agricultural Employment by Industry. Accessed June 16, 2011. http://www.nrf.com/modules.php?name=Pagesandsp_id=1242.

Ryan, A. and Kossek, E. E. (2008). Work-Life Policy Implementation: Breaking Down Or Creating Barriers to Inclusiveness. *Human Resource Management*, 47(2): 295–310.
▶

▶
Tilly, C. and Carré, F. (2011). Endnote: Retail Work – Perceptions and Reality. In I. Grugulis, I. and O. Bozkurt (eds) *Retail Work* (pp. 297–306). Basingstoke: Palgrave Macmillan.

U.S. Department of Labor, Bureau of Labor Statistics. (2011) Occupational Outlook Handbook, 2010–2011 Edition. Accessed 16 June 2011. http://www.bls.gov/oco/oco2003.htm

van Klaveren, M. and Voss-Dahm, D. (2011). Employers' 'Exit Options' and Low-Wage Retail Work. In I. Grugulis, I. and O. Bozkurt (eds) *Retail Work* (pp. 175–192). Basingstoke: Palgrave Macmillan.

Wright, P. and McMahan, G. (1992). Theoretical Perspectives for Strategic Human Resource Management. *Journal of Management*, 18: 295–320.

CHAPTER 10

Good Or Bad Jobs? Contrasting Workers' Expectations and Jobs in Mexican Call Centres

José Luis Álvarez Galván

Introduction

The central aim of this volume is to discuss to what extent bad jobs are inevitable in contemporary societies.* This chapter aims to contribute to this endeavour providing the perspective of a country of the global south. This task is undertaken by taking a step back from the central question and asking what would be a good or a bad job for Mexican workers and how the local context informs such an appreciation.

To analyse how Mexican workers perceive their employment conditions this chapter looks at the experience of work and employment conditions in Mexican call centres. Two central issues inform this analysis. On the one hand, it is argued that technology and managerial practices in mass customized services might erode workers' skills (Braverman 1974; Ritzer 1998). On the other hand, it is also argued that organizations might use numerical flexibility mechanisms as non-standard forms of employment to face competitive business environments (Harrison 1994). As a result, it seems inevitable that most workers in recently created mass service industries are likely to perform low-skilled jobs in precarious employment conditions (Frenkel 2004; Bazen and Lucifora 2005).

Overall, call centres are identified as a flagship industry of the new economy where workers are strictly monitored by IT systems and where non-standard forms of employment play a key role in reducing costs (Kinnie et al. 2000; Baldry et al. 2007). Nonetheless, it is also argued that customer segmentation practices are closely tied to differentiated managerial strategies where workers servicing high-income markets are more likely to experience high-involvement practices and enjoy better employment conditions than those workers servicing mass markets (Batt 2000; Frenkel 2004). This is to say that even in a context of highly standardized job designs and non-standard contracts relatively good jobs might be possible depending on the customer segment. In addition, important variations in human resources practices might arise when comparing in-house against outsourced call centres (Moss et al. 2008; Alvarez-Galvan 2010) and between call centres in rich and less developed countries (Miranda et al. 2006; Batt et al. 2007; Benner et al. 2007; Alvarez-Galvan 2010b).

Despite the rich empirical evidence about call centres, workers' own job expectations rarely play a central role in the analysis. It is true that workers' interpretation of managerial practices has been widely explored in the literature but these interpretations have been confined to the shop-floor terrain and rarely go beyond the boundaries of the organization. The evidence presented here suggests that more attention must be paid to the context where these employment relations take place as workers expectations are largely shaped by the local context, something that has been emphasized by other authors for the employers' side (Bazen and Lucifora 2005).

This chapter presents information collected through 65 in-depth interviews with call centre workers and managers about their work experiences in three outsourcing companies in Mexico City during the period 2006–2007. In order to protect participants' identities, their names and those of their organizations have been changed and appear here as Phonemex (a foreign firm, the largest call centre company in Mexico), Tecnotronics (also a foreign firm and the largest help desk in Mexico) and KPM (a large Mexican competitor). In addition, 18 additional interviews were undertaken with union representatives, officials of the Mexican Ministry of Labour, academics, consultants, industry representatives and other relevant informants.

Overall, the findings of this research indicate that local institutions matter when determining the quality of jobs and how this quality is perceived by workers. By local institutions, I refer not only to the institutional arrangements that shape employment relations (such as labour legislation or unions) but also the set of dynamic cultural and historical conventions that shape individuals and collective actions (such as perceptions about gender and age roles). The main conclusion of this chapter is that what can be considered as a good job in a highly competitive industry as such call centres is not necessarily perceived as such by workers, and the other way around for workers in apparently less attractive jobs in the same industry. The chapter is organized as follows. The first part presents workers' expectations in the context of labour market conditions in Mexico City. The following part presents the experience of those workers at the low-end customer segment category of call centre work while the next part presents the experience of workers at the high end of the spectrum.

Setting workers' expectations: overview of Mexico City's employment conditions and the call centre industry

It is important to understand what is not a good job but an acceptable job for Mexican workers. Many workers in Mexico do not have a 'formal' contract. In 2006, when the data for this research was collected, the proportion of workers without a formal or written contract was about 49 per cent of the total (Table 1). In these circumstances, the fear of having a job with no contract (or not having a job at all) seems to be the biggest concern in Mexico where the formal institutional setting is much weaker than in the US, Europe and other industrialized countries considered in this book. In this respect, the concern about the inevitability of bad jobs seems to be particularly strong in Mexico.

Table 10.2 provides more detail on job quality. At the national level, 41 per cent of Mexican female workers perform their activities in micro businesses in precarious employment conditions; almost 57 per cent had no benefits, 71 per cent lacked a permanent contract and nearly 87 per cent did not have a union. Having a job in Mexico City did not represent a significant advantage for women other than having less exposure to lower income jobs.

Overall, there is no major difference between Mexican women and men in their exposure to low income jobs. At the national level the situation of Mexican men is significantly better than that of women in two respects: men are considerably less likely to work in precarious conditions in micro-businesses and are less likely to hold involuntary part-time jobs. On the other hand, at the national level, men are more likely to have a job with no benefits, without a permanent contract and without collective representation (Table 10.2). Again, the greatest advantage for men of having a job in Mexico City is less exposure to low-income jobs than if they work in other parts of the country. In sum, Mexican workers live in a context of precarious employment conditions that largely shapes their expectations about the quality of the jobs available.

Table 10.1 Job contracts in Mexico, 2000–2006 (percentages)

	2000	2006
Permanent jobs	49	42
Temporary jobs	7	9
Without contract	44	49
Unemployment rate	2.2	3.5

Source: Presidencia de la República 2006.

Table 10.2 Mexico and Mexico City: employment for women and men, 2006

	Employed at precarious micro-businesses (a)	With low income (b)	Involuntary part-time job (c)	Without benefits (d)	Without permanent contract	Without union (e)
Women						
Mexico	41	50	36.3	56.9	71	87.2
Mexico City	41.4	36	32.7	52.3	65.6	86.6
Men						
Mexico	31.1	50	19.1	60.8	73.6	90.6
Mexico City	38.9	39.1	14.9	54.1	66.6	89.2

(a) People employed in small establishments (1–5 people in retail trade and services and 1–16 in manufacturing) without formal regulation, contracts or benefits.
(b) Wages per hour lower than the national median for males (approximately 1.8 USD per day in 2006).
(c) Less than 35 hours per week.
(d) Without end-of-the-year bonus, paid holidays or medical coverage.
(e) Not affiliated to any union.

Source: Adapted from Garcia (2009) based on the National Survey of Employment and Occupation (ENEO), second quarter.

The call centre industry is a large and rapidly growing sector of the Mexican economy (Table 10.3). In general, the typical call centre worker in Mexico City could be described as a young person (8–24 years old), with unfinished college education, and belonging to a household with a medium to lower-class income (about 6000 Mexican pesos monthly, the equivalent of approximately $500US). They are typically the children of manual workers, low-level bureaucrats and people employed in the informal economy (Bensusán and Rendón 2000). But as will be discussed below, there is substantial variation in worker characteristics.

Most call centre workers are in front-line jobs requiring relatively low skills and minimal autonomy, subjected to rigid scripts and constant monitoring from supervisors (either directly or through IT), although there is also a variation in conditions (Taylor and Bain 1999; Taylor et al. 2002; Frenkel 2004). Women and men seem to be evenly distributed in Mexico City's call centres where there is a roughly 50–50 per cent distribution (IMT 2007), unlike the industry at global level where call centre work is dominated by female workers (Batt et al. 2007).

Workers' social capital is the most important way in which call centre jobs are filled in Mexico City. Workers' social networks play a fundamental role in disseminating information about vacancies and, very importantly, about the quality of jobs available. To some extent, it is surprising that call centres, one of the flagship industries of the new economy, still relies on traditional forms of recruitment.

Table 10.3 Mexico: general indicators of the call centre industry, 2007

Dimensions		
No. of workstations	214,000	
Total employment	341,000	
No. of companies	21,262	
Proportion of the Latin American industry	29.5%	
2006 employment growth		
Mexico	21%	
Latin America	15%	
Worldwide	6%	
Establishment size		
No. of workstations	Companies	%
< 20	16,500	77.6
21–100	4,400	20.7
> 100	362	1.7
Total	21,262	100.0
Cost structure		
Human resources	63%	
Telephone lines and internet	19%	
Technological infrastructure	9%	
Other utilities	9%	
Industry structure	Companies	Employees
In-house	21,142	246,000
Outsourcing	120	95,000
Outsourcing segment: No. of workstations	20,885	
Turnover rate	40%	
The outsourcing segment as % of the total call centre industry:		
Employment	31.2%	
Sales	33%	
Workstations	9.8%	
Outsourcing workstations for offshoring services	34%	

Source: Mexican Institute of Tele-services (2007).

When recruiting, call centres usually look for 'students' in order to meet their needs for part-time employees hired through non-standard contracts. However, it is interesting that workers also 'play' this game and see themselves as 'students' even if they are no longer pursuing any kind of education or academic degree.

In this respect, when talking about the quality of their jobs, Mexican call centre workers expressed their opinions in relation on how far they feel they are from their 'ideal' situation pointing in three different directions: first, in relation to their employment conditions (understood as the set of HRM policies, organization of work and compensation levels); second, in relation to the working environment; third, in relation to the context.

Not surprisingly, workers' interpretations of the objective elements of their employment conditions were in line with HRM strategy in the two sections of the industry. On the one hand, those workers servicing *mass market* segments recognized that they fell at the low-end spectrum of HRM practices: their jobs were highly standardized and low-paid. Nonetheless, workers always said that their jobs were adequate in terms of the social atmosphere and given the context of precarious employment in Mexico. On the other hand, workers servicing relatively *high-income markets* recognized that they fell at the high-end spectrum of HRM practices with good wages and relatively high levels of autonomy at work. However, these workers also seem frustrated given the gap between their personal expectations and their current status at work.

In sum, in call centres in Mexico City, workers associated with mass markets seem to be relatively satisfied with their jobs while workers associated with higher income services seem unsatisfied. The next two sections discuss the experiences of these workers and potential explanations for their evaluation of working conditions.

The low-end experience: servicing mass markets

In call centres, jobs associated with services for mass markets have the lowest status (Batt 2000; Taylor et al. 2002; Frenkel 2004; Batt et al. 2007). Workers servicing mass markets usually perform semi-autonomous work, require minimum experience in sales and basic grammar and speaking skills, and do not need more than a rudimentary knowledge of computer software (to fill in forms) and telephonic devices (enabling them to carry out the simple tasks of dialling a number or transferring a call) (Taylor and Bain 1999). The training period tends to be short (about a week or so) and it is focused on product information. In this type of work, there is almost no interaction with the client firm on the job and the relationship with client firm representatives is focused on the evaluation of the quantitative components of service level agreements (Taylor et al. 2002; Taylor and Bain 2005). Finally, mass market agents frequently receive the lowest salaries in the industry and productivity bonuses are an important part of their wages (even up to 75% of their income). Conditions in these jobs are summarized in Table 10.4.

During most of the interviews workers described themselves as college students in part-time jobs. However, as the interviews progressed, many of

Table 10.4 Basic characteristics of the jobs analysed in this chapter

Market & task	Skills & Education	Typical Compensation
Mass markets: credit card and airline ticket sales and customer services (inbound/ outbound calls)	Semi-autonomous work & high school/ unfinished college education	– 150–250 USD monthly; – Up to 75% of the salary might depend on productivity bonuses; – Contract for services; – Few opportunities for promotion.
High-income markets: software and electronic equipment sales and customer services (inbound/outbound calls)	High-skill work & engineering degrees	– 400–500 USD monthly; – Up to 20% of the salary might depend on productivity bonuses but it is common to see employees with a 100% fixed salary; – There are also some employees with permanent contracts; – Some opportunities for promotion within the subcontracted firm or even in the client firm.

them revealed that, in fact, they did not study anymore and that they had dropped out from college some time ago. Most of these employees got the job shortly after dropping out from the school or they dropped out of school shortly after getting the job. Crucially, having a part-time job seems to them a reasonable excuse to justify their poor academic performance. Moreover, when asked whether they needed the job to secure financial resources at home, an overwhelming majority answered, 'No'. It seems that most of these workers simply did not find their way in school and found call centre work as a way to compensate for their academic failure before their parents. Most of the time, these workers said that they used their pay as pocket money for holidays or shopping as they didn't need money for rent and food because they lived at home.

In the call centres analysed, agents at the low-end categories held temporary contracts with a six-hour, five-day schedule, organized in two shifts: the first from 9am to 3pm and the second from 3pm to 9pm. Work was organized individually and agents were assembled in groups of no more than 15 individuals headed by one supervisor.

The managerial approach used in these accounts is clearly one of a 'piece-rate' system in which little autonomy and discretion is expected from workers (Fernie and Metcalf 1998). On paper, these jobs oriented to mass markets seem highly standardized and low-paid; in other words, they can be categorized as bad jobs.

Nonetheless, there were relatively high levels of job satisfaction among workers servicing mass markets, something that contradicts the findings obtained by other researchers in developed countries (Taylor and Bain 1999; Baldry et al. 2007) but seems in line with results for other less developed countries such as India, South Africa or Brazil (Miranda et al. 2006; Batt et al. 2007; Benner et al. 2007; Alvarez-Galvan 2010b) where the economic conditions are more difficult. It seems that workers systematically judge their own conditions taking a more general context into consideration:

> I mean, you know, this is not my dream job, I do not want to do this for the rest of my life but it is OK for the time being. My wage gives me money for my personal things, my holidays...also, I can see that other people *around* me, friends and classmates, are suffering a lot finding jobs. (Outsourcing agent, Phonemex)

Therefore, despite being subjected to strict surveillance and performing highly standardized work, workers in these job categories displayed unexpectedly high levels of job satisfaction. There are three explanations for such an unexpected finding. First, the difficulties of the local labour market make these jobs a 'reasonable' choice for many young workers. Importantly, the wages these workers received are not necessarily used to support a family or even an individual but rather as a complement to household income. This situation represents a fundamental factor in understanding workers' experiences in workplaces such as call centres in Mexico City. Most workers in these jobs seem to tolerate bad jobs and low wages due to the job's temporary nature and the lack of better opportunities in the labour market.

Second, the use of workers' social capital in recruitment allows employers to build an environment of social cohesion that discipline workers:

> Of course you feel the pressure of IT systems monitoring you all the time, the pressure of chasing selling targets everyday but, at the same time, the working atmosphere is great. I have a lot of friends here, actually, one of my best friends invited me to join the company. You can see many people hanging out together after work. (Outsourcing agent, KPM)

Social ties at work represent a fundamental element in disciplining workers in these Mexican call centres, a practice that is hardly new in the organization of work and seems to be persistent even in industries of the new economy.

Finally, the third reason explaining the relatively high level of workers' satisfaction in mass market services is related to the ambiguity of monitoring rules. On paper, workers are subjected to intense monitoring and supervision practices. However, evidence collected not just from interviews but also through non-participant observation indicated that, in practice, monitoring and supervision procedures were flexible and workers usually developed coping and resisting strategies that are tolerated by supervisors, strategies that have been largely documented by other researchers (Taylor and Bain 1999; Korczynski 2002).

These practices confirm the challenges and limitations of controlling front-line service work (Leidner 1993; Korczynski 2009). Here, workers 'break the rules' constantly. For instance, frequently sales staff devoted much effort to 'simulating' the validation of customers' information by calling friends and asking them to confirm real customers' data. Also, it is common to see agents breaking down families' airline ticket purchases into individual operations (one for each family member in order to get a larger bonus) despite the explicit prohibition to do so. Agents also often make extra effort (beyond the limits established by the rules) to find alternative solutions for customers in difficult situations.

However, if the labour market context, the use of workers' social capital, and the use of coping/resisting strategies help to understand high levels of satisfaction at work for agents servicing mass markets it does not explain the higher level of turnover in these jobs (about 40% per year). Perhaps, the single most important answer is related to the temporary expectations of these workers. These jobs are not supposed to last very long:

> Right now, this job is good for me. I am making good money for my things, my hobbies, my free time. Of course, I am not naive, I know that if I want to have a family I would need something better but this job is excellent for me right now! (Outsourcing agent, Phonemex)

Even though the turnover rate might be considered high it remains below that observed for other highly customer service-oriented services in Mexico, for example, retail jobs (with a turnover rate of about 110% every year) (Alvarez-Galvan 2010a). Therefore, workers' experiences at work largely depend on their own expectations that, in turn, are shaped by the general context.

At the end of the 1990s, when efforts for collective organization started in Mexican call centres, the expectations of these young workers (the bulk of the labour force in the industry) represented one of the main and more controversial challenges for unions. Inside the STRM (Telephone Workers Union of the Mexican Republic), some members did not want to pursue the unionization of call centre workers and they were perceived as less committed and immature. Instead, these union members suggested that it would be better to put more pressure on companies in order to re-internalize call centre services. In the end, a more inclusive position prevailed and the largest call centre company at that time was unionized. Importantly, members of the union recognized that providing younger workers with a solid idea about the relevance of their labour rights to improve their current conditions and career prospects, through close contact with older generations, was a key factor in convincing young workers that good jobs were possible through collective bargaining mechanisms.

The high-end experience: servicing high-income markets

Jobs oriented to relatively high-income markets and providing customized mass services (such as sales and customer services of software and electronic equipment) in call centres have relatively high status in call centres (Frenkel 2004; Alvarez-Galvan 2010b). However, it is worth mentioning that this group of workers represents only a tiny fraction of the jobs in the industry, no more than 10 per cent of the total (IMT 2007). On paper, these workers seem to have most of the ideal characteristics of service work in the new economy: higher skills, more autonomy and better education than the average worker. Agents servicing relatively high-income markets are the best paid in the sector by far. Most of these positions are filled by people with college degrees, many of them in engineering, including quite a few with master's degrees. The work performed usually requires higher skills and some firm-specific knowledge; basic experience in customer or sales services is highly desirable but not essential. As expected, workers in this category commonly display higher levels of autonomy when performing their tasks, but higher levels of dissatisfaction and tension were also observed in many cases.

A plausible explanation for this situation is that higher levels of education tend to be associated with higher expectations in the labour market. These workers do not seem very comfortable with the image of workers in call centres and hired by subcontracted companies. Not surprisingly perhaps, most agents in this category were aged 28 years and over, and, significantly older than those in the low-segment of the industry. The recruitment process still relies heavily on employees' social networks but companies also visit colleges and technical schools to encourage applications. The training period is lengthy: a week or two before starting work, a month of close supervision on the job and finally up to six or seven months to be proficient in the job.

In this research, one of the accounts providing technical support was located inside Tecnotronics, a Dutch company in Mexico City. This account was a helpdesk service for Sybase, a software company in the United States. The work schedule was eight hours, five days a week, and these workers were the only ones in the sample who had a permanent contract, which also included private medical insurance. In Tecnotronics workers did not receive any kind of bonus, just a salary related to their position in the organizational ladder. Entry-level workers received a monthly salary equivalent to about $400 US. In general, this situation was the case where workers had the best employment conditions – a good fixed salary, on-the-job training and opportunities for promotions.

The call centre manager of Tecnotronics, Daniel Gutierrez, insisted that the organization's goal was to retain workers for at least three years because this period of time was considered 'the minimum they need to become proficient with most of the firm-specific skills that they would need to stay even longer in Tecnotronics; I am saying so because we want them to stay with us after all the training they get here'. Despite this statement, technical support agents interviewed in this research were not entirely convinced about staying at Tecnotronics for long periods of time:

> Well, I know that the employment conditions we have here are good, especially if you look around and see how many people in Mexico are struggling to get a job, whatever job, even people with postgraduate education...but, I do not know, to be honest, I think it is a problem of expectations. We have invested a lot in our education and we dreamt of working for a huge and well-known company. Tecnotronics is good...but personally I would like to try to look for another company. (Outsourcing agent, Tecnotronics)

Agents in the Sybase account identified the workload as the main source of stress in the workplace, especially because most requests are labelled as 'urgent' (problems with software, hardware, networks, security measures etc.). Employees thought that they were acquiring useful skills through gaining expertise in managing the tools of a prestigious company while also improving their English language skills. Overall, workers in this account seem satisfied with their work and autonomy levels; they often recognize that they are in a better position than most call centre workers but, interestingly, they also expressed their need for a better status in the industry as a whole (something that they do not achieve at an outsourcing company).

In Phonemex, whose business profile seemed less prestigious than that of Tecnotronics, technical support agents were better paid, their salary included an important bonus proportion, and they seemed more satisfied than their counterparts in the Dutch outsourcer. At Phonemex, one account provides services to Microsoft. These agents had a separate, closed space, which workers from other accounts on the same floor were not allowed to enter. Each worker enjoyed a spacious desk, which contrasts with the often limited space other workers had in adjacent accounts. Most of the staff were single and male, with engineering degrees from public and private schools, and a middle-class background. Agents had a contract for services and their typical schedule was one of eight hours, five days a week. Microsoft was involved in their recruitment and demanded the right to having the last interview with candidates; in doing so, Microsoft controlled access into the account.

Microsoft also provided direct training to the agents, who received a monthly salary equivalent to $500US plus a bonus of up to 30 per cent depending on productivity and service quality standards. In this account, the bonus was assigned individually and agents did not have to compete to get it. Interviewees often said that they spent part of their free time helping other agents. Agents in this account looked for customers and, to do so, they needed to be familiar with the technical characteristics of the programmes and the 'financial' advantages of using these software products. Each agent was assigned particular geographical regions of Mexico as target markets with a list of potential customers; agents spent the day making outbound calls to technical and finance staff in different companies to introduce the product and make sales. Employees admitted that they did acquire new skills through performing this job as most of them did not have any sales skills before having the job:

> I believe that the biggest challenge for people in this account is finding new clients and making deals with them. This can be a long and arduous process and you need patience. This is something completely new for me, I mean, I am an engineer and I was not trained for this but I have to say that, if you want to be in business, you need to be good in sales. (Outsourcing worker, Phonemex)

Importantly, technical workers felt that they did not enjoy an extraordinarily high level of autonomy and discretion in this account, contrary to the relatively high-satisfaction experience of technical workers in the Sybase account at Tecnotronics. Technical workers in the Microsoft account felt pressure to hit sales targets at the end of the month and thought they were losing autonomy over the pace of work and breaks as the end of the month approached. Most of them acknowledged that they received better salaries and enjoyed higher levels of autonomy and discretion than most of their colleagues in the same organization but working on other accounts. Importantly, however, these technical workers also felt that, among workers performing the *same* kind of task for software companies, they were in a worse position because they worked in a subcontracted company:

> It depends, on paper the conditions are good, very good sometimes, especially if you look around and notice all those guys from college without

> any job or a very bad one. The problem for me is that I want to work in a better company, I do not want to provide services to Microsoft, I want to work at Microsoft! (Outsourcing agent, Phonemex)

It was expected that these workers servicing relatively high-income markets would report higher levels of satisfaction and commitment to their organizations and jobs as a result of their relatively higher autonomy and income. However, more technical workers expressed dissatisfaction with their jobs than those in low-segments. If only the pecuniary compensations were considered it would be very difficult to explain these manifestations of discomfort; they would be considered irrational. However, if one examines workers' expectations, then it is possible to understand their dissatisfaction. On the one hand, these workers had comparatively high levels of education and skills; consequently, they were expecting better salaries and bonuses and better opportunities for a good professional career within the organization. They believed that if the organization valued them they would be able to stay with the company and be promoted. If this did not occur, these workers believed that they were not important to the organization. However, most of them were in their early 30s and were becoming anxious about their career opportunities and job stability; they were starting (or already had) families and were looking for long-term contracts. According to the agents this level of frustration has an impact on the service delivered:

> There is a lot of frustration going on around here. Yes we have good pay; yes we are in a better position than those guys selling credit cards or airline tickets. Here you have your own desk and more autonomy to organise your work in the most efficient way for you. But, on the other hand, this job does not give you the status desired and this has a negative impact on our interactions with each other and with customers. (Outsourcing agent, Phonemex)

In sum, even when jobs seem good on paper, the experience of workers, shaped by contextual and personal circumstances, indicates that these positions are not perceived as good. The case of technical services for relatively high-income markets presented here indicates that multiple factors influence workers' perceptions.

Conclusions

The evidence presented in this chapter indicates that there is a consistent mismatch between workers' expectations and HRM practices in call centres in Mexico. Those workers servicing mass markets and having less attractive working conditions seem to have relatively higher levels of job satisfaction than those servicing high-income markets and enjoying better employment conditions and more autonomy at work. To explain this finding, it seems that workers' expectations play a crucial role in the way HRM practices are assimilated by workers.

In Mexico, a large proportion of workers perform their jobs under precarious working conditions, that is, they are likely to lack a written contract and collective representation, and to have minimal on-the-job training and reduced opportunities for long tenure at work (García 2009). Indeed, for labour-intensive industries these seem to be attractive pull factors to locate in Mexico. In this context, jobs oriented to mass markets in call centres are seen as competitive and good jobs for young workers despite the low compensation and lack of autonomy and discretion at work. For most of these workers, mass market call centre jobs seem a good opportunity to obtain 'complementary' earnings to spend on leisure activities rather than paying basic bills in their households. These findings seem to be in line with those observed in other developing countries. In addition, the working atmosphere in these services seems to be more relaxed and permissive than the one depicted in the US and European literature, and recruitment via workers' social capital is used to promote social cohesion and discipline in the workplace.

On the other hand, workers servicing high-income markets seem to be less satisfied with their working and employment conditions despite the higher levels of autonomy and compensation they enjoy. In many respects, it seems that these workers' expectations are not fulfilled by these jobs. These workers are older and have serious family responsibilities and call centre work does not seem to be very attractive for them.

This chapter has revealed the importance of considering other contextual factors when evaluating jobs. It is clear that a good job for workers is not only about material compensations (in the form of higher wages and better benefits) or job design (in the way work is organized and performed) but also about how these job characteristics stack up against perceived alternatives, and about social cohesion. These contextual factors become relevant when trying to explain the lack of a more militant collective response from workers in these industries. Call centre companies have been very successful in taking advantage of precarious employment conditions in the country and the existence of strong social cohesion at work as mechanisms to control and minimize workers' resistance in the shop floor.

These conclusions offer two different responses to the question about the inevitability of bad jobs in contemporary societies. If these workers were asked this question, on the one hand, agents at low-end categories would say that no better jobs are available for them, that in current circumstances, these bad jobs are valuable and even acceptable (this is why they are relatively satisfied with them). On the other hand, workers at high-end categories would say that better jobs are possible, that their frustration comes from the lack of opportunities for reaching better conditions and that they know these better jobs are somewhere else, in other companies, but not accessible to them.

Note

*This chapter was written while the author was a visiting researcher in the Department of Political and Social Sciences at Universitat Pompeu Fabra, Barcelona, Spain.

REFERENCES

Alvarez-Galvan, J. L. (2010a) *Liberalization and Retail: The Effects of Foreign Capital on Mexican Retail* (Saarbrücken, Germany: LAP Lambert Academic Publishing).

Alvarez-Galvan, J. L. (2010b) *Service Work and Subcontracting in the New Economy: Call Centres in Mexico City* (London: London School of Economics and Political Science).

Baldry, C., P. Bain, P. Taylor, J. Hyman, D. Scholarios, A. Marks, A. Watson, K. Gilbert, G. Gall and D. Bunzel (2007) *The Meaning of Work in the New Economy* (Basingstoke, England; New York: Palgrave Macmillan).

Batt, R. (2000) 'Strategic Segmentation in Front-Line Services: Matching Customers, Employees and Human Resource Systems', *International Journal of Human Resource Management*, 11(3), 540.

Batt, R., Doellgast, V., Kwon, H., Nopany, P. Nopany (2005) *Indian Call Center Industry Report: Strategy, HR Practices, and Performance* (Cornell: National Benchmarking Report).

Batt, R., D. Holman and U. Holtgrewe (2007) *The Global Call Centre Report: International Perspectives on Management and Employment* (Ithaca, NY: Authors).

Bazen, S. and C. Lucifora (2005) 'Employer Behaviour in the Low Wage Labour Market: Which Policies for Europe?' In Marx, I. and W. Salverda *Low-Wage Employment in Europe: Perspectives for Improvement* (Leuven: Acco).

Benner, C., Rahmat, O. and Lewis, C. (2007) *The South African Call Center Industry: National Benchmarking Report, Strategy, HR Practices & Performance* (Johannesburg: Sociology of Work Unit and LINK Center, University of Witwatersrand).

Bensusán, G. and T. Rendón, Eds. (2000) *Trabajo y Trabajadores en el México Contemporáneo* (México: Porrúa).

Braverman, H. (1974) *Labour and Monopoly Capital: The Degradation of Work in the Twentieth Century* (New York: Monthly Review Press).

Fernie, S. and D. Metcalf (1998) '(Not) Hanging on the Telephone: Payment Systems in the New Sweatshops'. (London: London School of Economics

▶

▶
and Political Science, Centre for Economic Performance, Discussion Paper No. 390).
Frenkel, S. (2004) 'Service Workers in Search of Decent Work', in S. Ackroyd, R. Batt, P. Tolbert and P. Thompson (eds) *The Oxford Handbook of Work and Organisation* (Oxford: Oxford University Press).
García, B. (2009) 'Los mercados de trabajo urbanos de México a principios del siglo XXI.' *Revista Mexicana de Sociología*, 71(1), 5–46.
Harrison, B. (1994) *Lean and Mean: the Changing Landscape of Corporate Power in the Age of Flexibility* (New York: Basic Books), p. 363.
IMT (2007) *La industria del call centre hoy* (Mexico: IMT).
Kinnie, N., S. Hutchinson, and J. Purcell (2000) '"Fun and Surveillance": The Paradox of High Commitment Management in Call Centres'. *International Journal of Human Resource Management*, 11(5), 967–985.
Korczynski, M. (2002) *Human Resource Management in Service Work* (Basingstoke: Palgrave Macmillan).
Korczynski, M. (2009) 'The Mystery Customer: Continuing Absences in the Sociology of ServiceWork' *Sociology*, 43(5), 952–967.
Leidner, R. (1993) *Fast Food, Fast Talk: Service Work and the Routinization of Everyday Life* (Berkeley: University of California Press).
Mexican Institute of Teleservices (IMT) (2007) *La industria del call centre hoy* (México: IMT), p. 46.
Miranda Oliveira, M., Hoyos Guevara, A. J. de, Nelmi Trevisan, L., Nogueira, A. J. F., Giao, P. R., Fatima Silva, M. de and Melo, P. L. R. (2006) *Brazilian Call Center Industry Report* (PUC-SP).
Moss, P., H. Salzman and C. Tilly (2008) 'Under Construction: The Continuing Evolution of Job Structures in Call Centers' *Industrial Relations*, 47(2), 173–208.
Presidencia de la República (2006) *Sexto informe de gobierno* (México: Presidencia de la República), p. 356.
Ritzer, G. (1998) *The Mcdonaldization Thesis: Explorations and Extensions* (London: Sage Publications).
Taylor, P. and P. Bain (1999) 'An "Assembly Line in the Head": The Call Centre Labour Process'. *Industrial Relations Journal*, 30(2), 101–117.
Taylor, P., G. Mulvey, J. Hyman, and P. Bain (2002) 'Work Organisation, Control and the Experience of Work in Call Centres', *Work, Employment and Society*, 16(1), 133–150.
Taylor, P. and P. Bain (2005) '"India Calling to the Far Away Towns": The Call Centre Labour Process and Globalization', *Work, employment and society*, 19(2), 261–282.

CHAPTER

11

Thirty Years of Hospital Cleaning in England and Scotland – An Opportunity for 'Better' Jobs?

Anne Munro

Introduction

This chapter presents an overview of hospital cleaning in the UK, drawing on material concerning hospital cleaners (also known as domestic service workers) from a series of research projects conducted in England and Scotland over a 30-year period. Cleaning work generally exhibits many of the features identified with 'bad jobs' – low pay, highly rationalized work systems with little individual autonomy, high levels of work intensity with tight supervision, unsocial hours, lack of career progression and lack of training opportunities.

By examining changes over 30 years, the chapter charts the impact on quality of work resulting from macro-level policy changes and the significance of local micro-level changes relating to work organization. It also points to the impact trade unions may have on the quality of work. An argument is made that in the hospital cleaning sector it is possible to organize work in such a way that the quality and experience of work can be improved. The chapter is divided into five parts. The first part provides an outline of the cleaning industry in general. The second and third parts draw on two phases of empirical research with hospital cleaners. The first phase of research includes a study of four hospitals in the Midlands of England carried out during 1982–84 and revisited during 1996–97. The second phase of research describes two case studies carried out during 2002–04 as a part of an ESRC Teaching and Learning Programme project.[1] The following part examines recent public and political concerns about hospital cleanliness and how the attempts to prevent hospital-acquired infections have led health authorities to reconsider how hospital cleaning is organized and managed. The chapter concludes by identifying the key drivers to job change in hospital cleaning and arguing that while certain features of hospital cleaning are likely to remain poor, there are a number of ways in which job quality can be improved.

'Bad jobs' in the cleaning industry in the UK

There are two national bodies which focus on the cleaning industry in the UK. The British Cleaning Council is the co-ordinating body for employers in the UK cleaning industry and Asset Skills is one of the Government's 25 Sector Skills Councils with responsibility for improving workforce skills. The cleaning industry as a whole includes both internal (for example offices, shops and hospitals) and external (for example shopping precincts, car parks) cleaning. By 2006 it was estimated that the whole industry accounted for 720,700 employees; of these 553,500 were employed specifically as cleaners or domestics (Asset Skills, 2009).

The sector is polarized between a large number of very small organizations and a small number of very large organizations, as well as encompassing a large proportion of informal working. Many private cleaning companies operate on low profit margins, with labour costs accounting for almost three quarters of total costs. As a result, the industry is characterized by low wages and unsocial hours. In 2003, staff turnover was estimated at 28.5 per cent, and employers reported significant difficulty in attracting recruits to cleaning jobs, particularly because of the unsocial working hours (Pye Tait, 2003a: 7). By 2009 Asset Skills found in their employer survey that this sample were reporting a turnover rate of up to 75 per cent in some instances and cleaners remaining in employment for an average of 12 weeks (Asset Skills, 2009).

In 2003, 80 per cent of the cleaning workforce was female, with 75 per cent of the total working part-time. The workforce was older and had a greater proportion of ethnic minority workers than for the UK workforce as a whole. Cleaning workers had fewer qualifications than the general UK workforce, although those in the public sector were more likely to hold some form of cleaning qualification (Pye Tait, 2003b: 6). In 2009 Asset Skills estimated that 74 per cent of employees held no qualification or a qualification below level 2 (Asset Skills, 2009). A cleaner is likely to be an older woman working unsocial hours, part-time, for low pay in a relatively low technology context. Significantly some of the main technological developments in the industry relate to monitoring staff rather than developments to the technology of the cleaning process itself. It is unsurprising that turnover rates are high and it is difficult to attract recruits; those who do apply to the sector frequently have few qualifications and are reported by employers as having a poor attitude and morale.

In this context, Asset Skills have identified investment in training as key to breaking out of the low skill/low pay trap. They have an action plan with four key aims: to make cleaning more attractive as a career option, to develop more attractive cleaning jobs, to encourage employers to offer more attractive cleaning packages and to make it more attractive for employers to undertake training and development activities (Asset Skills, 2009: 11). The challenge is that without regulation Asset Skills has no leverage with which to persuade employers to invest in staff.

Turning to health, hospital cleaners are responsible for cleaning all areas within the hospital including wards, offices, toilets and spaces with public access. The work may involve the use of chemical cleaning agents and mechanical tools, but primarily focuses on dusting, mopping, sweeping and polishing. The cleaners may also be responsible for the removal of non-hazardous waste and in some cases the service of meals in the ward. Hospital cleaning was historically under the control of the ward matron. Following the Salmon Report in the 1960s functional domestic service departments were formed with their own management structures (Manson, 1977). In 1966 female domestic service staff were low paid and earned less than male ancillary workers, but were better paid and had better terms and conditions than their female equivalents in the private sector (National Board for Prices and Incomes, 1966). Alongside the formation of functional domestic service departments, there was increased local collective bargaining around incentive bonus schemes (aimed primarily at male ancillary workers) which supported a significant growth in trade union membership. Union activity grew throughout the 1970s as public sector workers bore the brunt of income freezes amid soaring inflation, which culminated in the Winter of Discontent in 1978–79 and the election of the Thatcher Government in 1979. This chapter picks up the story of the development of hospital cleaning work following these events.

UNISON, the Transport and General Workers' Union (TGWU now part of UNITE) and GMB are the largest unions which recruit cleaners in the health sector.[2] TGWU and GMB have always recruited in the public and private sectors, although UNISON was initially a public sector union. All the unions now have collective agreements with a range of private companies with contracts for support services within the public sector. One main aim of the unions has been to keep public services within the public sector, and all have campaigned against the Private Finance Initiative (PFI) which enables private companies to build new facilities, such as a hospital, which is then leased to the NHS and the company retains the contact to provide all support facilities.

Where services have been sub-contracted to the private sector, a key concern of the unions has been the development of a two-tier workforce (those who had previously been employed by the public sector and those taken on by the private company after privatization). The Transfer of Undertakings (Protection of Employment) Regulations 1981 (TUPE) protected terms and conditions for transferred staff and the result was staff working alongside one another, doing the same job, on different terms and conditions. TUPE regulations were extended in 2003 and again in 2006 (Labour Research Department, 2003; 2011).[3]

In 2003 UNISON estimated the total value of contracted out facilities in the health service at around £1.1 billion (2003: 1). Cleaning accounts for the largest proportion of this figure (29 per cent) (UNISON 2003: 1). There has been a shift in recent years towards combined service agreements, for example including catering and cleaning. UNISON estimated that this development had risen from a negligible proportion of contracts in 1996 to 60 per cent in 2002 (2003: 1). It has been driven by the larger companies targeting large contracts to achieve economies of scale and by the growth of PFI contracts that include agreements to provide the whole range of support services (UNISON 2003: 1). As a result the larger, multinational companies have become more significant to the sector. UNISON has suggested that the top four companies (ISS, Compass, Sodexho and Rentokil) handle 51 per cent of contracted out services (2003: 2).

The re-organization of hospital cleaning during the 1980s and 1990s

This part of the chapter draws on research carried out in four hospital cleaning departments in the early 1980s and again in the late 1990s. Between 1980 and 1990, the number of domestic service staff in England (whole time equivalent) dropped from 68,579 to 33,861, a reduction of more than 50 per cent (Health and Personal Services Statistics 1991; 1993). Because of the frequency of part-time working this underestimates the actual scale of job loss. Between 1982 and 1986 alone, 30,000 hospital cleaning jobs disappeared or were moved to the private sector. A brief overview is given below of each hospital, then the main changes during the period are outlined and the implications for job quality are identified. All the hospitals were located in areas with large Asian communities.

During the first phase of research in 1982, cleaning was tightly supervised, although there was time to talk with patients and visitors and to complete various tasks for patients such as putting flowers in a vase. There was a hierarchy of preferred areas to work in – most cleaners prized the opportunity to work on a ward, where there was most patient contact. The importance of the relational aspects of the role, interacting with patients and

Table 11.1 Case study hospitals

Hospital	Domestic staff no.	Overview
City Hospital General hospital 190 beds + outpatients	98	97 of the staff were women working part-time. The one man was employed on a higher grade. No Asian women employed.
County Psychiatric Large rural psychiatric hospital 600 beds	106	103 of the staff were women – 59 part-time and 44 full-time; most of the full-time workers were Asian. The three men were employed on a higher grade.
Shire General District General hospital 290 beds + outpatients	63	All women, all working part-time on the lowest grade. Mix white (British, Irish, European) and Asian women.
Community Local General hospital 200 beds	58	All women on the lowest grade, of whom 36 worked part-time and 22 worked full-time (mostly Asian).

visitors, has been identified as a crucial factor in terms of domestic service staff's work satisfaction (Williams et al., 1977). Another significant aspect of work satisfaction appeared to be the widely shared feeling of doing a socially valuable and worthwhile job and cleaners frequently spoke about their commitment to the health service. Many of them had been in post for significant periods of time, often for more than 15 years, reflecting the relative security of employment.

Domestic service work is often organized around two shifts, one in the morning and one in the evening, although in the 1980s there were a vast range of start and finish times and women working a wide range of shift patterns – for example just weekends, just evenings, a couple of evenings and a couple of mornings. In two of the hospitals (City and Shire) shifts had been regularized removing some of the flexibility for staff and cleaning work had been established as a part-time job. In Community and County Psychiatric where about half of the jobs were full-time, most of the full-time jobs were held by Asian women. County Psychiatric was in a rural location some distance from a major conurbation, which meant that staff had to be 'bussed in', making short shift periods less attractive to staff and less economical to the hospital. Only men were employed in City and County Psychiatric. In these cases the men worked full-time, were given different job titles (team cleaners) and paid at a higher grade than the women. The men were not tied to a specific work area, but were given tasks throughout the hospitals and had much more physical mobility and autonomy. The manager from County Psychiatric claimed the need for a male employee was to use the larger polishing machine (needing technical and physical strength that was rewarded by higher pay); however, at nearby Shire Hospital women used the same machines with no extra pay. The picture in the 1980s was of a workforce divided by gender and race, but where there was some flexibility over work organization and hours of work (Munro, 1999; 2001). Work was highly supervised but there was space for interaction with patients and many of the women enjoyed doing what they felt to be an important job. One of the things most disliked about the work was the attitude of professional staff: many cleaners felt that doctors and nurses treated them as inferior beings.

From 1983 the government required all hospital cleaning services to be exposed to market testing, which meant that private companies could tender for the cleaning contracts. At City the contract remained in-house, although the number of staff were cut and the hours of the remaining staff were cut. At Shire General the number of staff remained constant, although the size of the hospital grew significantly and the contract remained in-house until 1996. Thus, the immediate impact of privatization was either the direct shift of services to the private sector or an intensification of work resulting from efforts to achieve an internal tender that could compete with the private firms, who were at this stage completely unregulated. With each wave of retendering, further attempts were made to find ways of cutting costs. At Community hospital managers repeatedly tried to move the full-time Asian women into part-time jobs in an effort to compete with private tenders. Tensions rose as the Asian women workers resisted this change – it was assumed that any woman worker should be prepared to move from full-time to part-time working (men were never expected to work part-time). When the tender went to a private contractor many other staff blamed the Asian women.

Another piece of legislation had an even more dramatic impact on County Psychiatric. The Community Care Act 1990 led to its eventual closure and the 600-bed hospital was replaced by a small 90-bed unit. Catering and cleaning departments were reorganized and a new generic role of Service Assistant was created. There were comparatively few jobs and all were part-time – none of the Asian staff from County Psychiatric went on to work in the new unit. In both cases the Asian women cleaners felt that the unions, dominated by male ancillary staff at Community and nurses at County Psychiatric, had let them down in the failure to save their jobs.

Hospital cleaning staff were amongst the first groups in the public sector to be identified as 'peripheral' to core activities, and as such suitable for competitive tendering, contacting out and rationalization. During this period the management focus was entirely on efficiency and cost cutting. Work was organized and reorganized in a gendered and racialized way. Unlike the cleaning sector as a whole, in these case studies there was a significant reduction in the number of staff from an ethnic minority background – full-time Asian women workers were to a large extent replaced by part-time white women workers. Overall, there was a reduction in the workforce and an intensification of work for those who remained. Shifts were increasingly designed to fit with the flexibility sought by managers rather than the flexibility needed by women with families. Alongside intensification work became more Taylorized and focused on core cleaning tasks, stripping out the emotional content of labour. Domestic service work has always had a mix of features associated with 'good' and 'bad' work quality, but during this period there is a clear shift toward the 'bad' factors.

Hospital cleaning in the 2000s

UK health policy in the 2000s emphasized the development of workforce skills for all, yet the continued prominence of the private sector narrows the focus of cleaning jobs. The second phase of research covers two case studies, which illustrate these trends – one of a hospital in Scotland which had been subject to competitive tendering and re-tendering; the second a case study of an NHS Trust in England which had successfully invested in staff development. The latter case demonstrates the benefits of the alternative approach of investing in cleaning staff. It also shows how local management have the scope to effect and improve the quality of working life.

St Mary's Hospital, Scotland

At the time of the research, cleaning at St Mary's hospital was contracted out to Clean Co, a non-UK-owned multi-national company with a Health Division of approximately 10,000 staff in the UK. It recognizes two trade unions, GMB and UNISON. Clean Co was the fifth private contractor to have gained the facilities contract at St Mary's since the services had first been subjected to competitive tendering. As a result staff in the domestic services unit were working on a range of different contracts – for some Clean Co was their sixth employer while doing the same job. The company gained the contract to provide full hotel services including catering, cleaning, portering, laundry and linen services, some driving and administration roles. It had its own centralized facility for the production of frozen meals which were delivered to the hospital and regenerated at ward level, with domestic staff serving meals. The cleaners were all female, the porters predominantly male and the catering assistants were mixed male and female.

Concerns about cleanliness and hygiene in hospital settings had become a subject of media and political concern following an unfavourable report from the Patients' Association in 2000 (Pallot, no date). This concern was followed by a focus on hospital cleaning in the Labour Government's NHS Plan later that year (Department of Health, 2000). Subsequently all bids for NHS cleaning contracts had to include reference to staff training and to demonstrate that cleaners were competent in key tasks, although formal qualifications were not compulsory. Reflecting new emphasis, every member of staff at Clean Co had a training card, and all training was tightly monitored and recorded. The main purpose of training was to ensure contract compliance and was focused on task-specific activities – food hygiene and mandatory training (health and safety, fire, manual handling, machinery, clinical waste management, cleaning materials and gases). Most training was provided by supervisors and all cleaners were tested on their knowledge of procedures through an annual exam. According to the unit manager all staff had personal development plans, and the company would train anyone to supervisory level if they wanted, although career progression within the company would require a move to another site with the company. He felt the company had excellent management training programmes and would train staff in non-task-specific areas, for example in IT, paying overtime for study after shifts. Despite these opportunities and the presence of internal career paths, those domestics who had considered career opportunities sought development routes into nursing assistant roles and direct employment by the NHS. None of the cleaners interviewed considered it an option to move out of the health service to gain promotion within Clean Co. Many of the cleaners had worked at the hospital for many years and, despite being Clean Co employees, articulated a commitment to the health service and a perception of doing an important job, as found in the earlier case studies.

At national level, management had identified generic working as key to its training strategy in the health sector. The move towards generic working involves both multi-tasking and an extension of flexible working hours. The company was developing the concept of the 'integrated worker' who would work in cleaning, catering and portering. It makes the further intensification of work possible by removing 'down time', especially in catering and portering – during lulls of work in one activity a worker could be transferred to assist in another activity. This strategy is only viable where a company has a contract for the whole range of hotel services and Clean Co's approach was a Rapid Response Team. This small group of staff were drawn from across the service areas, trained in the key activities for them all and paid at a higher grade. It was regarded by management as a new route for development and promotion, while bringing the ability to respond flexibly to the unexpected demands and events in any of the service areas. The main work of the Rapid Response Team turned out to be responding to unforeseen cleaning needs – accidents resulting in spillages, cleaning rooms after meetings and so on. Where cleaning becomes highly routinized and time managed, it leaves no space in which to respond to the inevitable unexpected events. Given that cleaning at this hospital was a wholly female activity, the one man in the team found it uncomfortable having to perform what was firmly established here as 'women's work'. This demonstrates how gender segregation may limit one form of reorganization and intensification.

The Clean Co contract was awarded in 1997 for five years but, when it came up for renewal in 2002, it was returned in-house.

East Coast Primary Care Trust

After the election of the Labour Government in 1997, there was a new focus on lifelong learning and the importance of training and development for all workers. Initiatives such as the proposals in 'Working Together – Learning Together' (Department of Health 2001) specifically identify a need for training and development for *all* staff within the NHS. East Coast Primary Care Trust is located in England serving a large geographical area with four local hospitals and a large number of small clinics and surgeries. Here senior management were committed to providing learning and development opportunities for all staff, including ancillary staff such as the domestic service workers. However, they felt that the government message was ambiguous:

> The Government is sending mixed messages. The NHS Plan indicates learning for all but more money is needed for training for ancillary staff. In the past ancillary staff have been neglected. But the Government also sets financial targets with patient care the bottom line – the ancillary side is where the cuts can be made – either the amount of time to do the job or their training... (Facilities Manager)

At East Coast a Training Manager had been appointed to lead development activities which went beyond the usual National Vocational Qualification (NVQ) and mandatory training for health and safety. Management were also working closely with the main trade union, UNISON. A number of union learning representatives had been elected, and they worked with management to identify and initiate a range of developmental learning opportunities for ancillary staff. Many cleaners were attending courses such as UNISON's Return to Learn or one of the 'Brush up Your Skills'[4] courses (for example on computing) as well as completing National Vocational Qualifications. As a result career pathways were being developed in which domestic service staff could progress to become healthcare assistants and a small number had gone on to qualify as nurses. While many cleaners did not want to take part in the new range of learning opportunities, an ethos had been created in this health service trust that opportunities were there and the chance of progression real.

One of the main benefits identified by both staff and managers of these programmes was the impact on staff confidence and their ability to work more autonomously. Staff spoke of their commitment to the Trust and of a realization of their potential to achieve more or progress in their career. Managers claimed that their training opportunities were an important aspect of their recruitment and retention strategy, with competition from local supermarkets for staff. While the job content had not changed significantly, the opportunity to develop was clearly an important factor in improving the quality of working life for the domestic service staff here.

Such an initiative had its challenges: any off-the-job training requires replacement staff as wards cannot be left dirty. Even where funds could be accessed to pay for replacements, a continual problem in the health service is having enough people available to do the work. In addition, staff who themselves have had a poor experience of formal education can be reticent about joining a course. It was the partnership with UNISON that was key to gaining staff acceptance and overcoming any initial suspicion about the courses available. Managers interviewed, who had staff on these courses, talked about the noticeable impact on the individual and on the way they worked. They clearly believed that staff who had been on these programmes delivered a better service. However, evidence tended to be anecdotal and did not convince all managers. Trainers expressed concern that clinical managers did not understand the value of such training for domestic staff, which was seen as a problem in the smaller clinics run by GPs:

> ... to train a domestic in communication skills requires a different culture. They [GPs] don't recognise the value of training people in non-specific skills – gives them confidence, motivates them. (Training Manager)

Wider developmental learning opportunities do not make work different or better, but may improve the experience of work for many and improve organizational environment.

The two case studies described here demonstrate two very different paths that can be taken in the management of hospital cleaning work. At St Mary's contracted out work was intensified and highly monitored, with the company's focus firmly fixed on maintaining the contract. In contrast at East Coast NHS Trust there was a desire to allow staff to achieve their potential, to become more confident and exercise greater autonomy in their jobs. The whole environment at East Coast was more positive and staff clearly happier in their work – investment in staff development had a significant impact on the way in which the women experienced the work. Events in both cases were driven initially by national government policy, although the way in which that policy is implemented at local level leaves significant discretion for local management.

The potential for 'better jobs'

Fear of hospital infections came to the fore of the political agenda again in the late 2000s with a number of high profile cases. This concern led to renewed attention on hospital cleaning. However, there is considerable debate about the causes of hospital-acquired infections: a consultant microbiologist has claimed that the first two key issues are insufficient hand washing and over-prescribing of antibiotics, followed in third place by ordinary cleaning (BBC News, 2011a). While not disputing such evidence, UNISON has claimed that cleaning plays a key role in the control of infections.

> Increases in MRSA rates in the UK hospitals coincided with the halving of the number of NHS cleaners and the impact of the introduction of competitive tendering and the contracting out of many hospital cleaning services to private sector providers. (Davies, 2009)

This position draws attention to both the number of cleaners employed and the way in which they are managed. The Labour Government had already championed the benefits of a return of control to nursing staff, using the rhetoric of a past golden age when the matron was in charge (Bently, 2007). The policy change led to the introduction of the ward housekeeper role in England. Such an approach may provide an opportunity for domestic staff to become part of the ward team, expanding the role and enhancing job quality. In contrast, cleaners themselves had frequently expressed concern about the way nursing staff treated them. In East Coast NHS Trust there was concern about proposals to give ward nurses greater control over the domestic service staff, removing them from the functional facilities department,

> [The] idea is to put cleaning under the nurses ... the difficulty is cover and training. We do all the things you need to have a well trained and efficient workforce. Could nurses do that? Nurses don't want management but do want control ... (Facilities Manager)

The outcome of increased nurse control could equally be a narrowing of the cleaning role alongside isolation from the functional department.

Gordon Brown, who took over as Labour Prime Minister in 2007, led an initiative for 'deep cleaning', a more comprehensive clean involving washing walls, beds, equipment and radiators (BBC News, 2011b). This process may involve particular chemicals or specialist equipment such as steam cleaners or ultrasound. This approach could bring the opportunity for job expansion, but past experience has been to retain basic cleaning as low skill routinized female activity, while giving the more technical or specialist tasks to other higher paid staff – often men.

As part of their response, in 2008, the Scottish Government announced that they were creating 600 new cleaning jobs in NHS Scotland and were bringing to an end the contracting out of cleaning services. It is difficult to identify in the workforce data whether these new jobs were actually created, but such an approach does lead to a greater possibility of improving jobs.

Conclusion

Researching one occupational group over such a long period of time provides insights into work organization and job quality and the factors that impact it over time. This research demonstrates that while cleaning work exemplifies 'bad work', there are significant differences between the public and private sectors. The latter is tied into a vicious circle of low investment, low skill, low pay and poor morale where employers chase ever-diminishing profit margins. Despite the efforts of the Sector Skills Council, it is difficult to see that situation changing without some form of regulation. Cleaning work in the public sector demonstrates superior extrinsic or objective features of work quality (pay levels, holiday and sickness entitlements and job security). Being a cleaner in the health sector also brings the potential for intrinsic rewards at a number of levels: working for the health service is seen by many workers as contributing to societal good through working in a socially useful institution; the activity of cleaning in a hospital setting is regarded as directly contributing to the safe delivery of healthcare, and dealing with patients and visitors provides an opportunity to help individuals directly. Not all cleaners have expressed such views, but these have been surprisingly constant messages from hospital cleaners over the years, many of whom are clearly proud of what they do. Hospital cleaning demonstrates that ostensibly bad jobs can have good aspects and that the context of work is central to its quality.

The tasks of hospital cleaning have changed relatively little over 30 years, but the organization of work has and the single major influence on this has been the introduction at a macro-level of competitive tendering and contracting out from 1983. Privatization and more recently PFI blur the divide between public and private sectors and have resulted in a worsening of the objective elements of work quality for those who find themselves employees of a private contractor *and* those who retain employment in the health service. The process of competitive tendering led to reduced working hours, less flexibility from an employee's perspective, greater work intensification, greater insecurity and poorer pay and benefits. Work intensification has in turn reduced the opportunity to interact with patients and visitors, limiting one of the opportunities to gain intrinsic value from the work. Nevertheless, even cleaners working for private contractors continued to express their commitment to the health service as an institution and the sense of value they attributed to their work.

In contrast national policies which support training and development for all staff have provided a potential route to enhance aspects of intrinsic job quality for cleaners. Developmental programmes such as Return to Learn contribute to greater confidence and self-worth as well as a willingness to work more autonomously. As Metcalf and Dhudwar (2010) suggest, managers do have choices about how far they are willing to implement such policies and how willing they are to collaborate with trade unions to achieve successful outcomes. At a micro level Facilities Managers have choices about the organization of work – whether they go down the route of job expansion and development for all cleaners, or maintain the majority of jobs as highly routinized with little discretion alongside a small number of 'expert' or generic staff.

There are relatively few levers to achieve improvements to the quality of hospital cleaning jobs, although the public concern over hospital-acquired infections has re-focused attention on the significance of cleaning, which can no longer be regarded as peripheral to core activities. This concern has already had an impact in Scotland on policy around privatization and funding for additional jobs. At every level trade unions are likely to have a key role in defending the objective elements such as pay, in supporting staff development initiatives, but they may also need to address issues at the micro level in terms of work organization.

Notes

1 The Network of five research projects on work based learning was coordinated by Helen Rainbird and this research was conducted as part of Project One 'The Regulatory Framework of the Employment Relationship'. The research team for this project included Helen Rainbird, Anne Munro and Jim Sutherland.

2 UNISON was formed in 1993 from three public sector unions – NUPE, the National Union of Public Sector workers; NALGO, the National And Local Government Officers; and COHSE, the Confederation of Health Service Employees.

3 The Transfer of Undertakings (Protection of Employment) Regulations 2006 implements the European Council Directive 2001/23/EC on the approximation of the laws of the Member States relating to the safeguarding of employees' rights in the event of transfers of undertakings or businesses.
4 Return to Learn (R2L) and Brush up Your Skills courses are programmes developed through UNISON'S Open College, designed for people coming back into education who want to improve their educational skills, often delivered in partnership with employers. They aim to develop life skills, writing and communication skills and build personal confidence.

REFERENCES

Asset Skills (2009) *A State of the Sector Report – The Cleaning Sector*, Asset Skills. Asset Skills web site www.assetskills.org (accessed 4.2.2010).

BBC News (2011a) *The Importance of Keeping Clean*, http://news.bbc.co.uk/1/hi/programmes/panorama/4673505.stm (accessed 10.11.2011).

BBC News (2011b) *Q and A: Deep Cleaning, http://news.bbc.co.uk/1/hi/health/7186799.stm* (accessed 2.5.2011).

British Cleaning Council web site, www.britishcleaningcouncil.org (accessed 10.11.2003).

Bently, D. (2007) 'Matrons and Nurses to Get More Powers', *Independent*, Monday, 17 September, http://www.independent.co.uk/life-style/health-and-families/health-news/matrons-and-nurses-to-get-more-powers-402590.html (accessed 6.8.2011).

Davies, S. (2009) *Making the Connections – Contract Cleaning and Infection Control*, London, UNISON.

Department of Health (2000) *The NHS Plan: a Plan for Investment, a Plan for Reform*, July, London, Department of Health.

Department of Health (2001) *Working Together – Learning Together*, London, Department of Health.

Health and Personal Social Statistics (1991 and 1993).

Labour Research Department (2003) *Law at Work 2003*, Labour Research Department Booklets: London, May.

Labour Research Department (2011) *Law at Work 2011*, Labour Research Department Booklets: London, June.

Manson, T. (1977) 'Management, the Professions and the Unions: a Social Analysis of Change in the NHS', in *Health and the Division of Labour* eds M. Stacey, M. Reid, C. Heath and R. Dingwell, London: Croom Helm.

Metcalf, H. and Dhudwar, A. (2010) *Employers' Role in the Low-Pay/No-Pay Cycle*, Joseph Rowntree Foundation.

Munro, A. (1999) *Women, Work and Trade Unions*, Mansell: London.

Munro, A. (2001) 'A Feminist Trade Union Agenda? The Continued Significance of Class, Gender and Race', *Gender, Work and Organisation*, 8:4, 454–471.

National Board for Prices and Incomes (1966) *The Pay and Conditions of Manual Workers in Local Authorities, the National Health Service, Gas and Water Supplies*, Report 29, HMSO Cmnd 3230.

▶

▶
Pallot, P. (no date) 'Cleaning Up the NHS', *Healthcare Solutions*, The Sodexho Healthcare Magazine, Issue 5.

Pye Tait (2003a) *The UK Cleaning Industry 2003 Labour Market Intelligence Update*, Pye Tait: Harrogate.

Pye Tait (2003b) *The UK Cleaning Industry 2003 Labour Market Intelligence Update – Executive Summary*, Pye Tait: Harrogate.

UNISON Bargaining Support (2003) *NHS Market Report*, UNISON: London, April.

Williams, A., Livy, B., Silverstone, R. and Adams, P. (1979) 'Factors Associated with Labour Turnover among Ancillary Staff in Two London Hospitals', *Journal of Occupational Psychology*, 52:1 (March), 1–16.

PART

III

Influences on Job Quality: The Role of Public Agency

CHAPTER

12

Unpacking the Logics of Labour Standards Enforcement: An Alternative Approach

Janice Fine and Jennifer Gordon

Introduction

For a developed nation with a functional legal system, longstanding and fairly comprehensive wage and hour laws at the federal and state levels, and stable inspectorates embedded in well-established civil service systems, the US has staggeringly low levels of compliance with wage and hour laws.* A recent study found that 26 per cent of low-wage workers in the nation's three largest cities suffered minimum wage violations in the week prior to its survey, and over 76 per cent of low-wage workers who laboured more than 40 hours in the prior week were not paid according to overtime laws (Bernhardt et al., 2009). In this chapter, we ask why US labour standards enforcement isn't working and what can be done to improve it. We begin by analysing the impediments to effective enforcement in low wage sectors today. We trace a set of 'logics' (Thornton and Ocasio, 2008) or theories as to how best to detect violators that have dominated state and federal-level wage and hour enforcement over the past century. We then move to our argument that the time has come for the revival of a different approach in low-wage industries, one proposed at the time of the New Deal but defeated before the final version of the Fair Labor Standards Act (FLSA) even began its journey through Congress. This alternative logic, somewhat akin to corporatist arrangements, called for workers' organizations as well as firms to partner with the government to detect violators, relying on the incentives of unions and high wage enterprises to patrol their industries and labour markets for unfair competition. We draw on this idea in laying out a vision for tripartism (Ayres and Braithwaite, 1992), a new enforcement regime that involves giving workers' organizations equal standing with government and employers to supplement complaint-driven and targeted inspections at both state and federal levels. In two cases, we find evidence of this approach in an emergent system that harkens back to the original idea of those with the greatest incentive and closest to the action working in partnership with government. After setting out those cases and analysing the lessons they offer, we conclude by reflecting on the prospects for a logic of worker organization involvement.

Why isn't enforcement working in the low-wage sector?

Decreasing funding with an expanding mandate

Although our interest is in wage enforcement at both state and federal levels, we focus on FLSA in this section , both because of its central importance and because many state wage laws are now patterned on the federal regime. When FLSA was enacted in 1938, it covered only about a third of American workers, predominantly in manufacturing. Among those excluded were agricultural, domestic, service and retail workers. In the decades following its passage, coverage gradually expanded, through incorporation of occupations and industries previously excluded from the Act and the inclusion of many small businesses by lowering the threshold volume of annual sales that determined whether a firm had to obey FLSA (Nordlund, 1997). It is not clear to us that the Department of Labor's (DOL) Wage and Hour Division (WHD) has ever had a theory about how to effectively patrol such vastly different industries.

Meanwhile, although funding for inspections initially increased following the extensions of coverage, it was not sustained. The past 30 years have seen a 55 per cent increase in the estimated number of workers and a 112 per cent increase in the number of establishments covered under FLSA (Bernhardt and McGrath, 2005). Although the number of WHD inspectors doubled from about 650 in 1960 to a high water mark of 1,343 in 1978 (Nordlund, 1997), by 1982 the inspectorate was down to 929. In 2008, WHD had only 709 investigative staff). Even when WHD reached its highest staffing level, the economy was expanding much more rapidly, increasing the number of firms covered under the law. As a result, the share of firms that WHD inspected fell from nine per cent in 1947 to two per cent by the late 1970s, and continued to decline afterwards (Wial, 1999). In the largest increase in many years, the Obama administration's 2012 congressional budget request proposes to field an inspectorate of 1,032 staff to monitor approximately 7,300,000 firms.

Growth in the hardest to police sectors and among the hardest to protect workers

As the preponderance of low wage jobs have shifted from manufacturing to service, long hours, low wages, high rates of injury and sweeping violations of workplace laws have followed workers there. Part of the problem lies with an increase in the number of small firms. Using Current Population Survey data on actual hours worked and wages received, Weil and Pyles generate a list of the 33 industries at highest risk of wage and overtime violations (Weil and Pyles, 2005). We refined their findings by analysing the composition of establishments in those industries. Our analysis demonstrates that most of the industries Weil and Pyles identify as being at greatest risk of FLSA violations are overwhelmingly composed of establishments of fewer than 20 employees.

The predominance of smaller firms and establishments in low wage industries is worth noting here not only because it seems to correlate with higher wage and hour violation rates, but because it introduces complications for the design of enforcement strategies. If the same number of workers are employed across a larger number of smaller enterprises, more personnel are required to locate the businesses, to travel to them and to inspect their records. Small businesses are also less likely than their large counterparts to have the sophisticated human resources departments and centralized record-keeping that facilitate proactive learning about the law, cooperation during inspections and participation in ongoing regulatory communities. On the very low-wage end of the ladder, small firms are also more likely to be mobile, short-lived and unregistered.

The growth of subcontracting as a business model introduces additional challenges for enforcement. The rise of the network supply chain model has resulted in the vertical disaggregation of firms across many sectors and in labour-intensive industries in particular. Even when small firms are embedded in subcontracting networks in which one large firm or a few firms set the terms of exchange, they are often not the employers of record for purposes of enforcement. Studies by a range of states as well as the federal DOL have found that up to 30 per cent of firms misclassify employees as independent contractors in order to avoid liability under FLSA as well as other workplace laws (US GAO, 2009). For some employers, subcontracting and misclassification are tactics in a larger strategy to evade detection of non-compliance.

A final factor making enforcement difficult in the low-wage sector is the high percentage of immigrants in the most at-risk industries. In 2009, foreign-born workers accounted for 15.7 per cent of the civilian labour force and 20 per cent of the low wage workforce. Two of every five low-wage immigrant workers are undocumented (US DOL, 2009) Immigrants constitute a significant share of many of the same industries. Weil and Pyles identify as having the highest violation rates. Immigrants may be unaware of their rights, afraid of deportation and hesitant to cooperate with government officials. The US government under George W. Bush and Barack Obama has implemented aggressive immigration enforcement policies that have rendered immigrants increasingly fearful of coming forward to report wage violations. The gap between immigrant communities and regulators is a serious impediment to effective enforcement of wage and hour laws.

The logics of enforcement

The state of low-wage work also suffers from a failure to match the logics of enforcement deployed by government agencies to the realities of low-wage work today. We identify four logics of detection that have dominated wage enforcement over the past century.

The logic of complaint-driven investigation

The logic that emerged in the early years of FLSA was a complaint-driven approach to detection, premised on the assumption that workers would come forward and inspections would be triggered by their complaints. Although during the 1940s and 1950s, WHD strongly embraced a proactive investigation strategy alongside the complaint-based approach, by 1960 the agency had begun an enduring reorientation toward complaints that would become the predominant approach.

Addressing worker complaints is clearly an important part of the work of a workplace enforcement agency. The question is whether this approach makes sense as the *predominant* aspect of the government's approach. An affirmative answer would be appropriate if the industries logging the largest numbers of complaints were also those with the worst underlying conditions. However, research by Weil and Pyles found little overlap between industries with the highest FLSA complaint rates and those with the highest wage and overtime non-compliance rates, suggesting that workers in industries with the worst conditions are much less likely to complain (Weil and Pyles, 2005).

The logic of proactive investigations

In the case of low wage industries, there is a strong case for federal and state departments of labour to use data on underlying levels of non-compliance to target specific industries in particular geographic areas. Since the 1940s, WHD has intermittently complemented its reliance on complaints with a focus on proactive inspections, the second 'logic' of enforcement. While this second logic has not taken root at the DOL as the predominant institutional model since the first decades of FLSA, the Obama administration is showing a strong renewed interest.

The logic of comprehensive coverage

For a time, at least in high wage industrial states, the number of federal inspectors was augmented by state labour departments that had their own sizeable inspectorates, and state-based federal wage and hour inspectors only really supplemented these larger state forces. Our interviews with state wage and hour officials reveal that some states had a large inspectorate that divided up the turf geographically and systematically patrolled it, on the theory that firms would comply in part because they would anticipate inspection. This is what we think of as the third logic. Resource constraints have taken this approach off the table. Today state wage and hour divisions are much smaller and take an overwhelmingly complaint-based approach (Fine 2009; Lurie 2010; Meyer and Greenleaf, 2011).

The logic of self-regulation

Over the past quarter century, the workplace has been a site for experimentation with various forms of 'new regulatory' practice. This is reflected in a trend toward self-regulation by firms in the arenas of health and safety standards, wage enforcement and discrimination, among others. We refer to the idea that employers should monitor themselves as the fourth logic of enforcement.

Scholars of self-regulation broadly recognize its limitations in a context of small employers and low-wage workers. We share these concerns about the turn towards self-regulation in the low-wage setting, where it seems likely that without a consistently enforced public regime of penalties for non-compliance, self-regulation would contribute to the further degeneration of standards in low-wage sectors (Ayres and Braithwaite, 1992; Estlund, 2010; Weil, 2001; Lobel, 2005).

To conclude, then, while the first and second logics of complaint-driven inspections and strategic targeting remain essential to any government enforcement strategy, they have proven insufficient to address the problem of non-compliance in low-wage sectors. The third logic of comprehensive coverage is no longer a realistic possibility, and the fourth logic of self-regulation has limited use in the context of the lowest-wage work.

One final note before moving on: in a series of articles, Michael Piore and Andrew Schrank highlight an emerging Latin American model of labour market regulation that features a high degree of discretion given to inspectors, permitting them in each case 'to judge the burden the regulations impose on the enterprise, and where this is excessive, or threatens the enterprise's very solvency, to balance particular regulations against each other and against the broader role of the enterprise in providing employment and goods and services' (Piore and Schrank, 2006: 12) and a requirement that violations be addressed through a plan to achieve compliance, rather than (or, in severe cases, in addition to) penalties (Piore and Schrank, 2006, 2007). Inspectors share information on best practices, suggesting efficient ways for the firm to comply with the law. Piore and Schrank note that these characteristics are typical of the French and Spanish systems, in which the Latin American approach has its roots. They characterize the original model as *unified* (in that all labour regulations are enforced by a single agency), *conciliatory* (in the sense that the goal is to bring the enterprise into compliance rather than to punish and deter deviations from the law) and *tutelary* (meaning that the inspector advises the business on achieving compliance over time) (Schrank and Piore, 2007: 10).

The consultative/tutelary model is gaining attention in the context of global supply chains as well. For example, Richard Locke et al. (2008) have recently argued that while traditional approaches to monitoring have largely failed to change working conditions in the global supply chain, close attention to interactions between global brands, inspectors and contractors reveals that a 'commitment' model in the relationship between the parties can have a real impact on working conditions. This model requires auditors to 'focus on remediation as opposed to coercion and engage in joint problem-solving, information-sharing, and mentoring' (p. 344), acting as consultants rather than police.

Although we applaud these efforts to think creatively about new methods of government enforcement, we have concerns about the translation of this model to the US low-wage context. To take Piore and Schrank's model, a number of their explicit and implicit assumptions about what makes the consultative approach work in Latin America, including about the motivations of employers and the frequency of inspections, do not appear to hold in low-wage sectors in the US. It seems unlikely that many employers in this country are unaware of the fact that they are required to pay minimum wages and overtime to their employees. The tens of thousands of straightforward violations of FLSA that occur annually, as restaurants pay immigrant dishwashers sub-minimum wages or residential construction companies hand out pay envelopes in cash containing straight time pay for overtime labour, appear often to be the result of a firm's deliberate attempts to compete more effectively by paying workers less, than of ignorance or mistake. Employers demonstrate intentionality in violating the law when they maintain two sets of payroll records or leave some workers off of payroll records and put others on, pay partly in cash and partly by cheque, require that workers use two different names (one for straight time and one for overtime hours), require that workers clock out after completing their straight time hours and work overtime hours off the clock, and engage in other practices to hide the number of employees they have, the number of hours worked or the amount of wages paid. Likewise, employer calculations about the efficiencies and cost of compliance seem quite likely to be accurate, in that a dollar saved from wages is a dollar into the coffers of the company.

Finally, it is only realistic to place so much weight on the role of labour inspectors in a society in which a substantial proportion of businesses are inspected with some frequency. In the US, as our earlier review of the statistics on labour inspections illustrates, the likelihood of inspection from the perspective of each low-wage employer is already staggeringly low.

Imagining a regulatory regime

Our proposal

How should we retool workplace enforcement? We believe that government must remain central to efforts to assure compliance with minimum workplace standards, despite serious resource constraints. Since there will never be enough government inspectors to cover all low-wage businesses, we propose the creation of a system that draws on the complementary strengths of government and civil society organizations.

We root our proposal in Ayres and Braithwaite's robust system of tripartism, in which, along with the government regulator and the firm, a 'public interest group' such as a union or some other community-based worker organization is given a formal role in the regulatory process, and in the theoretical ground seeded by Joshua Cohen and Joel Rogers, whose theory of Associative Democracy calls for government to draw on 'the distinctive capacity of associations to gather local information, monitor behaviour and promote cooperation among private actors' by assigning enforcement duties as well as other roles to third party groups (Cohen and Rogers, 1992: 426). Cohen and Rogers identify the situation where the government has adequately set standards but is unable to monitor compliance because the affected sites are too diverse, numerous and unstable – precisely the case in the low-wage sector – as a situation where the participation of third party associations is particularly urgent.

Our vision for the partnerships

What we offer here, first in the abstract and then in our case studies, is a closer examination of what it might mean for the government to collaborate with worker organizations in a sustained way to enforce wage and hour laws, in order to complement its existing partnerships with employers. We believe that much of what we propose could be implemented administratively, without any amendment of FLSA.

We start with the presumption that to have a meaningful impact on government enforcement, collaborations must be ongoing and robust, by which we mean partnerships must be *formalized* (the parties openly negotiate their expectations of and commitments to each other, including regarding the distribution of resources; this is also important to render the partnerships less vulnerable to changes in agency leadership or political regime), *sustained* (relationships between the staff of the agency and the organizations have time to build, increasing the resiliency of the bond in the face of conflict; lessons learned from each joint effort can enrich the next stages of the collaboration) and *vigorous* (the role of the third party partners is not symbolic, marginal, or merely consultative, but fully integrated into the work of the agency). The partnerships must also be adequately resourced – states must allocate enough staff to be able to mount a credible effort and must provide a threshold level of financial support to partner organizations that need it to fully participate.

With regard to *outreach*, workers' organizations might target local firms and groups of workers for informational visits and trainings. With regard to the *detection of violations*, worker centres are particularly qualified due to the trust that they command in immigrant communities, their links to immigrant networks, their linguistic and cultural competency and the credible assurances they can provide that a complaint to DOL funnelled through the centre will not reach the ears of immigration authorities. With regard to the *filing and investigation of complaints*, one strategy would be to designate civil society groups as sites where workers could register complaints with the DOL. In the fullest version of the model, workers' organizations could file claims with the government on behalf of workers who remained anonymous, triggering an investigation without putting specific workers at risk. With regard to *designing proactive strategies for enforcement that reflect the characteristics of specific industries*, workers' centres could use the knowledge of their members to help identify the industry-specific leverage points necessary to move forward with strategies to increase compliance that are retrofitted to the structure of particular industries. With regard to *ongoing deterrence*, ultimately we believe that monetary penalties must be drastically increased and applied frequently, license revocation must be a meaningful possibility and statutes of limitations must be either abolished or dramatically extended.

These ideas also hearken back to a logic of enforcement proposed during the debate about institutional design and modes of enforcement at the time of FLSA's drafting (O'Brien, 2001; Farhang and Katznelson, 2005). The original architects of FLSA argued that the law should be enacted not 'to provide workers with affirmative rights, but because the lack of such regulation violated trade practices, giving sweatshop employers an unfair competitive advantage'. To enforce the law, they proposed the establishment of a quasi-judicial agency, modelled after the Fair Trade Commission, which would work with 'enlightened employers and unions' who would 'band together and help police sweatshop employers'. Continuing concern on the part of Roosevelt administration officials about how the Supreme Court would interpret the Commerce Clause (Mettler, 1994), pressure from Southern Democrats and farm state Republicans to restrict coverage and opposition from American Federation of Labour (AFL) and Congress of Industrial Organizations (CIO) national leaders who feared DOL's wage-fixing powers would weaken private collective bargaining agreements, all contributed to the promulgation of a much weaker bill. Lawmakers removed the unfair trade provisions, and provided no regulatory role for unions. They established a weak quasi-legislative body under the Department of Labor appointed by the President, made WHD dependent upon funds provided from the general budget of the DOL and appointed inspectors through the civil service rules, giving the WHD administrator little control over them. WHD had no authority to issue cease and desist orders against employers and fines were set extremely low. While the enforcement provision of FLSA as passed by Congress allowed for opt-in class action suits and a possible role for unions as worker representatives, Congress amended this section in 1947, effectively barring unions from bringing class actions under FLSA (Linder, 1991).

How likely is it that what we propose here could be executed in reality and at a meaningful scale? As a first step in answering this question, we identified some cases of formalized partnerships between workers' organizations and government agencies that seek to raise levels of compliance with prevailing wage or minimum wage laws.

Two case studies

Los Angeles Unified School District (LAUSD) and Board of Public Works (LABPW) deputization programmes

Since 1996, the LAUSD has administered a program that trains *and deputizes* business representatives of building trades unions to enforce the prevailing wage on District projects, which are funded by nearly $30 b in school construction bonds. The programme grew out of an agreement with the building trades unions. In 2004, a similar program was established by the LABPW, which in that fiscal year had oversight over 308 projects with a value close to $339m.

The in-house Labour Compliance Program of the LAUSD trains union business agents as Work Preservation Volunteers ('WPVs'), provides them identification badges and business cards, and authorizes them to enter school sites to 'conduct labour compliance site visits, interview workers on District property...and assist with audits, hearings, and review conferences'. The LABPW's deputized inspectors, called Compliance Group Representatives ('CGRs'), are similarly trained and badged (indeed there is significant overlap between the groups). WPVs and CGRs interview employees about hours worked, hourly wage, job classification, official duties and problems receiving pay, filling out wage complaint forms with workers on the spot where violations are found. The availability of CGRs has been especially valuable for weekend coverage. They do not determine violations or assess penalties, but provide the raw data that city inspectors use to put together cases. They must attend trainings and renew their badges each year.

To forestall objections that business representatives would take advantage of their position to advance a union organizing agenda, they are required to sign an agreement prohibiting using the program to promote or gather intelligence for the union, disparage non-union contractors or review project data not associated with a pending complaint. Union representatives have overwhelmingly complied with these prohibitions. Government administrators believe that business agents view the ability to combat unfair competition as a strong enough incentive (and the risk of having their badge withdrawn a strong enough disincentive) to avoid abuse. Since initiation of the LAUSD program, the non-union proportion of repeat contractors working with the LAUSD continues to be one-third.

CGRs and WPVs have been extremely proactive, effectively operating as LAUSD and LABPW's directed enforcement team. The programs have significantly extended the capacity of the city inspectorate, traditionally focused on quality of workmanship rather than labour compliance. In 2009, the 85 CGRs expanded the LABPW inspectorate of 244 by more than 30 per cent. Over four years the Office of Contract Compliance has had 742 requests from CGRs to visit 168 worksites, granting 559 of them. These visits resulted in 1,155 interviews, which turned up 161 cases of possible underpayment-of-wage violations.

Inspectors' attitudes towards the CGRs have shifted dramatically, according to Chris Jenson, a top official who has been at the Bureau of Contract Administration from the beginning of the programme. 'When the program began, one of the inspectors said to me there is no way in hell I will ever let one of these guys come onto one of my jobsites...now I get calls from the inspectors asking can you send one of those guys out? Can you send someone who speaks Spanish or Korean?' In one wage underpayment claim, for example, CGRs were able to expand the case from two workers to twelve: 'My case went from fair to phenomenal,' said Jenson.

The LAUSD and LABPW programs in many ways represent the strongest version of what we call for. They are ongoing rather than campaign-driven, with the feel of deputies walking an industrial beat. That the programme is enshrined in public law, rather than operating as a project of a particular administration, augurs well for its permanence. In addition, these programmes are retro-fitted to the specific dynamics of the industry: they benefit from business representatives' knowledge of sector-specific dynamics, are contoured to the set of rules and regulations that apply to public construction and have access to vast quantities of information due to the requirement that contractors register with the City and submit copies of their payroll weekly, as well as through the public bidding process, which makes detailed data about labour and materials costs available for each bid. What is most exciting about the L.A. Joint Labour Compliance Monitoring programmes is the formal power wielded by the labour volunteers as a result of deputization.

Our principal concern is that it is difficult to tell whether the programs have reduced the number of prevailing wage violations in Los Angeles. There is no clear pattern in the annual data before and since the creation of the labour compliance programs. On the other hand, while LABPW officials were more equivocal, LAUSD government administrators were absolutely certain that compliance had increased significantly as a result of the program. An additional concern relates to the fact that, historically, building trades unions have excluded African-Americans and other people of colour from their ranks. Although the trades in LA have begun to address this problem, tensions persist. In many cities this is still a major issue that could impede the legitimacy and effectiveness of deputies.

Partnership between the California Labor Commission's Janitorial Enforcement Team and the Maintenance Cooperation Trust Fund

In 2006, California's Division of Labor Standards Enforcement (DLSE) established the Janitorial Enforcement Team (JET). The argument for JET was that policing the janitorial sector required inspectors with specific knowledge of industry structures and strategies. JET has a close working relationship with the Maintenance Cooperation Trust Fund (MCTF), a janitorial watchdog organization established in 1999 by Local 1877 of the Service Employees International Union and its signatory contractors. MCTF is employer funded.

The 40 union employers who participate in MCTF have a self interest in policing the industry. Employers, who also include non-union contractors, are strongly engaged in the programme.

JET alone represents an important innovation, but it would not have succeeded without the MCTF, whose 12 inspectors – many of them long-time janitors – more than quadruple JET's investigative capacity. MCTF provides state inspectors with specialized knowledge of industry structures and subcontracting arrangements.

MCTF plays a critical role in helping to assemble the documentation necessary for the state to bring cases. Understanding that few workers will come either to them or to government, MCTF inspectors routinely go out to worksites at night, during janitors' peak working hours. They identify the full scope of the subcontractor's operation, and build cases through systematic 'reconstruction' when workers lack pay stubs, identifying and interviewing each worker, determining which contractor employed them, and establishing the dates and hours worked. They use the state's formula to create a 'wage audit', their estimate of what the worker is owed.

While JET's inspectors must still carry out independent investigations, MCTF provides them with much of the raw material. JET investigators now accept cases from MCTF as opposed to requiring that workers approach DLSE directly. This is a significant departure from the past, when the overwhelming message was that investigators were not supposed to accept information from organizations or work cooperatively with them.

Since the partnership began, there have been an unprecedented number of administrative, civil and criminal actions brought against unscrupulous employers, resulting in more than $38m in back pay for janitorial workers. In 2007, the State Labor Commissioner and the Attorney General filed charges for $5m in non-payment of wages against two janitorial contractors for several restaurant chains. In 2008, the Labor Commissioner filed suit against a major building service company for close to $2m, and in 2009, the Labor Commissioner sued Corporate Building Services and its subcontractors for approximately $7.4m. As an indication of the impact JET has had, the lead investigator points to large companies that provide janitorial services to the hotel industry, which have abandoned contractors that JET has found in violation of the law, and now 'look for companies that are in compliance'. Lilia Garcia, MCTF Executive Director, also points to the partnership's work in the supermarket sector, which cost stores $22m and ultimately resulted in 3,000 janitorial jobs being brought back into the formal sector, as supermarkets, too, began to closely scrutinize contracts.

This partnership provides a compelling picture of how ongoing collaboration between a state agency and knowledgeable third-party organization can work on the ground, *without deputization* but with intensive collaboration and mutual trust. Just as the LAUSD and LABPW examples violated an old taboo against deputization, this partnership challenges ingrained agency opposition to close cooperation, including accepting documentation developed by third parties.

Conclusion

Just as there is nothing inevitable about bad jobs, there is nothing inevitable about faulty regulation. In this chapter, we have tried to understand the different systems of labour standards inspection that have emerged over the past 70-plus years and to identify promising contemporary strategies for improved compliance. Our case studies ratify the logic of direct participation in enforcement by organizations with the greatest incentive to police their labour markets. We find that worker centres and unions have access to information about sectors that are otherwise hard for the government to penetrate, knowledge about industry structures and the capacity to reach workers and document complicated cases. Our examples illustrate they have the incentives to want to be helpful, and that when entrusted with authority, organizations wield it responsibly.

Ultimately, whether these programs are enacted and whether they are successful will depend to a large extent on politics. Political power is how the Los Angeles Building and Construction Trades Council was able to create the LAUSD and Public Works programmes and how JET came to be established. In asserting that politics is the bottom line, however, we do not mean to imply that the challenges stop at the agency door. A new mayor or governor must bring about change within the bureaucracy. We know that organizational cultures can be major barriers to innovation, and that road-blocks to implementation arise based upon failures of communication and from competing sets of interests and power differentials within agencies. If attention is not paid to radically rethinking protocols and shifting incentives on the inside, change at the top will never be enough.

We understand that what we propose may be viewed by some as too large a pill to swallow. We stand strong for tripartism as a part of the package of approaches available to government agencies, but we do not see wholesale deputization as required in every case. Partial versions of our proposal could have a significant impact. The bottom-line is that absent creative strategies nested within clear logics of detection and deterrence at both state and federal levels, rates of compliance with minimum wage and overtime are likely to remain where they are.

Note

*The authors would like to thank Deborah Axt, Annette Bernhardt, Brian Burgoon, Sue Cobble, Jeff Eichler, Cynthia Estlund, Andrew Friedman, Lilia Garcia, Terri Gerstein, Rae Glass, Karin Johnsrud, Jack Metzgar, Karen Orren, Mike McCarthy, Michael Piore, Carmine Ruberto, Gay Seidman, Susan Silbey, Thomas Tighe, Chris Tilly, David Weil, Fordham research assistants Sarah Borsody, Jessica Jenkins, Carolyn Kim, and Nicholas Rosado, and Rutgers research assistants Martha Guarnieri and Salma Chand. A fuller development of the ideas and cases in this chapter first appeared in *Politics & Society* 38: 4, 2010.

REFERENCES

Ayres, I. and J. Braithwaite (1992) *Responsive Regulation: Transcending the Deregulation Debate* (New York: Oxford University Press).

Bernhardt, A., R. Milkman and N. Theodore (2009) *Broken Laws, Unprotected Workers: Violations of Employment and Labor Laws in America's Cities* (Chicago, New York, and Los Angeles: Center for Urban Economic Development, National Employment Law Project, and UCLA Institute for Research on Labor and Employment).

Bernhardt, A. and S. McGrath (2005) 'Trends in Wage and Hour Enforcement by the US Department of Labor, 1975–2004' (New York, NY: Brennan Center for Justice Economic policy Brief No. 3, September)

Cohen, J. and J. Rogers (1992) 'Secondary Associations and Democratic Governance', *Politics & Society*, 20(4): 393–472.

Estlund, C. (2010) *Regoverning the Workplace: From Self-Regulation to Co-Regulation* (New Haven, CT: Yale University Press).

Farhang, S. and I. Katznelson (2005) 'The Southern Imposition: Congress and Labor in the New Deal and Fair Deal,' *Studies in American Political Development*, 19(1): 1–30.

Fine, J. (2009) Unpublished Survey of State Departments of Labor (New Brunswick, NJ: Rutgers University Department of Labor Studies and Employment Relations).

Linder, M. (1991) 'Class Struggle at the Door: The Origins of the Portal to Portal Act of 1947', *Buffalo Law Review*, 39: 167–172.

Lobel, O. (2005), 'Interlocking Regulatory and Industrial Relations: The Governance of Workplace Safety', *Administrative Law Review*, 57: 1104–1115.

Locke, R., M. Amengual and A. Mangla (2008) 'Virtue out of Necessity? Compliance, Commitment and the Improvement of Labor Conditions in Global Supply Chains', *Politics & Society*, 37(3): 319–351.

Lurie, I. (2010) 'Enforcement of State Minimum Wage and Overtime Laws: Resources, Procedures, and Outcomes', Nelson A. Rockefeller Institute of Government State University of New York.

Mettler, S. B. (1994) 'Federalism, Gender, & the Fair Labor Standards Act of 1938', *Polity*, 26(4): 643–645.

▶

▶
Meyer, J. and R. Greenleaf (2011) 'Enforcement of State Wage and Hour Laws: A Survey of State Regulators', by the Columbia Attorneys General Project.

Nordlund, W. J. (1997) *The Quest for a Living Wage: The History of the Federal Minimum Wage Program* (Westport, CT: Greenwood Press).

O'Brien, R. (2001) 'A Sweat Shop of the Whole Nation: The Fair Labor Standard [sic] Act and the Failure of Regulatory Unionism', *Studies in American Political Development*, 15(1): 33–52.

Piore, M. and A. Schrank (2006) 'Trading Up: An Embryonic Model for Easing the Human Costs of Free Market', *Boston Review*, 31(5): 11–14.

Schrank, A. and M. Piore (2007) *Norms, Regulations, and Labour Standards in Central America*, Mexico City: Economic Conference on Latin America and the Caribbean.

Thornton, Patricia H. and William Ocasio (2008), 'Institutional Logics', pp. 99–129 in R. Greenwood, C. Oliver, R. Suddaby and K. Sahlin-Andersson, eds, ch. 3 in *The Sage Handbook of Organizational Institutionalism* (London: Sage).

US Department of Labor, Bureau of Labor Statistics (2009) 'Labor Force Characteristics of Foreign Born Workers – Summary', news release, 26 March (Washington, DC), http://www.bls.gov/news.release/frbrn.nr0.htm

US Government Accountability Office (US GAO) (2009) *Employee Misclassification: Improved Coordination, Outreach and Targeting Could Better Ensure Detection and Prevention*, Report to Congressional Requesters (Washington, DC, August).

Weil, D. (2001) 'Assessing OSHA Performance: New Evidence from the Construction Industry', *Journal of Policy Analysis & Management*, 20(4): 651–674.

Weil, D. and A. Pyles (2005) 'Why Complain? Complaints, Compliance, and the Problem of Enforcement in the US Workplace', *Comparative Labor Law and Policy Journal*, 27(1): 59–92.

Wial, H. (1999) 'Minimum-Wage Enforcement and the Low-Wage Labor Market', Institute for Work and Employment Research Working Paper #11, Massachusetts Institute of Technology, Cambridge, MA.

CHAPTER

13

Under the Radar: Tracking the Violation of Labour Standards in Low-Wage Industries in the US

Nik Theodore, Annette Bernhardt and James DeFilippis with Ruth Milkman, Douglas Heckathorn, Mirabai Auer, Ana Luz Gonzalez, Victor Narro, Jason Perelshteyn, Diana Polson and Michael Spiller

Introduction

At the start of the twenty-first century, core employment and labour laws are failing to protect low-wage workers in the US.* These are laws that place a floor under wages, safeguard worker safety and maintain decent working conditions. They are also designed to level the playing field for businesses in competitive industries. Employers must pay workers at least the minimum wage, and time and a half for overtime hours. They must follow regulations to protect workers' health and safety, and carry workers' compensation insurance in case of job-related illness or injury. They may not discriminate against workers on the basis of age, race, religion, national origin, gender, sexual orientation or disability. And they must respect workers' right to organize and to bring complaints about working conditions.

There is increasing evidence, however, that employers routinely break these core laws in a wide range of low-wage industries, from residential construction to retail, restaurants, janitorial services and home health care (Bernhardt et al. 2008; Bobo 2008). The full extent of the problem has been difficult to measure, and reliable estimates of the proportion of workers experiencing workplace violations, or the proportion of employers committing them, have not been available.

This chapter summarizes research findings that begin to fill the gap. In 2008, research teams surveyed 4,387 workers in low-wage industries in the three largest US cities – New York City, Los Angeles and Chicago – using a rigorous survey methodology that allowed researchers to reach vulnerable workers who are often missed in standard surveys (Bernhardt et al. 2009). The survey was designed to answer the following questions: How common are workplace violations, such as the percentage of workers earning less than the minimum wage or working overtime without pay? Which industries and occupations have the highest concentration of violations? And who are the workers most affected?

This chapter summarizes the findings from this survey. The next section briefly reviews the methodology used to conduct the survey. It is followed by a presentation of key research findings. We then explore the economic context within which workplace violations occur, as well as the policy environment surrounding workplace enforcement efforts. We conclude by offering a set of recommendations to shore up labour standards in low-wage industries.

Measuring the prevalence of workplace violations in low-wage industries

To assess the extent of employer compliance with core employment and labour laws, research teams in Chicago, Los Angeles and New York City administered the 2008 Unregulated Work Survey – an in-depth survey of workers who are employed in low-wage industries. Researchers incorporated two key innovations into the survey design. First, we used an innovative sampling methodology – Respondent-Driven Sampling (RDS) – to identify and sample from the full range of workers in the low-wage labour market, including unauthorized immigrants and off-the-books workers. Respondent-Driven Sampling is a network-based method for sampling hard-to-reach populations and generating statistically valid population estimates. It uses a chain-referral approach that is similar to 'snowball' sampling but it incorporates mathematical models to correct for bias that is introduced by network-style recruitment (see Heckathorn 1997, 2007). Over the past decade, RDS has become a favoured approach for sampling 'hidden' populations, particularly in cases where the sampling frame is unknown. It is a method that is well suited for recruiting workers who may be employed off the books or who might otherwise be missed in standard labour market surveys. Second, researchers developed an extensive questionnaire that allowed them to rigorously assess whether employment and labour laws were being broken, without relying on workers' own knowledge of those laws. The survey instrument mirrored the various employment and labour laws that are in place in Chicago, Los Angeles and New York City, allowing violation rates to be calibrated according to the particular state and local laws that govern employment relations in each city.

The survey was administered to 4,387 frontline adult workers (those holding non-managerial or non-professional positions) whose primary job was in a low-wage industry in Chicago (Cook County), Los Angeles (Los Angeles County) and New York City (the five boroughs). Workers in low-wage industries comprise approximately 31 per cent of all frontline workers and 15 per cent of all workers in the three cities. Following the RDS methodology, recruiting began with a small number of workers who fit the study criteria; after these workers were interviewed they recruited other workers from within their social networks; those workers in turn completed the survey and then recruited others; and so on. As part of the RDS methodology, the resulting data were weighted to adjust for differences in respondents' social network size and recruitment patterns, and to ensure that the distribution of industries and occupations in our sample reflected the composition of each city's low-wage labour market. Research teams were in the field for approximately six months during the spring and summer of 2008, conducting in-person interviews at multiple sites, including community colleges, service providers, community-based organizations and churches. The surveys were conducted in 13 languages.[1] Finally, we should note that while the recession in the United States officially began in late 2007, it deepened significantly in autumn of 2008, after we had completed our fieldwork, and thus our findings should not be read as a function of the severity of the economic downturn.

Violations of core employment laws

Workplaces in the United States are governed by a core set of employment and labour laws that establish minimum standards for wages, heath and safety on the job, fair treatment at work and the right to organize. This section summarizes some of these laws and presents findings on the prevalence of workplace violations experienced by survey respondents.

Minimum wage violations

Minimum wage laws are the bedrock standard that places a floor under pay for frontline workers in the US labour market. Covered employees must be paid at or above the minimum wage set by federal or state law, whichever is higher. At the time of the survey, the states of California, Illinois and New York each had minimum wage rates above the federal standard. In 2008, the hourly minimum wage was $8.00 in California, $7.50 in Illinois and $7.15 in New York. Minimum wage rates apply to workers regardless of whether they are employed full- or part-time, or whether they are paid by the hour, by the job, by the piece or in some other manner. Minimum wage laws also cover unauthorized immigrant workers, as do all the other laws reported in this chapter.

Fully 26 per cent of the workers in our sample were paid less than the minimum wage in the previous workweek (see Table 13.1). Moreover, these minimum wage violations were not trivial in magnitude: 60 per cent of respondents who suffered a minimum wage violation were underpaid by more than $1 per hour, and the median amount of underpayment was $1.43 less than the legally required minimum wage. We also measured minimum wage violations for tipped workers, who in Illinois and New York have lower statutory minimum wages than do non-tipped workers. Of the tipped workers in our sample – restaurant workers, car wash workers, hotel workers and the like – 30 per cent were paid below the legally required tipped-worker minimum wage.

Table 13.1 Workplace violation rates

Violation	Percentage of workers with a violation, of those at risk
Minimum wage violations in week prior to survey	
Worker was paid below the minimum wage	25.9
*Overtime violations in week prior to survey**	
Worker had unpaid or underpaid overtime	76.3
*Off-the-clock violations in week prior to survey**	
Worker not paid for off-the-clock work	70.1
*Meal break violations in week prior to survey**	
Worker had any of the below meal break violations	69.5
Worker was denied meal break	21.8
Meal break was interrupted by employer or supervisor	15.6
Worker worked through meal break	16.7
Meal break was shorter than legally required	50.3
*Retaliation violations for most recent complaint or organizing effort**	
Worker experienced retaliation by employer for making complaint or organizing a union	42.8
*Workers' compensation violations for most recent on-the-job injury**	
Worker experienced an illegal action by employer	50.3

* Starred violations are only measured for workers at risk of a violation; for example, only those who worked more than 40 hours in the week are at risk of an overtime violation, and only tipped workers are at risk of a tipped minimum wage violation.

Source: Authors' analysis of 2008 Unregulated Work Survey.

Overtime violations

The Fair Labor Standards Act of 1938 (FLSA) stipulates that covered employees must be paid 'time and a half' for all hours worked over 40 during each week for a single employer. Over one quarter of survey respondents worked more than 40 hours for a single employer during the previous workweek and therefore were at risk for an overtime violation. More than three quarters (76%) of these workers were not paid the legally required overtime rate by their employer. Like minimum wage violations, overtime violations were far from trivial; employees with an overtime violation worked an average of 11 overtime hours in the previous week, and 12 per cent had worked more than 20 overtime hours. Most of these workers (73%) were paid just their regular pay for these hours, but a sizable minority (19%) was not paid at all for these hours.

Off-the-clock work

In addition to unpaid overtime, many frontline workers in the low-wage labour market perform 'off-the-clock' work that takes place before or after a regularly scheduled shift and for which no pay is provided. Off-the-clock work is technically a minimum wage violation, but we chose to analyse it separately because it involves employees not being paid at all for time worked. We asked workers whether they came in before their shift officially began or stayed after their official ending time and, if they did, whether they received payment for this time.

Nearly one-quarter of workers (22%) reported that they had worked before and/or after their regular shifts in the previous workweek, and were thus 'at risk' for an off-the-clock violation. Of these workers, 70 per cent did not receive any pay at all for the work they performed outside of their regular shift. Those who experienced this violation worked a median of one hour per week without pay, and thus the magnitude of this violation is less severe than those pertaining to minimum wage or overtime laws.

Meal break violations

California, Illinois and New York each have laws that require employers to provide workers an uninterrupted meal break during their shift (although the length of the required meal break, as well as the minimum shift length after which a break must be provided, varies from state to state). The law does not require the employer to pay for the meal break, but if the employee works during the break, he or she must be compensated. Based on each state's regulations, we determined whether workers received all of their required meal breaks and whether these breaks were of the required length.

The vast majority of respondents (86%) worked enough consecutive hours to be legally entitled to a meal break. However, more than two-thirds of these workers (69%) experienced a meal break violation in the previous workweek. Nearly one-quarter (22%) of respondents with this violation received no meal break at all at some point during the previous week. Half (50%) had a meal break that was shorter than the legally mandated length. Workers also reported being interrupted by their employer during the break (16%) and working during part of their meal break (17%).

Illegal retaliation

Workers who complain to their employer or to a government agency about their working conditions, as well as those who attempt to form a union, are protected by law from retaliation by their employer for these activities. We asked respondents whether they had made a complaint in the past year to their employer, to their supervisor or to a government agency, or whether they had attempted to organize a union.

Of the 20 per cent of workers in our sample who either complained about a workplace issue or attempted to form a union in the previous 12 months, 43 per cent experienced retaliation from their employer or supervisor as a direct result of their most recent complaint or organizing effort. Employers illegally retaliated against workers by, for example, cutting workers' hours and pay, threatening to call immigration authorities, firing workers and increasing workloads.

Another 20 per cent of workers in our sample reported that they chose not to make complaints, even when they encountered substandard conditions in the workplace, such as dangerous working conditions, discrimination or not being paid the minimum wage. Of these workers, over half (51%) said that they did not make a complaint because they were afraid of losing their job, another 10 per cent were afraid they would have their hours or wages cut, while 36 per cent thought it would not make any difference if they complained. Fear of retaliation and expectations of employer indifference, then, figure strongly in workers' decisions about whether to make a complaint.

Workers' compensation violations

Workers' compensation insurance provides at least partial wage replacement and coverage of medical costs for workers who are injured on the job or who become ill in the course of employment. However, our survey reveals that the workers' compensation system is ineffective in reaching workers employed in low-wage industries. Twelve per cent of survey respondents experienced an on-the-job injury requiring medical attention in the previous three years.

However, only 8 per cent of these injured workers had filed a workers' compensation claim for their most recent injury.

Our data suggest that this low rate of filing is due in part to the ways in which employers respond to on-the-job injuries. Forty-three per cent of seriously injured respondents reported that they were required to work despite their injury; an additional 30 per cent reported that their employer refused to help them with the injury; 13 per cent were fired shortly after the injury; and others were threatened with deportation or notification of immigration authorities, or were explicitly told by their employers not to file a workers' compensation claim. Not all of these employer responses are illegal. However, fully 50 per cent of those respondents who suffered an on-the-job injury experienced a violation of workers' compensation law for their most recent injury.

Wage theft in US cities

The survey documented widespread violations of core employment and labour laws in low-wage industries in Chicago, Los Angeles and New York City. More than two-thirds (68%) of workers in the sample experienced at least one pay-related violation in the previous workweek. The average worker lost $51, out of average weekly earnings of just $339. Assuming a full-time, full-year schedule, we estimate that these workers lost an average of $2,634 annually due to workplace violations, out of total earnings of $17,616. This amount translates into wage theft of 15 per cent of earnings. Furthermore, we estimate that in a given week, approximately 1,114,074 workers in the three cities combined experience at least one pay-based violation. Extrapolating from this figure, frontline workers in low-wage industries in Chicago, Los Angeles and New York City lose more than $56.4 million *per week* as a result of employment law violations. The largest portion of these lost wages are due to violations of minimum wage laws (58%), followed by overtime violations (22%), rest break violations (10%) and off-the-clock violations (8%).

The spread of workplace violations

So far, this chapter has documented pervasive violations of core employment and labour laws in the three largest US cities. These violations emerge from the spread of substandard employment conditions throughout many low-wage industries, and they contribute to the increasing problem of working poverty, as well as to rising levels of economic insecurity among low-wage workers (Standing 2002; Hacker et al. 2010). Women, immigrants and people of colour are disproportionately affected by substandard employment conditions (Bernhardt et al. 2009). Two distinct dynamics are at play: women, immigrants and people of colour are disproportionately found in jobs in the low-wage labour market, and within that labour market, they are more likely to experience workplace violations.

At the same time, our analysis of the demand- and supply-side correlates of workplace violations shows that demand-side factors are far stronger than supply-side variables in predicting violation rates. Using logistic regression models to test for the unique contribution of job/employer characteristics on the one hand, and workers' demographic characteristics on the other, we found that job/employer characteristics were four times stronger than demographic variables in predicting minimum wage violation rates; ten times stronger in predicting overtime violation rates; 1.8 times stronger in predicting off-the-clock violation rates; and 12.8 times stronger in predicting meal break violation rates (for more detail see Bernhardt et al. 2009).

These findings lend credence to the conclusion that the extensive violations documented in this chapter ultimately are the result of employer decisions about whether to comply with the law. In some sectors, widespread employer evasion and violation of employment and labour laws have created new industry conventions that serve to normalize substandard jobs. This pattern can clearly be seen in the restaurant industry, for example, where low wages and lean staffing models predominate (Liu and Apollon 2011), as do violations of overtime and minimum wage laws. Employer practices and the design of workforce systems in a range of low-wage industries have incorporated various low-road tactics for holding down wages and reducing other employment-related costs (Appelbaum et al. 2003; Bernhardt et al. 2008; Hanson and Pratt 1995; Peck 1996; Waldinger and Lichter 2003), including the non-payment of legally mandated wages.

These practices are not confined to marginal businesses or to a small number of rogue employers. In fact, widespread violations are found in some of the largest and fastest growing industries in the country, such as retail trade and home health care. And although our research found that large companies have lower violation rates than small businesses (for example, 29% of workers in companies with fewer than 100 employees were paid less than the minimum wage, compared with 15% of workers in companies with 100 or more employees), violations are by no means limited to 'mom and pop' stores or to establishments in the 'underground economy.'

Instead, it appears that violations are occurring, albeit to varying degrees, in industries where the economic restructuring of the past three decades has been most intense, resulting in the dominance of low-wage, cost-cutting business models over high-wage, high-productivity models (see Table 13.2). The drivers of this shift are multidimensional, and they vary

Table 13.2 Workplace violation rates by select industries

	Percentage of workers with violations			
Industry	Minimum wage	Overtime*	Off the clock*	Meal break*
Apparel & textile manufacturing	42.6	71.0	48.4	73.2
Food & furniture manufacturing, transportation & warehousing	18.5	51.9	66.0	66.8
Grocery stores	23.5	65.0	75.2	57.3
Home health care	12.4	76.3	87.5	82.7
Personal & repair services	42.3	91.8	76.8	75.2
Private households	41.5	88.6	82.6	83.6
Residential construction	12.7	70.5	72.2	54.9
Restaurants & hotels	18.2	69.7	74.2	75.7
Retail & drug stores	25.7	83.4	62.7	63.8
Security, building & grounds services	22.3	62.6	70.0	50.7

*Violation rate measured only for workers at risk of the violation; i.e. those who worked more than 40 hours last week; who came in early or stayed late; or who were eligible for a meal break.

Source: Authors' analysis of 2008 Unregulated Work Survey.

by sector. In industries such as retail, grocery stores and trucking and warehousing, this shift has been driven by de-unionization and government deregulation. In industries such as health care and child care, this shift has been driven by the continued shrinking of public funding streams and the privatization of the welfare state. Additionally, in a growing number of industries such as building maintenance and apparel manufacturing, this shift has been driven by subcontracting and other arm's-length employment arrangements.

In particular, the externalization of work – through various outsourcing arrangements such as subcontracting, temporary staffing, independent contracting, and the like – has obscured employers' responsibility for the well-being of their workforces and it has blunted efforts to hold employers accountable when they pursue low-road forms of competition based on the degradation of labour standards (see Beynon et al. 2006; Cappelli et al. 1997; Vosko 2010). This decentralization and devolution of production and service provision has principally been motivated by employers' twin desires to lower wages and to avoid mandatory social payments, such as those associated with unemployment insurance and workers' compensation, as well as by their interest in evading legal liabilities for workplace injuries and discriminatory hiring practices. As employment arrangements have been restructured through increasingly elaborate and geographically dispersed subcontracting chains, growing segments of local economies are rendered opaque to workers, government enforcement agencies, labour unions and workers' rights advocates, making it difficult to design effective enforcement initiatives.

In practice, the ways that the drivers of economic restructuring contribute to the pervasiveness of workplace violations in low-wage industries are through the re-emergence of wage suppression as a key competitive strategy and an important means for securing market share (see Appelbaum et al. 2003; Weil 2010a, 2010b). Employers are increasingly organizing work in ways that obscure both the lines of legal (and normative) accountability in the employment relationship and the extent to which violations of wage and hour laws are being perpetrated. Competitive conditions contribute to, rather than counteract, employer inclinations to suppress employment costs, and unscrupulous employers have exhibited considerable ingenuity in devising ways to reduce wage costs and other liabilities. Employer tactics for holding down wage payments and blurring lines of accountability include paying workers a flat weekly rate, regardless of the exact numbers of hours worked that week; having workers 'clock in' using different timecards, or having workers begin their shift before clocking in; paying workers 'straight time' when overtime pay is mandated by law; misclassifying workers as independent contractors; employing workers who are supplied by day labour staffing agencies; and failing to provide pay documents as required by law.

The data presented in this chapter, as well as additional interviews of low-wage workers by the team, reveal a range of employer practices aimed at reducing total wage payments, a competitive strategy that often is enabled because transparency in employment arrangements has been dramatically reduced. Employers in these industries often have considerable leeway to suppress wages and to violate workplace laws, in part because union density in most low-wage industries is negligible. In fact, this lack of union density meant that our survey included very few unionized workers, too few for us to estimate the effects of unionization on violation rates. High levels of union density in an industry provide a mechanism for monitoring employment standards from within the workplace itself and throughout an industry. However, in the absence of high union density, pressures to raise wages and improve working conditions are dampened. Likewise, the ability to initiate enforcement actions instigated through worker complaints is significantly diminished (Weil 2009). Complaint-driven enforcement is further undermined when employees are vulnerable to employer retaliation, because of unauthorized immigration status or other forms of labour market marginalization, such as having a criminal record. These combined forces have meant that in most low-wage industries, there are few worker-led means of regulating employment conditions.

The absence of a viable within-industry means of safeguarding labour standards in the low-wage labour market, either through inter-firm competition or through unionization and other forms of employee voice at work, means that the task of monitoring and enforcing workplace laws falls on government enforcement agencies. However, in recent years, there has been a marked erosion of government enforcement of core employment and labour laws. An investigation by the US Government Accountability Office (2008) into employer compliance with wage and hour laws found that enforcement actions by the federal Wage and Hour Division (WHD) of the US Department of Labor have been decreasing despite an increase in the number of worksites. Furthermore, although WHD had recognized that low-wage workers are the segment of the workforce most vulnerable to violations of wage and hour laws, for much of the reporting period, the Division was unable to effectively identify and target low-wage industries. Furthermore, even when the data were made available, WHD did not use the information to redirect enforcement resources to high-violation industries. Diminished enforcement efforts have had a perverse effect on employer behaviour because, when the likelihood of detection is low, employers in low-wage industries have little incentive to comply with the law. Thus, the low risk associated with noncompliance renders basic worker protections weak and ineffective.

The combined effects of economic restructuring, employers' use of wage-suppression tactics, and the erosion of government enforcement of core employment and labour laws have created a regulatory void in low-wage labour markets. These circumstances have led to intensifying downward pressures on wages in a range of industries, while the reorganization of work has reduced the degree of transparency in employment relationships. These developments, in turn, have exacerbated the downward drag on compensation and workplace conditions, creating a vicious cycle of cost cutting and labour exploitation. In the absence of effective workplace enforcement, wage theft has become a key cost-saving measure and a standard business practice in many low-wage industries.

Conclusion: restoring labour standards in low-wage industries

This chapter has documented widespread violations of employment and labour laws in low-wage industries in Chicago, Los Angeles and New York City. In the final section we explore ways to restore labour standards and conclude by emphasizing the need for government to make the protection of labour standards a priority. The high rates of workplace violations that we have documented in this chapter are evidence that US employment and labour laws are failing millions of workers in low-wage industries. Our analysis, in this chapter and elsewhere, suggests that these violations are the outcome of a set of economic drivers and policy enablers. Economic changes in trade and competition, some economy-wide and some specific to individual industries, have interacted with public policies that either enable or fail to mitigate the negative impacts of economic restructuring on workers and working conditions. In particular, policy failures over the past several decades in three areas – weak workplace laws, weak enforcement of these laws and a dysfunctional immigration policy have combined to enable, and even encourage, the type of systematic violations documented in this chapter. The policy challenge, then, is to move forward on three fronts: improved enforcement, updated standards and immigration reform.

Improved enforcement

For reasons we outlined in the previous section, government enforcement must be the cornerstone of any viable response to workplace violations. However, in recent years, enforcement efforts at both the federal and state level have weakened, creating a significant enforcement gap. There is a pressing need for new approaches to addressing the reality that workplace violations are becoming standard business practice in many low-wage industries (see National Employment Law Project (2010) and Weil (2010) for detailed policy recommendations). To counteract this trend, enforcement policy in the US should,

- move towards proactive, 'investigation-driven' worksite enforcement, rather than primarily reacting to worker complaints as they come in. This means identifying industries where violations are systemic, conducting strategic, repeated and well-publicized workplace audits, and cracking down on employers who are repeat offenders. The goal should be to send industry-wide signals that the government will vigorously pursue violators, thereby strengthening the deterrence function of enforcement measures by increasing the likelihood of inspection and showing that agencies are prepared to levy meaningful penalties on violating employers.
- increase the number of workplace investigators. Between 1980 and 2007, the number of inspectors enforcing federal minimum wage and overtime laws declined by 31 per cent, even as the labour force grew by 52 per cent (National Employment Law Project 2008). Similarly, the budget of the Occupational Safety and Health Administration was cut by $25 million in real dollars between 2001 and 2007; at its current staffing and inspection levels, it would take the agency 133 years to inspect each workplace just once (AFL-CIO 2007: 6). Such staffing levels mean that government enforcement agencies lack a credible deterrence function.

- increase the reach and effectiveness of enforcement by partnering with worker centres, unions, service providers and legal advocates. Government alone will never have enough staff and resources to monitor every workplace in the country on a regular basis. Community partnerships can help to identify industry segments where workplace violations are most common and what types of methods employers use to evade detection. Worker centres, in particular, have developed their capacity to understand industry dynamics and employer practices, and these organizations can be effective partners with government agencies.
- strengthen penalties for violations. Currently, penalties for many workplace violations are so minimal that they fail to deter many employers. For example, the savings to employers from paying employees less than the minimum wage often outweigh the costs, even for those few who are apprehended. More substantial penalties are central to enhancing the deterrence function of enforcement initiatives.

Updated legal standards

Strengthened enforcement is important, but so too are strong legal standards that recognize the changing organization of work. Changes are needed on three fronts:

1. *strengthen legal standards*. Raising (and indexing) the minimum wage, updating health and safety standards, extending coverage of overtime laws higher up the income distribution and reaffirming the right of workers to organize through labour law reform are key improvements. Such policy changes would compel employer compliance, improve the competitive position of businesses that play by the rules and maintain labour standards.
2. *close coverage gaps*. Some occupations, for example, home health care aides and domestic workers, are excluded from key workplace protections. Closing gaps in coverage must be a priority for policymakers if standards in low-wage labour markets are to be substantially improved.
3. *hold employers responsible for the workers they employ*. Some unscrupulous employers evade their legal obligations by misclassifying workers as independent contractors or by subcontracting work to fly-by-night operators who then break the law. Employers should be held responsible for the workplace standards they control, whether directly or indirectly through subcontracting relationships.

Immigration reform

Although unauthorized immigrants are covered by most employment and labour laws, in practice, they are effectively disenfranchised in the workplace by their lack of legal status, their fear of deportation and the willingness of many employers to exploit their vulnerability. Any comprehensive policy initiative to reduce workplace violations must therefore,

- Prioritize equal protection and equal status in national immigration reform. Immigration reform without close attention to labour market impacts and workers' rights will push more workers into the underground economy, leading to greater insecurity for immigrant families and less economic integration. A guiding principle for reform must be that immigrant workers are guaranteed the full protection and remedies of employment and labour laws, and enforcement agencies must aggressively pursue workplace violations suffered by unauthorized immigrants.
- Ensure status-blind enforcement of employment and labour laws by maintaining a 'firewall' between workplace and immigration inspections. Agencies enforcing minimum wage, prevailing wage, health and safety, and other worker-protection laws can and should maintain a firewall between themselves and immigration authorities, so that unauthorized workers will not fear deportation if they make a wage claim or file a workplace grievance.

The research findings presented in this chapter show that many low-wage industries are effectively positioned beyond the reach of government enforcement of core employment and labour laws. The corresponding spread of workplace violations has significantly undermined the economic standing of workers in the labour market, reducing already low annual earnings while also eroding employment standards in leading industries of urban economies. Our findings show that violations are widespread in major low-wage labour markets, with more than two-thirds of workers experiencing at least one pay-based violation in the previous workweek. Lousy jobs may not be inevitable. However in the current context, industry dynamics reinforce low-road employer practices and workers face tangible barriers to defending their rights (not least of which is their financial dependence on substandard, insecure jobs and employer retaliation against workers who contest these conditions). In this situation workplace violations are certain to spread without a renewed government commitment to safeguarding labour standards through improved laws backed by stronger enforcement.

Notes

*This chapter is based in part on Annette Bernhardt, Ruth Milkman, Nik Theodore, Douglas Heckathorn, Mirabai Auer, James DeFilippis, Ana Luz Gonzalez, Victor Narro, Jason Perelshteyn, Diana Polson and Michael Spiller (2009) *Broken Laws, Unprotected Workers: Violations of Employment and Labor*

Laws in America's Cities, available at www.unprotectedworkers.org. The research was supported by the Ford Foundation, the Haynes Foundation, the Joyce Foundation, the Rockefeller Foundation and the Russell Sage Foundation.

1 For more information on the methodology for this study, see Spiller et al. (2010).

REFERENCES

AFL-CIO [American Federation of Labor-Congress of Industrial Organizations] (2007) *Death on the Job: The Toll of Neglect*. Washington, DC: AFL-CIO.

Appelbaum, E., Bernhardt, A. and Murnane, R. J. (eds) (2003) *Low-Wage America: How Employers Are Reshaping Opportunity in the Workplace*. New York: Russell Sage Foundation.

Bernhardt, A., Boushey, H., Dresser, L. and Tilly, C. (eds) (2008) *The Gloves-off Economy: Workplace Standards at the Bottom of America's Labor Market*. Ithaca, NY: Cornell University Press.

Bernhardt, A., Milkman, R., Theodore, N., Heckathorn, D., Auer, M. DeFilippis, J., Gonzalez, A. L., Narro, V., Perelshteyn, J., Polson, D. and Spiller, M. (2009) *Broken Laws, Unprotected Workers: Violations of Employment and Labor Laws in America's Cities*, available at www.unprotectedworkers.org

Beynon, H. Grimshaw, D., Rubery, J. and Ward, K. (2006) *Managing Employment Change: The New Realities of Work*. Oxford: Oxford University Press.

Bobo, K. (2008) *Wage Theft in America: Why Millions of Workers Are Not Getting Paid and What We Can Do About It*. New York: New Press.

Cappelli, P., Bassi, L., Katz, H., Knoke, D., Osterman, P. and Useem, M. (1997) *Change at Work*. New York: Oxford University Press.

Hacker, J. S., Huber, G. A., Rehm, P., Schlesinger, M. and Valetta, R. (2010) *Economic Security at Risk*. New York: Rockefeller Foundation.

Hanson, S. and Pratt, G. (1995) *Gender, Work and Space*. New York: Routledge.

Heckathorn, D. D. (1997) 'Respondent-Driven Sampling: A New Approach to the Study of Hidden Populations', *Social Problems*, 44(2): 174–199.

Heckathorn, D. D. (2007) 'Extensions of Respondent-Driven Sampling: Analyzing Continuous Variables and Controlling for Differential Recruitment', *Sociological Methodology*, 37(1): 151–207.

Liu, Y. Y. and Apollon, D. (2011) *The Color of Food*. Oakland, CA: Applied Research Center.

Peck, J. (1996) *Work-Place: The Social Regulation of Labor Markets*. New York: Guilford.

National Employment Law Project (NELP) (2010) *Just Pay: Improving Wage and Hour Enforcement at the United States Department of Labor*. New York, NY: NELP, available at http://www.nelp.org/page/-/Justice/2010/JustPayReport2010.pdf?nocdn=1

National Employment Law Project (NELP) (2008) *Rebuilding a Good Jobs Economy: A Blueprint for Recovery and Reform*. New York, NY: NELP, available at http://www.nelp.org/page/-/Federal/NELP_federal_agenda.pdf?nocdn=1

▶

Spiller, M., Bernhardt, A., Perelshteyn, J. and Heckathorn, D. (2010) 'Sampling, Fielding, and Estimation in the 2008 Unregulated Work Survey'. Technical Report, Center for the Study of Economy and Society, Cornell University, Ithaca, NY.

Standing, G. (2002) *Beyond the New Paternalism*. London: Verso.

US Government Accountability Office (2008) *Fair Labor Standards Act: Better Use of Available Resources and Consistent Reporting Could Improve Compliance*. Washington, DC: US Government Accountability Office.

Vosko, L. H. (2010) *Managing the Margins: Gender, Citizenship and the International Regulation of Precarious Employment*. Oxford: Oxford University Press.

Waldinger, R. and Lichter, M. I. (2003) *How the Other Half Works: Immigration and the Social Organization of Labor*. Berkeley, CA: University of California Press.

Weil, D. (2009) 'Rethinking the Regulation of Vulnerable Work in the USA: A Sector-based Approach', *Journal of Industrial Relations*, 51(3): 411–430.

Weil, D. (2010a) 'Fissured Employment', working paper, Boston University, Boston.

Weil, D. (2010b) *Improving Workplace Conditions through Strategic Enforcement*. A report to the Wage and Hour Division, Boston University, Boston.

CHAPTER 14

Employment Standards 'Modernization' in Canada

Mark P. Thomas

> The workplaces and workers of Ontario are flexible, modern and adaptable. Employment standards legislation should be equally so.
>
> (Ontario, 2000, p. 4)

> Our government is committed to helping businesses focus on what they do best – creating jobs for Ontario families. We can protect the public interest without creating unnecessary barriers to business. The *Open for Business Act* will save businesses both time and money.
>
> (Ontario, 2010a)

Introduction

Minimum employment standards (ES) legislation – laws that establish a base in a labour market for fundamental workers' rights, including those in the areas of wages, working time, paid time away from work and severance pay – lie at the heart of debates about bad jobs.* Minimum employment standards regulate the employment rights of the most vulnerable workers, primarily those engaged in non-unionized jobs in low-wage labour markets (Fairey, 2007; Pollert, 2007, 2009). Moreover, in establishing minimum conditions within a labour market, they also set the base for collective bargaining (Mitchell, 2003). Recently, such standards have become targets for neo-liberal policy initiatives as governments in high income labour markets seek to encourage labour market 'flexibility'. At the same time, as unionization rates decline and more workers become reliant on legislated standards, scholars and workers' rights advocates have begun to consider how reforms to legislated minimum standards could alleviate some of the harshest conditions of bad jobs as a first step towards promoting decent work (Thomas, 2009; Vosko, 2010).

In 2007, the Toronto-area Workers' Action Centre issued a report on precarious employment in Ontario (WAC, 2007). The persistence of conditions characteristic of bad jobs is clearly articulated in the stories collected from a wide range of low-wage workers. These stories document the continuing problems of unpaid wages and overtime, workers being misclassified as self-employed and therefore exempt from minimum standards, expectations to work hours well in excess of legislated standards, and a general lack of enforcement of minimum employment standards.

This report on the persistence of bad jobs was bookended by two phases of reforms to employment standards legislation in Ontario. In 1999, the neo-liberal Progressive Conservative provincial government announced its intention to dramatically reform – to 'modernize' – the province's employment standards legislation. The government had been elected on a platform that included promises to substantially re-write Ontario's labour and employment laws in order to make the province 'open for business'. In its platform, (the *Common Sense Revolution)*, it pledged to remove barriers to economic growth created by 'ideologically-driven legislation and over-regulation' (PCPO, 1995, p. 14). Businesses needed greater flexibility to respond to increasing global competitive pressures. To balance the competing demands of work and family, employees needed greater flexibility through alternative scheduling arrangements. A comprehensive package of reforms to the province's employment standard was introduced in 2001.

A decade later, with the province governed by a Liberal party determined to introduce a series of austerity measures in response to the ongoing global financial crisis, Ontario's employment standards legislation was targeted for 'modernization' once again (Fanelli and Thomas, 2011; Ontario, 2010a). Rather than focus on the legislated standards themselves, however, these reforms targeted the complaints and enforcement process. In particular, the government sought to introduce efficiencies into these processes that would enable the Ministry of Labour to address a backlog of employment standards complaints.

This chapter examines the period of employment standards reform in Ontario between 2001 and 2010, drawing its analysis from key informant interviews, legislative and policy documents produced by the Ontario MoL and documents produced by organizations engaged in lobbying efforts to influence employment standards reforms. Interviews were conducted with a range of key informants engaged in employment standards policy development and advocacy, including policymakers from the Ontario Ministry of Labour, community legal workers who assist non-unionized workers with employment standards complaints, as well as representatives from Canadian unions and non-unionized workers' organizations that have lobbied for improvements to employment standards legislation.

The chapter situates these periods of reform within the context of a neo-liberal public policy agenda and a labour market characterized by increasing levels of precarious forms of employment. Ontario is Canada's most populous province, with high levels of immigration and cultural diversity, and employment in a wide range of manufacturing and service economy jobs. While the primary focus is on employment standards reforms in Ontario at the turn of the twenty-first century, the Ontario case helps illustrate the connections between neo-liberal labour law reforms and labour market insecurity for those workers most reliant on employment standards. The chapter argues that these periods of employment standards reform in Ontario reproduced and intensified the employment conditions characteristic of bad jobs.

Regulating employment standards in Ontario, Canada

In Canada, employment standards include legislated standards in the areas of minimum wages, hours of work, overtime, leaves, and paid vacations and holidays. These standards are largely regulated at the provincial level, although some employees fall under the jurisdiction of the federally regulated *Canada Labour Code*. Ontario's *Employment Standards Act* (*ESA*) came into effect in 1969. It combined previously existing minimum standards legislation regulating minimum wages, maximum hours of work, overtime rates and arrangements and paid vacations into a comprehensive legislative framework that set minimum standards for Ontario's labour market and provided legislative protection for those most vulnerable to exploitation.

The core standards of the *ESA* were altered through minor reforms during the 1970s and 1980s;[1] however, while specific standards were improved incrementally, the overall model of regulation – a secondary form of protection for workers outside collective bargaining arrangements – remained intact (Thomas, 2009).

Despite the shortcomings of employment standards legislation – both in terms of low standards relative to those set through collective bargaining, and poor enforcement of the legislated standards (*discussed below*) – many workers rely on these standards as a primary means of labour market protection, particularly the growing segment of the labour force engaged in non-unionized, low-wage work. While employment standards were developed to provide legislative protection against the deterioration of employment conditions, the trajectory of employment standards reform followed by successive Ontario governments in the early years of the twenty-first century created the potential to exacerbate, rather than alleviate, employment conditions characteristic of 'bad jobs'.

Neo-liberalism and 'modern' employment standards

Through the 1980s and 1990s, neo-liberal governments in many high income countries emphasized the need for public policy to promote economic competitiveness, prompting shifts from welfare state to workfare state models of labour market regulation (Harvey, 2005; Jessop, 1993). Underlying this discourse is the assumption that regulatory interventions that run counter to short-term profitability interests will inhibit the competitiveness of markets. This initiative not only a project of policy reform but also involves reshaping the social expectations workers have about employment (Peck, 2001; Sears, 1999). These processes influenced labour law reforms across the advanced capitalist economies. In the United States, beginning in the 1980s labour laws became increasingly oriented towards promoting economic competitiveness and individual rather than collective rights (Befort and Budd, 2009). In Australia neo-liberal re-regulation of labour laws brought about shifts from industry-wide agreements on wages and work rules towards legislated minimum standards and enterprise-based negotiation as a way to heighten labour market flexibility (McCallum, 2005). Neo-liberal policy discourses connected the reform of employment standards to the necessity of encouraging emergent patterns of labour flexibility in order to promote competitive advantage. The adoption of neo-liberal policy frameworks, articulated and promoted through policy discourses of competitiveness, lay at the heart of employment standards reform processes that would unfold in the late 1990s in Ontario and elsewhere.

Neo-liberal principles of labour market re-regulation – emphasizing market-based mechanisms to promote both economic competitiveness and labour discipline – were brought to Ontario's employment standards in 1995, with the election of a Progressive Conservative provincial government committed to making the province 'open for business' by providing employers greater 'flexibility' through a thorough rewriting of the provinces' labour laws. Specifically, the government claimed the need to modernize employment standards through a discourse that tied reform of the *ESA* to the government's general economic commitment to 'improve the province's competitive status as a place to invest' (Ontario, 2000, p. 4). This commitment was rooted in the government's assertion that 'flexible' labour policies were needed to promote economic competitiveness in a global economy.

The government formed the Red Tape Review Commission (RTRC) to review existing regulations that affected Ontario's businesses and related institutions and to make recommendations regarding the need to change or eliminate 'inappropriate regulatory measures' (RTRC, 1997, p. xii). Rooted in neo-liberal ideology rather than evidence of the constraints of regulation, the government claimed that such unnecessary rules and regulations deterred job creation and reduced economic competitiveness by adding excessive costs to Ontario's businesses. The RTRC produced numerous recommendations regarding the province's employment standards legislation, which was defined as being 'outdated' and unable to provide 'the flexibility required to meet the needs of the modern workplace'. These recommendations included that weekly maximum hours of work be increased and that exemptions from the legislation be broadened (RTRC, 1997, pp. 92, 96).

The government then embarked on a three-phase programme of employment standards reform grounded in these principles. First, it ended the annual increases to the minimum wage that had been occurring since the 1980s, freezing the general rate at $6.85.[2] The minimum wage freeze, which lasted for nine years, was a significant change in direction as, minimum wage increases had been implemented regularly in order to protect wage rates of workers with little bargaining power.

Second, it turned its attention to the complaints processes. In 1996, the *Employment Standards Improvement Act* reduced the time limit for workers to register formal complaints from two years to six months and placed a $10,000 limit on monetary awards for *ESA* violations, regardless of the value of lost wages.[3] To claim more, an employee would have to do so through civil court, but could not file an ESA claim *and* take a civil action simultaneously. The *Act* also introduced a provision preventing unionized employees from filing employment standards complaints with the Ministry of Labour, requiring employees with union representation to resolve employment standards complaints through the grievance arbitration process, thus placing the cost of administering *ESA* complaints in the hands of unions, rather than the Ministry of Labour.[4]

According to the provincial government, these amendments were meant to encourage 'self-reliance' between employers and employees in resolving *ESA* complaints.[5] The practice of self-reliance reflects a privatization of employment standards regulation by situating them in the context of direct negotiation between employers and employees. This, in effect, reduces the state's role in administering employment standards enforcement. Reducing the time limit for filing complaints and the ceiling on financial compensation placed restrictions on employees' abilities to secure protection from employment standards violations, indicating that underlying the stated goals of self-reliance lay the intention to curtail workers' rights.[6]

The amendments were highly favoured by employer associations. The Retail Council of Canada (RCC) stated that '[t]he challenge of ESA reform is to facilitate...diversity and flexibility in the best interests of both parties', and considered Bill 49 to be a 'good first step' in this process (RCC, 1996, p. 4). Similarly, the Canadian Federation of Independent Business 'commended the Ontario government for its resolve to undertake a two-stage overhaul of the... ESA' and 'supported Bill 49... as the first stage in that reform' (CFIB, 2000, p. 1).

In July 2000, the Ministry of Labour issued a consultation paper outlining its proposals to modernize Ontario's employment standards. The *ESA* was described as being 'filled with language, concerns and approaches of an earlier era' and thus no longer relevant to the contemporary Ontario economy (Ontario, 2000, p. 3). In *Time for Change*, the government committed to modernizing the *ESA* so that it would 'improve workplace flexibility' and thereby encourage growth and innovation (Ontario, 2000, p. 3).

Time for Change proposed a wide-ranging package of reforms. The hours of work and overtime proposals were perhaps the most controversial. The government proposed to increase the maximum allowable hours of work per week to 60 (from 48), to allow for this weekly maximum to be calculated by averaging hours over a three-week period, and to allow for overtime (hours in excess of 44 hours) also to be averaged over a three-week period. Proposals on vacation pay and public holidays submitted that, subject to employer–employee agreement, vacations could be scheduled in daily increments, and employees could work public holidays with either additional pay or a substitute day off. *Time for Change* also emphasized the need to encourage greater self-reliance on the part of employers and employees in standards enforcement.

These proposals represented the most significant re-writing of employment standards legislation since the introduction of the *ESA*, and signalled the government's willingness to enhance further the employer-oriented flexibility contained within the *ESA*. Unsurprisingly, the proposals met with widespread support from employer associations, who emphasized strongly the need to introduce greater flexibility into the *ESA* in order to 'recognize and accommodate the trend towards more varied work arrangements and allow greater choice in designing those arrangements' (CFIB, 2000, p. 2).

While the reactions of employer associations were largely favourable, the proposed changes received across the board criticism from organized labour and community organizations working with non-unionized workers (employment standards Work Group (ESWG), 2000). These organizations claimed that the proposed changes would only benefit employers and would lead to a reduction in workers' rights across the province. Further, labour and community organizations expressed concern that the standards in the *ESA* were already insufficient and that the proposed changes would take employment standards back in time rather than forward. The consultation process itself was viewed with scepticism due to its short notice and its limited scope.[7]

As an alternative, labour and community organizations called for a reduction in the weekly hours maximum, and for stronger enforcement mechanisms to improve the regulation of employment standards. These calls framed a campaign of opposition, focusing in particular on the 60-hour workweek. While the campaign was not expected to stop the proclamation, it was designed to raise awareness about the ways in which the new legislation would lower the floor of workers' rights.[8]

Time for Change was, with few amendments, adopted in new employment standards legislation effective from 2001.[9] Increases to the weekly maximum hours of work (up to 60) remained the same, although the proposal to allow for the averaging of weekly hours maximums over three weeks was dropped. The overtime averaging proposal was extended to allow for averaging over a four-week period. Both these provisions formally required 'employee consent' to alternative hours arrangements. The *Act* also indirectly set a 13-hour limit on maximum daily hours in its stipulation that an employee was to be entitled to 11 hours' free from work each day (Fudge, 2001). Proposals to introduce greater flexibility into the vacation and holiday provisions of the *Act* were maintained.

Notwithstanding government claims that the legislation would benefit employers and employees, the model of labour market regulation developed through the policy reforms process offered nothing to alleviate the situation of heightened labour market vulnerability experienced by workers in precarious employment; rather it supported the normalization of neo-liberal labour flexibility. Specifically, the policy reforms introduced through the *ESA* 2000 reduced direct government involvement in regulating workplace standards, promoted increased employer control over work time, facilitated the normalization of non-standard and low-wage employment relationships and further entrenched a privatized model of the regulation of workplace standards (Fudge, 2001; Mitchell, 2003; Thomas, 2009).

The reduction of government regulation of workplace standards and the increased capacity for employers to control working time stemmed from the transition from a permits-based system for extra hours to a system based on 'employee consent' in the increase in allowable weekly hours and the system of overtime averaging. The *Act* enabled employers to increase the work time of those workers already working long hours. Overtime averaging arrangements permitted instances where employees could work over 44 hours without compensation at time-and-a-half for those hours, if the total hours of work for the four-week period were less than 176 hours. This measure enables significant reductions in the cost of, and thus encourages greater use of, overtime labour. Combined, these provisions shifted the regulation of working time standards back to the private relations between employers and employees, and implicitly created the means for employers to exhibit greater control over the scheduling of extra work hours.[10]

Financial insecurity experienced by low-income employees reinforced this enhanced employer power as the minimum wage was frozen from 1995 until 2004[11] increasing the economic insecurity of those already in precarious employment relationships. Moreover, the freeze held clear implications for conditions of racialized income inequality (Thomas, 2010). Poverty rates amongst racialized groups continued to increase through the late 1990s into the early twenty-first century. Through the 1990s, while approximately 25 per cent of Canadians earned under $10 an hour, 41 per cent of recent immigrants were in this earnings category. Longstanding racialized labour market trends in Canada, including an overrepresentation in low-wage, low-status occupations, meant that workers from racialized groups were among those most directly affected by the minimum wage freeze.[12]

The employment standards reforms supported the normalization of precarious employment relationships. The potential for increased working hours and reduced overtime costs (through averaging arrangements) discourages employers from hiring additional workers. Thus, the ability to schedule longer hours of work encouraged trends towards a model of employment whereby core groups of workers take on longer hours, and are supplemented by a contingent of contract and part-time workers working irregular hours and shorter work weeks. In this way, employers secure greater capacity to maintain lean staffing levels (which are supplemented by contract/temporary workers), and to construct flexible and nonstandard employment relationships characterized by a lack of hours stability.

The impacts of the 2001 *ESA* reforms have been clearly documented (WAC, 2007). Conditions characteristic of precarious employment, including low-wages, unpaid wages, excessive hours of work, unpaid overtime, lack of public holidays, and termination without notice or severance pay were exacerbated in the following years. These conditions were particularly pronounced in sectors of the labour market where racialized workers predominated, indicating that racialized communities were disproportionately impacted by the deterioration of legislated standards (Thomas, 2010).

The Conservative government was defeated in 2003 and replaced by a Liberal government. Amendments to Ontario's employment standards legislation in 2004 did not alter the general tendencies set by the previous reforms. The most noted reform, *The Employment Standards Amendment Act (Hours of Work and Other Matters) 2004*, purported to eliminate the 60-hour work week; however, it simply introduced a government approval process for employer/employee agreements for extra hours and overtime averaging arrangements.[13] The legacy of the 2001 legislation remained largely intact, even after the defeat of the government that brought it into effect.

Enforcing employment standards

Minimum employment standards are meaningless without effective enforcement. Yet such standards are often very poorly enforced, leaving many workers who rely on them vulnerable to employer power (Pollert, 2007). Poor enforcement conditions were endemic to the Ontario case, particularly in the years following the 2001 reforms. Many conditions of bad jobs persisted due to poor enforcement practices (WAC, 2007). One of the factors inhibiting a more comprehensive enforcement effort was the staffing levels of the Ministry of Labour's Employment Standards Branch. The broader neo-liberal regulatory paradigm emphasizes the need to reduce so-called red tape and eliminate inefficiencies, which may include downsizing of public sector workforces. Adherence to this perspective resulted in general downsizing across the Ontario public sector with approximately one-quarter of the Employment Standards Officer (ESO) posts terminated, thereby contributing to the implicit deregulation of employment standards (USWA, 2000).[14]

From 2001, the Ministry of Labour regularly proclaimed its commitment to increasing the number of ESOs and to improving the proactive inspections process. Indeed, between 2003 and 2009, the number of proactive inspections was increased from 151 to 2,100. Nevertheless, the longstanding reliance on individualized employee complaints remained the primary enforcement mechanism of the *ESA*, with the aim of promoting employer–employee 'self-reliance' being the key emphasis. As illustrated in Table 14.1, during this period, the number of complaints from workers has grown dramatically, leading to a significant gap between complaints received and those resolved. A steadily growing number of claims has produced a backlog of some 14,000 unaddressed employment standards complaints (Gellatly et al., 2011).

Table 14.1 Employment standards claims, investigations and inspections, 2003–2009

Year	New claims	New claims & previous year's outstanding claims	Claims with investigations completed	Claims investigated of total claims in that year	Unpaid wages & ESA entitlements recovered for workers	Proactive inspections
2003–04	16,175	19375	15,771	81%	$15.5 mil	151
2004–05	18,301	21,532	15,950	74%	$15.7 mil	2,355
2005–06	18,972	23,496	15,776	67%	$13 mil	2,515
2006–07	22,623	29,197	15,955	55%	$17 mil	2,500
2007–08	20,789	34,031	18,533	54%	$11.7 mil	1,250
2008–09	23,276	38,774	21,304	55%	$11.6 mil	2,100

Sources: Gellatly et al. (2011); Ontario Ministry of Labour Fiscal Year Reports 2003–2007; Ontario Ministry of Labour Results Based Plans and Ontario Annual Reports; Employment Standards Program, Annual Report 2007–2009.[15]

Emphasizing self-reliance as a primary enforcement mechanism de-emphasizes pro-active enforcement mechanisms (such as targeted inspections) that would address power imbalances in the workplace. Other enforcement strategies, such as routine investigations which have been successful in detecting violations, have been given a secondary priority This individualized, complaints-based process places the onus of reporting employment standards violations on employees who may be reluctant to complain due to fear of employer reprisal (Fairey, 2007; WAC, 2007). These types of power imbalance were exacerbated through the 200 reforms.

Moreover, the timeline to file a complaint, which was reduced from two years to six months, was identified by many community legal workers as insufficient to cover the potential violations a worker may experience in a workplace, particularly in forms of precarious employment. Such violations may occur over a period of years but workers may not report them until they are able to find another job.[16] Thus, the insufficient time limit to file complaints creates further barriers to effective enforcement.[17]

While the government claimed a commitment to 'fairness' for workers, an analysis of the reformed administrative and enforcement practices reveals that the re-regulation of employment standards through new legislation, which provided increased employer control over workplace standards, was accompanied by other forms of 'flexibility' through disputes resolution practices that privatized the complaints process through the promotion of 'self-reliance'. Alongside poor enforcement practices, these 'modern' employment standards potentially eroded employment conditions instead of providing legislative protection from bad job conditions.

Creating 'efficient' and 'modern' enforcement practices

Reforms to legislated standards that favour business over workers are one way in which neo-liberal governments have sought to introduce labour market 'flexibility'. Employment standards 'modernization' may also include changes to enforcement practices that further reduce government regulation of the employment relationship and that heighten the vulnerability of workers reliant on legislated standards to forms of employer power. For example, in the early 2000s, the UK government introduced a series of reforms to workplace disputes resolution that place new burdens on employees aiming to defend their workplace rights, all under the guise of 'modernization' (Pollert 2005). Despite an official policy discourse that claimed the reforms were designed to promote 'fairness at work', these reforms compromised the workplace rights of unorganized workers reliant on legislated standards, exacerbating 'the inequality between capital and labour by setting basic statutory requirements for employers...but a complex new regime for employees, with further obstacles to overcome' (p. 238).

Following a similar model, the Ontario government passed the *Open for Business Act 2010* (OBA) as part of a larger government initiative to create a climate favourable for business. As in 2001, the discourse of 'modernization' framed the package of employment standards reforms. Unlike in 2001, however, these latest reforms focused not on standards themselves, but on the *ESA* complaints and enforcement procedures. According to the Ontario Ministry of Labour, the aim of employment standards modernization was to 'establish services that achieve fairness for workers, while helping business to be increasingly competitive in the global economy' (Ontario, 2010c).

Once again, Ontario's business community supported the *OBA* policy reforms. The President and CEO of the Ontario Chamber of Commerce claimed that the reforms 'will allow our members to spend more of their money advancing productivity and creating jobs...rather than dealing with onerous and sometimes contradictory regulations' (Ontario, 2010a). Similarly, the Vice President of Canadian Manufacturers & Exporters Ontario echoed these sentiments stating 'these reforms will ensure Ontario is open for business by removing outdated processes and unnecessary red tape' (Ontario, 2010a). Opposing such claims, community organizations drew attention to the ways in which the OBA could 'add additional barriers and burdens' by placing the onus of enforcement increasingly on workers themselves, rather than Ministry of Labour inspectors (WAC, 2010, p. 1).

The *OBA* amended employment standards enforcement procedures fundamentally. It introduced a requirement that workers who experience employment standards violations first approach their employer seeking resolution before being eligible to submit a claim to the Ministry of Labour. And it gave new powers to ESOs to facilitate settlements between workers and employers, including new and unprecedented discretion over monetary compensation for workers.

The amendments to the employment standards complaints process contained within the *OBA* increase the pressure on individual workers in at least two ways. First, employees are required to notify their employer before the Ministry of Labour will initiate an employment standards claim (Ontario, 2010b). The assumption behind this is that '[m]ost employers want to do the right thing and they will often remedy the situation promptly and voluntarily, if they agree there is a valid claim' (Ontario, 2010c). In putting the onus on an individual worker to initiate the complaints process directly with their employer, however, this requirement heightens the opportunity for employer pressure to deter a complaint from going forward to the Ministry. Second, the amendments place responsibility on individual workers to collect the information for their complaints, reducing the requirements on the investigative procedure itself. Where an officer determines that there is insufficient evidence provided by an employee, the officer may determine there is no violation.

The amendments to the ESA through the *OBA* also promote a voluntary approach to employment standards regulation, specifically through amendments that give ESOs a role in bringing employers and employees to a mediated settlement. This approach creates potential for employers to resist the process if they feel it will not work in their favour. Moreover, it privileges a mediated settlement over an actual award by an officer, which may expedite the claims process but could reduce the value of the settlement achieved by a worker.

In addition, the Ministry of Labour established an employment standards Task Force to address the backlog of 14,000 employment standards complaints, giving the Task Force a two-year mandate to clear this backlog (Gellatly et al., 2011). The Task Force is to investigate these existing claims 'based on an officer's review of written materials and through telephone discussions with parties' (Ontario, 2010d). The Task Force will utilize the new complaints procedures, in particular the potential for voluntary, mediated settlements to expedite the settlement process.

As the legislation was just passed at the time of writing, and as the Task Force has not yet completed its mandate, it is not yet possible to determine the longer term impact of the *OBA*. Nevertheless, the implications are clear, as these developments reflect a process of 'market regulation' (Standing, 1999), whereby neo-liberal policy reforms enhance the ways in which labour markets are regulated through market forces, in particular relations of commodification. In this neo-liberal context, labour legislation and labour market policies are often designed to 'weaken protective regulations, restrict collective institutions and strengthen pro-individualistic regulations' (Standing, 1999, p. 42). Standing's concept of market regulation draws attention to the fact that, through neo-liberal policies such as the *OBA*, labour markets may be re-regulated to promote the heightened commodification of labour power and increase workers' exposure to market forces. Market regulation can be seen in the specific aspects of the *OBA* that emphasize an individualized, privatized and voluntary process for regulating employment standards complaints and settlements. The implications of these shifts for workers in Ontario are that the market, rather than the state, becomes the enforcement mechanism.

Conclusion

This chapter has analysed two phases of employment standards reform in Ontario. These reforms were shaped by the principles of neo-liberalism, thereby contributing to a shift towards a model of labour market regulation that promotes market-based, privatized and individualized relations between employers and employees. In the context of workplace and labour market restructuring characterized by growth in forms of nonstandard and precarious employment, framed through a discourse of modernization, successive Ontario governments used employment standards reforms to further promote employer-oriented forms of flexibility, thereby increasing employee vulnerability at a time of growing insecurity.

The reforms implemented by the Progressive Conservative government in 2001 reduced the direct government involvement in the regulation of workplace standards, promoted increased employer control over work time, facilitated the normalization of nonstandard employment relationships and increased the vulnerability of workers in non-unionized workplaces. Almost a decade later, the *OBA 2010* further entrenched an individualized, complaint-based enforcement model that has the potential to heighten, rather than alleviate, conditions of precarious employment. Combined, these two phases of employment standards reform ensure that 'modern' employment standards in Ontario remain outdated and poorly enforced. In this way, reforms to employment standards legislation play a central role in much broader processes of labour market and workplace reorganization, and thereby contribute to the employment conditions characteristic of bad jobs.

These reforms to employment standards legislation in Ontario mirror developments in other jurisdictions where neo-liberal labour market policy reforms have weakened legislated standards and placed an increased burden on workers to enforce their rights. Legislated standards are not the only answer to defending workers' rights, as collective organization provides workers with greater capacity to challenge the power of capital. Nevertheless, minimum standards legislation can play an important role in raising the floor of the labour market, by both creating standards that alleviate some of the harshest conditions of bad jobs and providing a stronger base upon which collective bargaining can begin. Moreover, as discussed, legislated standards alone are insufficient. They must be accompanied by enforcement processes that effectively counterbalance the power of employers. Such measures, however, are a far cry from the direction taken under the aim of employment standards modernization in recent years.

Acknowledments

*Research for this paper was funded through the Social Sciences and Humanities Research Council of Canada. I would like to thank to Sarah Rogers for research assistance on the project.

Notes

1 Termination notice and pregnancy leave provisions were added in the early 1970s and severance pay was added in the 1980s. The minimum wage rose through incremental increases to $6.85 in 1994. In 1991, the Employee Wage Protection Program was introduced to provide employees with compensation for unpaid wages, overtime wages, vacation pay, holiday pay, and termination and severance pay (up to a maximum of five thousand dollars) in cases where employers had been found in violation of the ESA (Ontario, 1991).
2 AO RG 7-130, A Review of Ontario's Fair Wage Programme, Research Branch, January 1971.
3 See Bill 49 (c.23, SO 1996).
4 Jonathan Eaton, 'Province shifts ES responsibility. Changes put onus on unions to ensure rules are applied', *Toronto Star*, Monday, 2 December 1996, C3; David Ivey, 'Changes to basic employment rights affect all Ontarians', *Hamilton Spectator*, Saturday, 7 December 1996, B2.
5 Jonathan Eaton, 'Province shifts ES responsibility', *Toronto Star*.
6 Interview, CL1, September 2001. The Bill originally included a provision that would allow employers and unions to contract out of the *ESA*, or negotiate standards below those written in the *ESA* for hours of work, holidays, and overtime, vacation, and severance pay where any negotiated settlement, as a whole package, provided total benefits greater than those contained in the *ESA*.

   Jonathan Eaton, 'New law will gut workplace standards'; Canadian Press, 'Delay study of job rules, Tories urged. Hearings called a "sham" after major change is withdrawn', *Toronto Star*, Tuesday, 20 August 1996, B3.
7 Interview, CL2, September 2001.
8 Interview, CL2, September 2001.
9 Bill 147, the amended ESA, received third reading on 20 December 2000.
10 Interview, CL2, September 2001.
11 Under considerable pressure from labour and anti-poverty organizations, Dalton McGuinty's Liberal government introduced a series of increases to Ontario's minimum wage with the aim to raise it to $10.25 by 31 March 2010.
12 See 'Understanding the Racialization of Poverty in Ontario' (www.colourofpoverty.ca), Campaign 2000 et al. (2000), and WAC (2007) for an overview of these patterns.
13 Cavalluzzo, Hayes, Shilton, McIntyre and Cornish (2004) *Update: Ending the 60 Hour Work Week?* December 2004. Accessed on April 19, 2005, at http://www.cavalluzzo.com/
14 Interview, CL1, September 2001.
15 On file with authors.

16 Canadian Press, 'Labour Activists Compile "Bad Boss" Inventory', *Hamilton Spectator*, 10 September 1996, A2.
17 Interview, ER1, September 2001.

REFERENCES

Befort, S. F. and Budd, J. W. (2009) *Invisible Hands, Invisible Objectives: Bringing Workplace Law and Public Policy into Focus*. Stanford: Stanford Economics & Finance.

Campaign 2000 (2000) *Work Isn't Working for Ontario Families: The Role of Good Jobs in Ontario's Poverty Reduction Strategy*. Toronto: Campaign 2000.

Canadian Federation of Independent Business (2000) *CFIB Submission to the Ontario Government on its July 2000 Consultation Paper, Time for Change: Ontario's ES Legislation*. Toronto: CFIB.

Employment Standards Work Group (2000) *Time For Change: Tories Turn Back the Clock But Working People Want to Move Forward: A Response to Time For Change*. Toronto: ESWG.

Fairey, D. (2007) New 'Flexible' ES Regulation in British Columbia. *Journal of Law and Social Policy*, 21: 91–113.

Fanelli, C. and M. Thomas 2011. Austerity, Competitiveness and Neoliberalism Redux: Ontario Responds to the Great Recession. *Socialist Studies*, 7(1/2): 141–170.

Fudge, J. 1991. *Labour Law's Little Sister: The Employment Standards Act and the Feminization of Labour*. Ottawa: Canadian Centre for Policy Alternatives.

Gellatly, M., J. Grundy, K. Mirchandani, A. Perry, M. Thomas and L. F. Vosko 2011. 'Modernizing' Employment Standards? Administrative Efficiency, Market Regulation, and the Production of the Illegitimate Claimant in Ontario, Canada. *Economic and Labour Relations Review*, 22(2): 81–106.

Harvey, D. 2005. *The New Imperialism*. Oxford: Oxford University Press.

Jessop, B. 1993. Towards a Schumpeterian Workfare State? Preliminary Remarks on Post Fordist Political Economy. *Studies in Political Economy*, 40: 7–39.

McCallum, R. 2005. Plunder Downunder: Transplanting the Anglo-American Labor Law Model to Australia. *Comparative Labor Law & Policy Journal*, 26(3): 381–400.

Mitchell, E. 2003. The Employment Standards Act 2000: Ontario Opts for Efficiency over Rights. *Canadian Labour and Employment Law Journal*, 10: 269–286.

Ontario, 1991. *Employee Wage Protection Program*. Background # 91-05. Toronto: Ministry of Labour.

Ontario, 2000. *Time For Change: Ontario's Employment Standards Legislation, A Consultation Paper*. Toronto: Ministry of Labour.

Ontario, 2010a. Ministry of Labour News Release, 17 May, Ontario Is Open for Business: McGuinty Government's Proposed Act Will Deliver Results for Business, http://news.ontario.ca/medt/en/2010/05/ontario-is-open-for-business.html, date accessed 10 December 2010.

Ontario, 2010b. Ministry of Labour News Release, 17 May, Proposed Open for Business Act – What Others Are Saying, http://news.ontario.ca/medt/

▶

►
en/2010/05/proposed-open-for-business-act---what-others-are-saying.html, date accessed 10 December 2010.

Ontario, 2010c. Ministry of Labour News Release, 25 October 2010, New Legislation Modernizes Ontario's ES, http://www.labour.gov.on.ca/english/news/bulletin_ofba.php, date accessed 15 November 2010.

Ontario, 2010d. Ministry of Labour, Employment Standards Task Force, http://www.labour.gov.on.ca/english/es/pubs/is_estf.php, date accessed 15 November 2010.

Peck, J. 2001. *Workfare States.* New York & London: The Guilford Press.

Pollert, A. 2005. The Unorganised Worker: The Decline in Collectivism and New Hurdles to Individual Employment Rights. *Industrial Law Journal,* 34(3): 217–238.

Pollert, A. 2007. Britain and Individual Employment Rights: 'Paper Tigers, Fierce in Appearance but Missing in Tooth and Claw'. *Economic and Industrial Democracy,* 28(1): 110–139.

Pollert, A. 2009. The Vulnerable Worker in Britain and Problems at Work. *Work, Employment and Society,* 23(2): 343–362.

Progressive Conservative Party of Ontario (PCPO), 1995. *The Common Sense Revolution.* Toronto: PCPO.

Red Tape Review Commission (RTRC), 1997. *Cutting the Red Tape Barriers to Jobs and Better Government: Final Report of the Red Tape Review Commission.* Toronto: Red Tape Review Secretariat.

Retail Council of Canada (RCC), 1996. *Presentation to the Standing Committee on Resources Development.* Toronto: RCC.

Sears, A. 1999. The 'Lean' State and Capitalist Restructuring: Towards a Theoretical Account. *Studies in Political Economy,* 59: 91–114.

Standing, G. 1999. *Global Labour Flexibility: Seeking Distributive Justice.* London: Macmillan.

Thomas, M. 2009. *Regulating Flexibility: The Political Economy of Employment Standards.* Montreal & Kingston: McGill-Queen's University Press.

Thomas, M. 2010. Neoliberalism, Racialization, and the Regulation of Employment Standards. In S. Braedley and M. Luxton, eds. *Neoliberalism and Everyday Life.* Montreal & Kingston: McGill-Queen's University Press, 68–89.

United Steelworkers of America (USWA), 2000. *Time for Change: Ontario's Employment Standards Legislation, Consultation Paper.* Toronto: USWA.

Vosko, L. F. 2010. *Managing the Margins: Gender, Citizenship and the International Regulation of Precarious Employment.* Oxford: Oxford University Press.

Workers' Action Centre (WAC) 2007. *Working on the Edge.* Toronto: WAC.

Workers' Action Centre and Parkdale Community Legal Services (PCLS) 2010. Submission to the Standing Committee on Finance and Economic Affairs regarding Schedule 9, Bill 68, An Act to Promote Ontario as Open for Business by Amending Or Repealing Certain Acts. Toronto: WAC & PCLS.

CHAPTER

15

Are Skills the Answer to Bad Jobs? Incentives to Learn at the Bottom End of the Labour Market

Ewart Keep and Susan James

Introduction

Under the UK's New Labour government there was a strong belief that the existence of bad jobs was by no means inevitable. Indeed, New Labour's policy narrative assumed that bad jobs were being driven from the labour market by globalization and the resultant arrival of a knowledge-driven economy. Specifically, skills policy was believed to be the answer to a range of social and economic problems that extended well beyond low pay and bad jobs, for example, social mobility and productivity (Blair 2007; Brown 2010). To begin addressing these ills, a platform of minimum individual legal rights for workers, a National Minimum Wage and an associated regime of in-work tax credits to top up low wages were put in place. In addition, however, policy stressed that government could hasten the removal of bad jobs by supplying more skills to those at the lower end of the employment ladder (DfES 2003, 2007; HM Treasury 2002). Consequently, the focus became more and better education and training. The New Labour Government adopted a twin track approach to skills: firstly, with efforts to improve the quality and outcomes in initial compulsory and post-compulsory education and training; and secondly, a major push to up-skill poorly qualified adult workers via publicly funded training.

While skills undoubtedly have a role to play, on their own they fall well short of a panacea (Lloyd and Mayhew 2010): a skills-centric policy can expend large sums of public money to limited effect and divert attention from other issues that need to be tackled. In this chapter we argue that three factors served to undermine New Labour's policies on education and training as a route for workers to move out of bad jobs: first, the persistence of a substantial number of bad jobs; second, that adult skills initiative are costly and the evidence suggests somewhat limited impacts; third, the structure of the bottom end of labour market provides weak incentives to learn either in terms of current job or for progression (which in turn helps explain the second factor above).

These factors will continue to circumscribe the role that skills alone can play in tackling the problem of large numbers of bad jobs in the UK labour market. The first two factors will be dealt with briefly in what follows, with the bulk of attention reserved for the third. However, bad jobs are not inevitable, certainly not in the abundance in which they are found in the UK. In concluding, we argue that rather than a one-size-fits-all skills policy, a multi-level suite of policy interventions is required. These interventions involve labour market regulation and developing new labour market institutions.

The failure of the knowledge-driven economy 'vision'

In the late 1990s and early 2000s the vision of a knowledge-driven economy took root across the developed world. Its antecedents go a long way back (e.g. Drucker 1959) but in essence the work of Reich (1991) and Florida (2005) suggested human capital as the sole unique source of competitive advantage (for firms and nations). Consequently, notions of a future of work where workers' skills would imbue their activities with high levels of autonomy, 'authorship' and reward were developed (Michaels et al., 2001).

Unfortunately, as time passed it became clear that this 'happy ending' would not be universal and that while there are knowledge-driven sectors and firms, a substantial proportion of paid employment remains outside this sunny upland (Thompson 2004; Toynbee 2003). At present about 22 per cent of the UK workforce are low paid on EU definitions (less than two thirds median earnings), and almost a third of all female workers fall into the category (Lloyd et al. 2008). Projections of occupational growth show little sign that low paid employment in the UK is likely to fall this side of 2020 (Lawton 2009). Furthermore, if the new UK Coalition Government's plans to open nearly all public service provision to open competition by any willing provider come to fruition, it must be assumed that low waged work may well increase. In the past one of the main ways private providers have achieved 'efficiency gains' and cut costs when taking on public service provision has been via reduced terms and conditions for the workers (Toynbee 2003).

Adult skills initiatives – high costs and limited impact?

In order to combat bad jobs, the government's efforts have had two main policy foci. The first is adult basic skills – literacy and numeracy – in combination with up-skilling all adult workers to a first Level 2 qualification. Level 2 is assumed to be the equivalent of successfully completing UK lower secondary education, and the level the government deemed to be the minimum for employability. The evidence that is currently available, however, paints a mixed picture on the impact and value for money of attempts to boost skill and qualification levels among low paid workers. Evaluation of work-based efforts to tackle problems with adult basic skills (Wolf et al., 2010) identified two issues. First, that employers appear far less concerned about adult basic skills (particularly numeracy) than the policy rhetoric normally assumes, and employees were participating in government-funded adult basic skills learning largely for reasons that had nothing to do with work. Second, that work-based provision is extremely expensive to arrange and, while its impact on workers appears to have been positive in terms of confidence gained (Evans et al. 2009), for employers the legacy generated by public investment was often largely ephemeral. As Wolf et al. (2010: 400) observe in relation to employers, 'our longitudinal research found no stable legacies or outcomes at all, either in the form of ongoing provision, or in changes in employers' training activities.'

Furthermore, even the official evidence makes it fairly clear that the notion of a first Level 2 qualification as a minimum platform for employability is incorrect, and the difference in employment outcome between having a Level 1 qualification and a Level 2 is very small (especially for males) (BIS, 2010a). The reasons why demand for certified skill may be so low at the bottom end of the labour market are explored later in this chapter.

The second thrust to policy was a belief that government subsidy for training in the workplace, coupled with government-supported training brokerage services, could transform employer attitudes and practices around training. The main policy vehicle through which the New Labour Government tried to achieve this transformation was Train to Gain (T2G) (National Audit Office, 2009). T2G is a huge and complex topic, and cannot be analysed here in any detail, not least as provision under this brand or banner was constantly changing and evolving (NAO, 2009). However, in essence, T2G offered a government subsidy of 100 per cent to employers for some types of adult basic skills provision, as well as for training and accreditation to get workers who did not already possess a first Level 2 qualification up to that level.

A key point to note is that T2G had multiple policy objectives, some possibly in tension with others. It was designed to both encourage employers to undertake more training and boost productivity, and at the same time help to make individual low-qualified adult workers employable and enable their progression in the labour market. As a result, the choice of qualifications undertaken by trainees was made by their employer and was usually tied to their current job rather than to opportunities to progress or change career.

Under the Coalition Government T2G and its official evaluation have ceased, with the result that we will now probably never be able to determine what long-term impact it had upon the subsequent wages and labour market progression of those workers who had been through the programme. Moreover, given the current and likely future fiscal climate, the chances that any UK government in the foreseeable future will be willing or able to finance or return to this kind of heavily subsidized, blanket adult training provision seems slender.

Perhaps the key question to arise from the experiences of adult basic skills provision in the workplace and T2G is why such large-scale government initiatives were deemed necessary. The main answer is official belief in the prevalence of market failure (Keep 2006). The alternative explanation, which will be advanced below, is that the incentives to learn and to invest in learning created by labour market structures and opportunities, particularly for those workers destined for or already in low end employment, are limited, patchy and uncertain and that public money was used to fill this void and to act in lieu of stronger signals and rewards for skill from employers.

Weak incentives to learn? The official policy model

Official views about the incentives to learn at the lower reaches of the UK labour market have been founded on a distinctive reading of human capital theory that revolved around analyses of rate of (wage) return accruing to investment in different types and levels of qualification (Keep 2009a). In essence, the trap that policy-makers fell into was to seize upon figures on the average wage returns to acquiring higher level qualifications and then assume that if everyone gained qualifications at that level they too would garner similar reward (DfES/DWP 2006). Thus, if every single worker were to be helped to achieve a Level 4 (degree or equivalent) qualification they would on average earn the same graduate wage premium as when such qualifications were relatively scarce. This effect has been assumed to hold good irrespective of underlying occupational and sectoral wage structures.

The reasoning behind this belief was one whereby wages were believed to directly reflect employees' productivity levels and, as upskilling was deemed to automatically boost productivity (Keep et al. 2006), raising the skill levels of low paid workers would inevitably make them more productive, which in turn would lead to higher rates of pay. In as much as policy acknowledged that there were other aspects of lower end employment besides low pay that were disagreeable to workers, it assumed that skills offered an answer because it provided individual workers with the ability to quit bad work and find better jobs.

As a result, low paid employment came to be seen as being caused primarily by the workers' lack of (certified) human capital. Furthermore, in some cases the problem of low pay was portrayed as resting with individual defeatism and workers' failures of aspiration and self-betterment, rather than with the structure of the economy and firms' product market strategies and the resultant job hierarchies, work organization, and job design. Thus, insofar as workers and employers were failing to react to these perceived incentives in the ways intended or anticipated by policy-makers, the problem was usually deemed to lie either with negative cultural attitudes or with 'market failure' rather than leading to any questioning about the strength of the incentives themselves (see Keep 2006).

There are three points to note about this approach. First, its conception is extremely individualistic, with bargaining power residing with the individual worker whose stock of human capital empowers them in negotiations with employers. Collectivist answers around trade unions and bargaining power (the traditional route by which workers had been able to use skills to leverage gains) were seen as outdated. Second, it ignored and supplanted earlier approaches that suggested that low pay and bad jobs were rooted in the nature of occupations and their relationship with particular product markets and sources of competitive pressure, and with weak trade unions and the under-development or absence of collective bargaining arrangements (Mayhew and Bowen 1990). These complex, structurally embedded analyses were conveniently relegated from view, and the simpler, mono-causal theory around skills elevated in their stead. Consequently policy-makers avoided confronting the issues about labour market regulation, collective forms of employee representation and the actions and choices of employers, all of which were deemed to be 'off limits' (Keep 2009b). Third, the skills-based approach bears only limited congruence with reality. In the UK labour market the supply of good jobs is finite, and there remains a substantial reservoir of low paid employment, much of which is low skilled, and which often carries with it other characteristics of bad work: lack of task discretion, high levels of stress and very weak employee 'voice' (Lawton 2009; Lloyd et al. 2008). A result of the surfeit of bad jobs is the often weak demand for skill, the rewards for acquiring skills are often small or non-existent, the opportunities to escape such work are limited and the incentives acting on individuals to overcome any of these issues reduces accordingly. It is to these incentives that we now turn.

The incentives to learn

We have developed a structure for analysing the different types, causes and strengths of incentive acting on individuals to engage in learning (see Keep 2009a; Keep and James 2010a). In essence, there are three basic categories of incentive:

1. Type 1 – are generated inside the education and training system, and create and sustain positive attitudes towards the act of learning itself and towards progression within each student or trainee. In other words, many Type 1 incentives produce, or are the result of, intrinsic rewards generated through the act of learning;
2. Type 2 – are created in wider society and the labour market and the rewards they give rise to are external to the learning process itself (for example, the higher wages and more interesting work that the highly qualified can expect to access); and
3. Type 2b – government subsidies acting in lieu of strong enough Type 2 incentives. Education Maintenance Allowances, Learning Agreements and Adult Learning Allowances are three examples.

It is apparent that for many adult workers in bad jobs, the Type 2 incentives (wage gains, progression opportunities and chances for job enrichment) are too patchy and limited (Keep and James 2010a). We argue the reasons are bound up with the following mutually re-inforcing matrix of negative factors.

Some problems with incentives for workers in or entering bad jobs

Weak occupational identities and skill requirements: In comparison to many European countries, conceptions of learning for UK labour market entry have often been focused on acquiring the skills needed to undertake a particular job, rather than a broader set of skills that might be needed to enter and progress inside a particular occupation (Winch 2011). In general, broader notions of occupational identity and its formation have been restricted to those training for the traditional professions (law, medicine etc). This model in part simply reflects the reality of many lower end occupations in the UK, where levels of discretion and control are often very limited and the work is often reduced to simple repetition of very basic tasks (James and Lloyd 2008), and where the skills needed to do this kind of work are very limited. Models of work organization and job design that limit the need for discretion and skill are more prevalent in the UK relative to many north European countries (OECD 2010).

Narrow conceptions of vocational skill and learning: Lack of properly formed notions of broader occupations and occupational progression routes lead in turn to very narrow conceptions of what vocational skill and learning are required for entry and to hold down a given job. One of the key differences between UK initial vocational learning and that on offer in many other developed countries is the almost total absence in the UK of provision of any substantive element of general education above and beyond basic literacy and numeracy and some relatively low level Information and Communications Technology (ICT) skills (Wolf 2011). Consequently, those workers who follow a vocational learning pathway often find it difficult to return subsequently to any form of more academic learning or to progress (either immediately or later) into higher education. This model leads to narrowly defined programmes of skill acquisition. These programmes focus on qualifications, which as suggested below, are based around the acquisition of task-specific competences needed to perform a particular job rather than a more expansive model of learning aimed at entry into a broader vocation or occupation.

Vocational qualifications that generate weak wage effects: In the 1980s the UK pioneered the development of a system of vocational qualification (National Vocational Qualifications – NVQs) that was competence based and which was structured around breaking a job into a set of discrete tasks and then defining and supplying the competences needed to undertake these tasks. In other words, it was a model that exemplified and embodied the narrow conceptions of job and occupation outlined above. Often the occupational standards which the qualifications were supposed to support and reflect were established on the basis of a lowest common denominator approach among employers in a sector, with the least ambitious employers keeping skill demands low – though in some sectors, such as engineering, this approach was not the case.

The key point is that while this model of vocational qualification design may meet the immediate needs of some employers, it creates qualifications that offer little economic empowerment because, a) the skills being imparted are narrow and often low level; b) it fails to provide broad, coherent packages of learning that can support re-entry into learning or career progression; and c) it offers almost no foundation for the individual in developing their roles as citizens and members of the wider community, again in contrast to practice elsewhere in Europe (see Brockmann et al. 2011). Furthermore, the evidence suggests very clearly that the acquisition of many lower level vocational qualifications does not lead to substantial increases in workers' earning power (McIntosh and Garrett 2009). Insofar as training leading to lower level vocational qualifications does offer good returns, they tend to do so when provided by the employer rather than by colleges or other external agencies.

Hitherto the main policy response to this evidence has been to commission further analyses of the Rate of return data in the hope of finding a more favourable story. The question not posed, at least in public, by policy-makers until very recently has been whether the picture revealed by Rate of return suggests a number of problems: firstly, with the design, specification and learning contents of some low level vocational qualifications – a problem that the Wolf Review of Vocational Education (Wolf, 2011) does raise very directly; secondly, with the way recruitment and selection processes use and value such qualifications, and with the degree to which labour market regulation (for example licence to practice requirements) is absent; thirdly, with the structure of the labour market and of wages for workers in the occupations covered by such qualification. We would argue that policy is confronted by all three of these problems and that progress on any one of them requires intervention around the others, particularly as the first two problems are often consequences that flow from the third.

Limited and weak labour market regulation: The absence of widespread licence to practice requirements in the UK labour market stands in marked contrast to practice in some other Anglo-Saxon economies (for example, Canada, Australia and the US at the level of individual state), or in places such as Germany and Austria. The fact that people do not need to acquire a particular type and level of qualification in order to enter most forms of employment has three effects. First, it means that employers have considerable freedom about who they can recruit (for a review of the evidence see Keep and James 2010b). For many lower end jobs employers are looking for skills (and behavioural traits) that are not well-captured by formal qualifications. As a result of this freedom and of 'informal' recruitment and selection practices, the hold that qualifications have on the recruitment and selection process for some jobs is limited.

Second, the uncertain role of qualifications in recruitment and selection in turn reduces the incentives to individuals to invest time and money (directly or via wages foregone) in acquiring qualifications as the strong incentive that a licence to practice regime offers is absent (see Keep 2009a). Finally, the lack of labour market regulation and the freedom to 'aim low' when recruiting helps explain why the UK trails in many OECD league tables on education and training, and why relatively few young people acquire good levels of qualification in the UK. As Green (2009: 17) notes,

> Unfortunately, Britain has long been caught in a low-qualification trap, which means that British employers tend to be less likely than in most

> other countries to require their recruits to be educated beyond compulsory school leaving age. Among European countries only in Spain, Portugal and Turkey is there a greater proportion of jobs requiring no education beyond compulsory school.

Given this weak demand side pull from the labour market, Britain's distinctive and weak pattern of educational achievement, in terms of both initial and continuing education, is much easier to understand.

Limited opportunities for progression: For those workers in many lower paid jobs the opportunities to progress upwards into better paid work are often limited in scale and uncertain (Cheung and McKay 2010) and, insofar as opportunities do exist, the focus may not centre on the skills of the workers per se. For example, a willingness to work full rather than part-time may be critical (Lloyd and Mayhew 2010). Neither official policy nor mainstream human resource management debates has devoted much attention to progression for those workers at the lower end of the labour market; indeed much of the discourse around the types of jobs of these workers has centred on outsourcing, offshoring and other forms of dividing up work that have made robust internal labour markets ever harder to sustain. As Ben-Galim et al. (2011: 14) note, 'the "advancement vacuum" in employment policy means that the main framework for supporting progression in work is adult skills policy.' Unfortunately, the weak prospects for advancement out of many low paid jobs further serves to undermine adult skills policy by reducing the incentive on employers to train the bulk of their workforce for progression and also reduces the case for individuals to invest in their own skill, thereby creating a vicious circle.

More is not enough ...

Each of the above factors, on their own, would cause problems for policies aimed at boosting low-paid individuals' willingness to engage in training and of using skills as the answer to low paid work. However, as the foregoing exposition has hinted, the problems are in part mutually inter-dependent consequences of each other and are deeply rooted in the structure and regulation (or the lack thereof) of the labour market, making progress extremely problematic. Unfortunately, policy-makers have exhibited limited acknowledgement or comprehension of these issues, though as Johnson et al. (2009: 55) note, the implications are quite clear:

> Major surveys have consistently found that career progression and accessing better paid jobs are key motivators for people (including lower-skilled workers) participating in learning and training. Yet there is evidence that

> undertaking low level vocational training offers few immediate returns to the individual in terms of higher wages. If this remains the case, there may be little rational incentive for lower skilled workers to participate in such forms of training... entry level adult learning may act as a first step towards further skills development activities that carry a higher wage premium, but there is a need to ensure that such progression routes are clearly articulated and that even the most basic skills provision is clearly linked to improved job performance and/or opportunities for progression.

In particular, there seems to be very limited understanding within policy thinking about two fundamental points. The first is that skills generally imbue the holder with labour market power – in terms of choice between employers and the level of wages that can be commanded – only in relation to their scarcity relative to demand. Of themselves, qualifications and being skilled do not automatically command a premium or confer individual bargaining power if they are more or less ubiquitous, or where supply exceeds demand. The example of the rapid growth of low pay among German service sector workers is apposite. Nearly 80 per cent of low paid service workers in Germany now hold a Level 3 qualification (Bosch 2010). By comparison with many low paid UK workers German workers are more highly skilled, but this fact does them little good in sectors such as retailing and call centres, where collective bargaining is weak or has disappeared, and where qualified labour and skills are available in abundance.

Far from creating skills that are relatively scarce and highly valuable, much of the effort expended by public policy over the past three decades has been directed at creating a world where the supply of qualified labour now outstrips demand and where over-qualification is a growing problem (Felstead et al. 2007). Furthermore, the main thrust of skills policy for those workers in low end employment has been around supplying them with qualifications chosen by their current employer, which are now known to have limited currency and wage effects in the labour market, and where rather than paying to supply such workers with new skills, much of the public support has gone into formally accrediting skills already possessed.

The second point, as we have argued in more detail elsewhere (Keep 2009a; Keep and James 2010a), is that workers or prospective workers at the bottom end of the labour market are the ones who face the weakest, patchiest, most complex and uncertain (and hence risky) incentives to invest in learning and skills, and who normally have the most limited resources to invest. A common perception among policy-makers is that insofar as there are problems with individuals' investment in skills, the issues are either to do with lack of ambition and aspiration or are the result of barriers to learning, for example lack of time. The assumption is then made that if such barriers can be removed, the natural outcome will be more learning. In reality, even if all the barriers to learning that research has identified (see Spielhofer et al., 2010) were removed, it is unclear whether the incentives to invest in learning would be strong enough to lead to much higher levels of activity. Unless and until learning is seen as likely to pay off in terms of better wages, more interesting and varied work, and opportunities for progression, individual investment in skills may well remain smaller than hoped.

Conclusion

The New Labour experiment around adult learning as an answer to bad jobs and limited progression in the labour market ended with the UK general election of May 2010. In the ensuing era of fiscal austerity and reduced public spending T2G was an early casualty; in addition government funding to support adult learning in further education for those low income workers is about to be reduced sharply, with the expectation that individuals will now pay up to half the cost of the course (Linford 2011). Volumes of government-funded adult learning among the low paid look set to fall dramatically.

Under the new Coalition Government there is still a policy push around adult basic skills but expectations around what this policy can deliver in terms of labour market outcomes at the lower end appear more muted, not least because the Conservative and Liberal Democrats who form the coalition have other concerns and priorities. These policies centre on getting more unemployed, disabled and economically inactive persons into paid employment and on making work 'pay' (as compared to being on state benefits) against a backdrop of high and still rising unemployment. Although the rhetoric often still echoes the EU's Lisbon Strategy of 'more and better jobs' slogan, the suspicion has to be that, with two-and-a-half million workers unemployed, the emphasis in the immediate future is on the 'more' rather than the 'better'. At the same time, the focus for adult learning policy has, to some extent at least, swung back to wider, non-work related learning (BIS 2010b).

The other key determinants of training policy are the twin imperatives of reducing state spending and voluntarism. The first means that a New Labour style attempt to spend and subsidize a way to 'victory' in the OECD education and skills league tables, even if such was still deemed a desirable goal, is no longer available as the resources to support it have vanished. The expectation is that in a freed up marketplace for education and training, where the state has largely 'got out of the way', workers and their employers, separately or together, will decide to invest in human capital from a responsive range of providers (public and private) (BIS, 2010b).

The second imperative around voluntarism means employers are not to be compelled via regulation to do more training or to offer it more widely across their workforces, which has been a central and consistent theme of education and training policy in the UK since 1981 and the announcement of the abolition of the statutory Industrial Training Boards (Keep 2009b). Although some minor incremental changes in terms of mandating health and safety training have been made, the only substantive attempt to make inroads into a largely voluntaristic training system came with New Labour's belated granting of a statutory right for individual workers to request time off for training. On election, the Coalition Government swiftly put this recently passed legislation under review and, at the time of writing, it was announced that it would be revoked for all employers with less than 250 staff. The volume, type, level and pattern across the workforce of employer-provided training thus remains almost wholly at the discretion of the individual employer.

Research, not least that conducted for the Russell Sage Foundation's low waged Europe project (Gautie and Schmitt 2010; Lloyd et al. 2008; Lloyd and Mayhew 2010), suggests that solutions to the problem of bad jobs lie beyond skills, and in part depend on new ways of configuring labour market institutions such as collective bargaining, and labour market regulation (for a fuller discussion see Bosch et al. 2010). Insofar as enhancing the skills of low paid workers can play a part in addressing the problem of bad jobs, it is liable to be able to do so only as one component within a much more broadly framed set of policies concerned with innovation, organizational development, work organization and job redesign (OECD 2010) or, as Ben-Galim et al. (2011: 3) observe, 'whether efforts to improve the nation's skills lead to more and better jobs will depend on improving how employers invest in and utilize the skills of the workforce'. Unfortunately, the design and development of interventions in these areas is extremely problematic because UK governments, of all mainstream political persuasions, have hitherto disliked and avoided intervening in the 'black box' of the workplace (Keep et al. 2006; Keep 2009b). In some senses, the official obsession with upskilling as an answer to bad jobs has thus been a form of displacement activity that has allowed government to avoid confronting structural problems in the labour market and the workplace.

REFERENCES

Ben-Galim, D., Krasnowski, K. and Lanning, T. (2011) *More Than a Foot in the Door*, London: IPPR.

Blair, A. (2007) *Our Nation's Future – The Role of Work*, www.number-10.gov.uk/output/Page11405.asp (accessed 04 May 2007).

Bosch, G. (2010) personal communication with the authors.

▶

▶
Bosch, G., Mayhew, K. and Gautie, J. (2010) 'Industrial Relations, Legal Regulations and Wage Setting', in J. Gautie and J. Schmitt. (eds) *Low-Wage Work in the Wealthy World*, New York: Russell Sage Foundation, 91–146.
Brockmann, M., Clarke, L., Hanf, G., Mehaut, P., Westerhuis, A. and Winch, C. (eds) (2011) *Knowledge, Skills, Competence in the European Labour Market: What's in a Vocational Qualification?* Oxford: Routledge.
Brown, G. (2010) *Prime Minister's Podcast* – 17 January, www.number10.gov.uk/Page 22142 (accessed 19 January 2010).
Cheung, S. Y. and McKay, S. (2010) *Training and Progression in the Labour Market*, DWP Research Report No 680, London: Department for Work and Pensions.
Department for Business Innovation and Skills (BIS) (2010a) *Supporting Analysis for 'Skills for Growth: the National Skills Strategy'*, BIS Economics Paper No. 4, London: BIS.
Department for Business Innovation and Skills (BIS) (2010b) *Skills for Growth*, London: BIS.
Department for Education and Skills (DfES) (2003) *21st Century Skills – Realising Our Potential*, London: HMSO.
Department for Education and Skills (DfES) (2007) *Post-16 Skills: Government Response to the the Ninth Report of Session 2006-7*, House of Commons Education and Skills Committee, HC 1101, London: HMSO.
Department for Education and Skills/Department for Work and Pensions (DfES/DWP) (2006) *DfES and DWP: A Shared Evidence Base – The Role of Skills in the Labour Market*, Nottingham: DfES.
Drucker, P. (1959) *Landmarks of Tomorrow*, New York: Harper.
Evans, K., Waite, E. and Admasachew, L. (2009) 'Enhancing 'Skills for Life'? Workplace Learning and Adult Basic Skills', in S. Reder and J. Bynner (eds) *Tracking Adult Literacy and Numeracy*, London: Routledge, 242–260.
Felstead, A., Gallie, D., Green, F. and Zhou, Y. (2007) *Skills at Work 1986–2006*, SKOPE, University of Oxford.
Florida, R. (2005) *The Flight of the Creative Class*, New York: Harper Business.
Gautie, J. and Schmitt, J. (eds) (2010) *Low-Wage Work in the Wealthy World*, New York: Russell Sage Foundation.
Green F. (2009) *Job Quality in Britain*, UKCES Praxis Paper No. 1, Wath-upon-Dearne: UK Commission for Employment and Skills.
H M Treasury (2002) *Developing Workforce Skills: Piloting a New Approach*, London: HM Treasury.
James, S. and Lloyd, C. (2008) 'Supply Chain Pressures and Migrant Workers: Deteriorating Job Quality in the UK Food Processing Industry', in C. Lloyd, G. Mason and K. Mayhew (eds) *Low-Wage Work in the United Kingdom*, New York: Russell Sage Foundation, 211–246.
Johnson, S., Sawicki, S., Pearson, C., Lindsay, C., McQuaid, R. and Dutton, M. (2009) *Employee Demand for Skills: A Review of Evidence and Policy*, UKCES Evidence Report 3, Wath-upon-Dearne: UK Commission for Employment and Skills.
Keep, E. (2006b) 'State Control of the English Education and Training System – Playing with the Biggest Train Set in the World', *Journal of Vocational Education and Training*, 58(1): 47–64.
▶

Keep, E. (2009a) *Internal and External Incentives to Engage in Education and Training – A Framework for Analysing the Forces Acting on Individuals*, SKOPE Monograph No. 12, SKOPE, Cardiff University.

Keep, E. (2009b) *The Limits of the Possible: Shaping the Learning and Skills Landscape through a Shared Policy Analysis*, SKOPE Research Paper No. 86, SKOPE, Cardiff University.

Keep, E., and James, S. (2010a) *What Incentives to Learn at the Bottom End of the Labour Market?* SKOPE Research Paper No. 94, SKOPE, Cardiff University.

Keep, E., and James, S. (2010b) *Recruitment and Selection – A Review of Extant Research and Some Thoughts on Its Implications for Education and Training Policy*, SKOPE Research Paper No. 88, SKOPE, Cardiff University.

Keep, E., Mayhew, K. and Payne, J. (2006) 'From Skills Revolution to Productivity Miracle – Not as Easy as It Sounds?' *Oxford Review of Economic Policy*, 22(4): 539–559.

Lawton, K. (2009) *Nice Work If You Can Get It*, London: IPPR.

Linford, N. (2011) 'Great Idea: Let's Put Education Out of Reach of Those Who Need It Most', *Guardian*, Education supplement, 29 March, 5.

Lloyd, C., Mason, G. and Mayhew, K. (eds) (2008) *Low-Wage Work in the United Kingdom*, New York: Russell Sage Foundation.

Lloyd, C. and Mayhew, K. (2010) 'Skills: the Solution to Low Wage Work?' *Industrial Relations Journal*, 41(5): 429–445.

Mayhew, K. and Bowen, A. (eds) (1990) *Improving Incentives for the Low-Paid*, Basingstoke: Palgrave Macmillan/National Economic Development Council.

McIntosh, S. and Garrett, R. (2009) *The Economic Value of Intermediate Vocational Education and Qualifications*, UKCES Evidence Report 11, Wath-upon-Dearne: UK Commission for Employment and Skills.

Michaels, E., Handworth-Jones, H. and Axelrod, B. (2001) *The War for Talent*, Boston MA: Harvard Business School Press.

National Audit Office (2009) *Train to Gain: Developing the Skills of the Workforce*, HC 879 Session 2008–2009, London: TSO.

Organisation for Economic Cooperation and Development (OECD) (2010) *Innovative Workplaces: Making Better Use of Skills within Organisations*, Paris: OECD.

Reich, R. (1991) *The Work of Nations*, New York: Vintage.

Spielhofer, T., Golden, S., Evans, K., Marshall, H., Mundy, E., Pomati, M. and Styles, B. (2010) *Barriers to Participation in Education and Training*, DfE Research Report RR009, London: Department for Education.

Thompson, P. (2004) *Skating on Thin Ice – The Knowledge Economy Myth*, Glasgow: Big Thinking.

Toynbee, P. (2003) *Hard Work – Life in Low-Pay Britain*, London: Bloomsbury.

Winch, C. (2011) 'Skills – a Concept Manufactured in England?' in M. Brockmann, L. Clarke, G. Hanf, P. Mehaut, A. Westerhuis and C. Winch (eds) *Knowledge, Skills, Competence in the European Labour Market: What's in a Vocational Qualification?* Oxford: Routledge.

Wolf, A., Aspin, L., Waite, E. and Ananiadou, K. (2010) 'The Rise and Fall of Workplace Basic Skills Programmes: Lessons for Policy and Practice', *Oxford Review of Education*, 36(4): 385–405.

Wolf, A. (2011) *Review of Vocational Education – The Wolf Report*, London: Department for Education.

Author Index

Subject Index